What is Political Economy?

Eight Perspectives

What is
Political Economy?

Eight Perspectives

edited by
DAVID K. WHYNES

Basil Blackwell

First published 1984
Basil Blackwell Publisher Ltd,
108 Cowley Road, Oxford OX4 1JF, UK

Basil Blackwell Inc.
432 Park Avenue South, Suite 1505,
New York, NY 10016, USA

1472184

British Library Cataloguing in Publication Data
What is political economy?
1. Economics
I. Whynes, David K.
330.1   HB171

ISBN 0-85520-746-9

Typeset by Katerprint Co Ltd, Oxford.
Printed in Great Britain by
Page Bros, Norwich.

Contents

Biographica

Norman Barry is Reader in Politics at the University of Buckingham. He previously taught at the City of Birmingham Polytechnic and at the Universities of Exeter and Queen's, Belfast. He is the author of *Hayek's Social and Economic Philosophy* (1979) and *An Introduction to Modern Political Theory* (1981), as well as of many articles on classical liberalism, political philosophy and political economy. He is presently researching into the philosophical foundations of classical liberalism and libertarianism.

Arun Bose took his Economic Tripos from Trinity College, Cambridge, where he returned in 1960 to spend a year under the Commonwealth Universities Interchange. He has been Lecturer in Economics at Kirori Mal College, Delhi University and has published articles in *The Economic Journal, History of Political Economy* and other journals. His major books are *Marxian and Post-Marxian Political Economy* (1975), *Political Paradoxes and Puzzles* (1977) and *Marx on Exploitation and Inequality* (1980). As a member of the central leadership of the Indian communist movement (1941–50), Arun Bose was engaged in full-time political activity at the national level. Since the late 1960s he has concentrated on research and teaching of the analytical foundations of Marxian political economy without affiliation to any political party.

Roger Bowles is Lecturer in Economics at the University of Bath and Visiting Research Associate at the SSRC Centre for Socio-Legal Studies, Wolfson College, Oxford. He is co-author of *The Economic Theory of the State* (1981), author of *Law and the Economy* (1983) and has published articles in both law and economics journals. He is presently researching into enforcement and efficiency in the criminal justice system and also into economic aspects of the law relating to foreign money liabilities.

John Elliott is Professor of Economics at the University of Southern California, Los Angeles. He has written extensively on many areas of political economy and economic thought and has lately edited *Marx and Engels on Economics, Politics and Society* (1981). His more recent journal articles have focused on the thought of Marx and Schumpeter. His current projects include a study of Yugoslavian Marxism and *Comparative Economic Systems and Political Economy* (forthcoming).

Bruno Frey is Professor of Economics at the University of Zurich. He is Managing Editor of *Kyklos* and has lately held visiting appointments at the Universities of Stockholm, Vienna and Oxford. His more recent publications include *Modern Political Economy* (1978), *Democratic Economic Policy* (1983) and *International Political Economics* (1984).

Alan Hamlin studied at the Universities of Wales and York and is presently Lecturer in Economics at the University of Southampton. He is Joint Managing Editor of *The Economic Review*. In 1982 he was Visiting Research Fellow at the Centre for the Study of Public Choice, Virginia. His research interests include public choice and industrial economics and he has published articles in these areas. He is currently working on a book on the ethical basis of economics.

Shaun Hargreaves-Heap is a Lecturer in Economics in the School of Economic and Social Studies, University of East Anglia. He has published articles in the fields of macroeconomics and political economy. In 1981–2 he was Visiting Assistant Professor at Concordia University, Montreal.

Martin Hollis is Professor of Philosophy in the School of Economic and Social Studies, University of East Anglia. He is co-author of *Rational Economic Man* (1975), author of *Models of Man* (1977) and co-editor of *Philosophy and Economic Theory* (1979) and of *Rationality and Relativism* (1982). He has published many papers in the philosophy of the social sciences and is presently working on a book about rational choice.

David Whynes lectures in Economics at the University of Notting-
ham, having previously been a Research Fellow at the University of
York. He is the author of several books, most recently *Comparative
Economic Development* (1983) and *Invitation to Economics* (1983).
His interests centre on public economics, political economy and
economic thought.

Introduction

In 1957, Paul Baran published *The Political Economy of Growth*, a study of accumulation and economic development. Nowadays regarded as a formative contribution to modern Marxist analysis this book is of interest for one further reason. According to the *Cumulative Book Index*, the world bibliography of publications in the English language, it was the only book on political economy to be published in that year. Indeed, it was only the third new publication on political economy to have been produced since 1953. Three books in five years might appear an appalling indictment of a profession's productivity but the explanation is simple. The label 'political economy', so common in the English-speaking world during the nineteenth century, had fallen from grace by the middle of the twentieth. Turn to that section of the *Cumulative Book Index* headed 'economics' and you will find dozens of new titles listed each year, all evidence of the exemplary industry of economists, political or otherwise.

Moving forwards to the present day, political economy seems to be back in fashion. In 1983, over 50 new volumes in English were launched, each with a title beginning *The Political Economy of. . . .* The subjects covered ranged from innovation to socialism, from world poverty to big business, from demographic change to drug trafficking. The year was not special; even the most cursory examination of British and American publishers' catalogues over the past decade will reveal the increasing use being made of the 'political economy' label in parallel with, and sometimes at the expense of, 'economics'. Quite a few publishers now run 'political economy' series. Some are issuing editions of their books formerly entitled *The Economics of. . .* under the new designation.

These simple observations prompt a host of questions. What should we make of this trend? Does the burgeoning political economy literature indicate a renewal of interest in the approaches to social analysis employed by writers of political economy in the nineteenth century and earlier? Alternatively, are we witnessing the emergence of a new political economy, one posing a threat to the established paradigm of orthodox or mainstream economics? Perhaps the truth lies at a far less profound level, for we might conclude that the gradual change in terminology is little more than the manifestation of a shift in literary fashion. Perhaps publishers are seeking new ways of marketing the same old economics books! In short, is there any real difference between economics and political economy?

It was questions of this nature which came to mind when my publisher first confronted me with the problem directly, What is political economy? Guessing that the term was likely to mean different things to different people, I was not long in concluding that any search for an answer was not one best conducted alone. This explains a final report with nine authors. In fact, the volume which has eventually appeared is, in many respects, the consequence of my passing the original question on to others who were encouraged to provide their own personal reactions within a particular context. It was therefore my intention to end up with a collection of essays in which each contribution could stand as an independent view on an aspect of the central question whilst simultaneously providing a link in a chain of argument.

Before the structure of the book is outlined, one point requires clarification. Fundamental to the whole enquiry is whether there exists any difference of substance between the connotations of the two terms 'economics' and 'political economy' and it is abundantly clear that, in certain contexts, there does not. In such cases, the terms can be taken as interchangeable, and our enquiry is at an end! Some authors, for example, clearly view the latter term simply as an archaic form of the former. In their interpretation, 'political economy' is to 'economics' what 'mead' is to 'meadow'. The employment of the older term in some modern book titles can therefore be accounted for by the contemporary modes or stylistic mannerisms. The deliberate usage of obsolete or 'old-fashioned' phrases as a literary form is popular and is not confined to academic writing – in most British holiday resorts you will come across 'Ye Olde Englishe Tea-Shoppe'. Of the two terms, it is 'political economy' which has the more pleasing metre and, to our modern jargon-assaulted ears, the more impressive ring. At the same time, certain economists see economics and political economy as being on opposite sides of the same coin. An example here is Lord Robbins (1981) who interprets political economy as the 'application of Economic Science to problems of policy'. To Robbins, it seems, 'economics' is the central body of scientifically-established doctrine whereas 'political economy' embraces 'all the modes of analysis and explicit or implicit judgements of value which are usually involved when economists discuss the assessment of benefits and the reverse or recommendations for policy' (p. 8). At various times, other economists have designated this area a branch of 'economics', either normative, welfare or applied, or 'economic policy'. Irrespective of the differences in nomenclature, all see the two ideas as essentially complementary; one is the application of the other.

It is not the concern of the present volume to prescribe or to proscribe definitions. I have neither the right nor the inclination to compel a fellow writer to use, say, my preferred 'economic policy' in place of his 'political economy'. A difference of opinion on the grounds of terminological convention is, however, intellectually trivial and does not concern us here. The essential point is that the contributors to this volume do see political economy and contemporary economics as being conceptually distinct and *this* distinction *does* concern us.

To understand why writers feel the need to emphasize the difference as profound, a word or two must be said about 'economics'. The united front which the profession tries to present to the layman is, as all economists know, merely a thin veneer concealing deep divisions. There is, we are regularly told, a 'crisis' in economic theory. Indeed, over the past 20 years this crisis has been almost permanently evident because it seems to have been the favourite theme for the Presidential Addresses to the Royal Economic Society and the American Economic Association. No less a man than Wassily Leontieff has chastised his colleagues for the over-zealous use of abstraction and algebra. Joan Robinson has lamented economics' stunted development in certain areas of social relevance, whilst J. K. Galbraith has admitted to finding the basic axioms of economic theory beyond belief (Routh, 1975). The economic theory in which the crisis is seen to be occurring is the 'contemporary economics' of the preceding paragraph, also referred to as 'orthodox', 'mainstream', 'positive' and 'neo-classical' economics.

As formal statements about the subject must remain the province of the book proper I shall provide here only a simple caricature.

Orthodox economics is the stuff of textbooks used in the more respectable of undergraduate courses. It is equilibrium in restricted logical systems, it is deductive speculation. Orthodox economics recognizes 'micro' and 'macro'; it proceeds marginally and it reasons mathematically. Orthodox economics is Walrasian general equilibrium, Cobb-Douglas production functions, Hicks-Hansen IS/LM analysis and the Hecksher-Ohlin theorem. Most important of all it is, for a number of people, quite unsatisfactory and hence the crisis.

The dissatisfaction has, I think, two related origins. First, it is only relatively recently – since the 1940s and 1950s – that the present orthodoxy in Western economics has become orthodox. Contemporary economics owes far more to Lausanne than it does to Cambridge yet Marshall's influence was undoubtedly more dominant than that of Walras in the earlier part of this century. Even then, however, Marshallian economics did not possess the monopoly of interpretation – in Europe, coherent Austrian and Marxian approaches were being evolved and a powerful American challenge was in preparation. This being the case, we can consider the present controversy involving the orthodoxy and its critics simply as a continuation of a long-running and, as yet, unresolved debate. The second origin of dissatisfaction has been the orthodoxy itself because a necessary consequence of its ascendancy has been its exposure. Critics, having become conscious of inadequacies, have been driven to develop alternative approaches, approaches often rooted in a reappraisal of methodologies which had, in earlier times, fallen from favour.

These two themes – dissatisfaction with orthodox economics and corresponding interest in alternative forms or methods of analysis – recur regularly throughout the papers appearing in this volume. The organization of the book reflects the variety of approaches to the original question about the nature of political economy which appeared feasible. The opening paper by Shaun Hargreaves-Heap and Martin Hollis represents an investigation at perhaps the most abstract level, for it examines the philosophical underpinnings of the issue. It demonstrates the existence of a 'need for political economy' as a mode of analysis arising out of the logical inadequacies of the orthodox economic approach. The need having been established, the paper then explores the specific form which such a political economy ought to take, and this involves it in an examination of some of the variants to be discussed in the following section.

If one peruses the literature on economic matters couched in broader rather than narrower terms one comes across several groups of writers, all of which take pains to make regular and consistent use of the 'political economy' label. Clearly, these are self-professed political economists and an analysis of their ideas thus provides a second possible route to the answer for our original question. Under the general heading 'Approaches to Political Economy' the views of four schools are examined. First, Norman Barry looks at the Austrian School whose adherents include Böhm-Bawerk, von Mises and Hayek. Barry highlights the distinctive motivational and behavioural assumptions which characterize Austrian thought and he demonstrates the close correspondence between Austrian economic analysis and political values. Second, John Elliott discusses the American 'institutionalist' school of which Thorstein Veblen is perhaps the best-known member. Elliott identifies a number of themes in institutionalist thought, such as the analysis of capitalist development and the nature of collective action, and attention is focused particularly on the work of Commons and Galbraith. Third, modern developments in Marxian political economy are explored by Arun Bose. He is especially interested in the role of the labour theory of value in Marx's model, particularly in relation to modern Cambridge capital theory. Bose also indicates the prospects for future advances in the area. Finally in this section, Alan Hamlin examines the work of the 'public choice' school which includes writers such as James Buchanan. Hamlin's particular concern is to contrast the contractarian nature of the public choice approach with the more utilitarian stance of orthodox economics.

The final avenue to the original question is the exploration of 'Themes in Political Economy'. This involves the examination of particular subject areas in general terms, either to understand how different analytical approaches have actually been made or to investigate the relevance of a theme for any or all of the schools of political economy. This section of the book opens with Bruno Frey's appraisal of the current state of politico-econometric modelling. He is interested particularly in the modelling of government policy behaviour and comparisons are made between the performances of econometric and politico-econometric models. My own paper is concerned with international analysis. It compares the neo-classical paradigm with that currently being used by political economists, examines current foci of concern and appraises the strengths of the international political economy approach. Finally, Roger Bowles examines the nature of property and its significance in the context of the operation of an economic system. The relation of property to law, and law to markets, is discussed, as is the origin and enforcement of property rights.

When I initially solicited the contributions for this volume I had little idea as to what the eventual outcome might be. Such was indeed the intention for, as I have explained, I hoped for individual responses rather than papers prepared along preconceived or prearranged lines. Each paper (my own included) was written with only minimal guidance regarding the likely content of the others. On reading through the completed volume it becomes abundantly clear that differences of opinion exist. Given economists' reputation for disagreement this is perhaps not at all surprising. I confess to having come across arguments which seem to me to be unacceptable and others about which I remain uncertain; I am sure that each individual contributor is going to feel the same. Editors are not censors, however, nor are they referees. Such contradictions as are contained herein must remain, if only to demonstrate that we are still a very long way from an homogeneous political economy. These differences notwithstanding there are, it seems to me, certain parallels between the various perspectives offered and I shall say more on this matter in the concluding section of the book.

1

Bread and Circumstances:
The Need for Political Economy*

SHAUN HARGREAVES-HEAP AND MARTIN HOLLIS

Microeconomic textbooks bristle with alert maximizers. Shoppers adjust the utility of the mth apple to that of the nth pear. Businessmen skate along cost curves in a finely tuned zest for profit. Preferences are fully ordered, information perfect and calculations faultless. Markets clear to the mutual benefit of firms and households. This is the ideal-type case. If actual economies are more sluggish, then they should be made more ideal. Perhaps, for instance, their public sectors are too large or their workers mistaken about the future rate of inflation. This is in the spirit of the monetarism and supply-side economics which many governments are pursuing. Critics are startled to find a theory so distant from real life in its abstractions given such power to shape it in practice. Their doubts about both its truth and its uses sum to a disquiet about the whole basis of the neo-classical or positive economics, which are our academic orthodoxy.

The centre of unease is the set of highly schematic assumptions, which abstract from the bustle of a living economy and translate the business of production and exchange into logical space. The broad complaint is of lack of realism and, in what follows, we shall fasten on two aspects of it. One is the abstraction by which men and women become utility-maximizing individuals and the other is the artifice, which sets a boundary between their economic activity and the rest of their social and political lives. Our aim is to demonstrate the need for political economy. The groundwork will be laid in the first section and brought to life with an example from labour economics in the

*We should like to thank Ian Steedman and our colleagues at the University of East Anglia, especially Steve Rankin, for comment on an earlier draft.

second. By then the boundary between the economic and the political or social will have been breached, in readiness for the final section, where we shall try to suggest what sort of political economy we need.

I

We begin with some definitions, partly to make it clear what we mean by terms like 'orthodoxy' and partly as a way of introducing some issues in economic theory, where we believe that economics and philosophy come together in the service of political economy.

By 'orthodoxy' we refer to the kind of economics, especially to the kind of microeconomics, commonly taught in the schools and universities of Western Europe, America and other places where Walras, Marshall and Samuelson are celebrated. Readers will know roughly what we mean but precision is not easy. Common labels are 'neo-classical economics' and 'positive economics' but that sets a puzzle at once, since it is not plain that they label quite the same thing and there is no entirely standard practice to follow. So, without contradicting the textbooks, we shall use the labels for two distinct components of the orthodoxy, which are combined in the familiar approach. Economic science (like others) attempts to produce a true picture of its world by applying a proper scientific method. We shall use 'neo-classical economics' to name the broad orthodox picture and 'positive economics' to name the orthodox account of proper scientific method. This is a device for separating an economic from a philosophical angle of vision but, since we shall not be trying to breed dissent by playing one off against the other, it should not be a contentious device. For, although denying that orthodoxy can be defined by its method alone, we shall specify only as little of an orthodox ontology as we need to start us off.

The neo-classical picture is of the economy as an interplay between utility-maximizing individuals and profit-maximizing firms. Crucial are the exogenous or 'given' elements in these optimizing activities. These are individuals' preferences, the production technology and the institutional context of the interplay. Shadings and qualifications could be added but the central message is constant: individual preferences determine economic outcomes within a given market structure, subject to constraints imposed by the available technology. The message says nothing of social and political influences. They belong to the frame, not to the picture, and the course of economic transactions can be understood from within accordingly.

That is too baldly stated to be more than a reminder; but we are confident of it, because of the individualism at the core of neo-classical economics. Economic agents are separate individuals, who act on their given preferences and choose rationally from the options available whatever will best satisfy those preferences. Whatever shapes the preferences or constrains the options is an externality. Society and politics function as precursors of preference and as parameters of choice but agents once in the market do (or try to do) the rational economic thing. A transaction is a set of individual economic choices and can be understood as such. This individualism has moral and political overtones but at bottom it is a factual thesis: people are individuals; they act through rational choice; and agency is a relation between preference, choice and expected outcome.[1] To question it, as we shall later, is to doubt the whole neo-classical picture.

The picture goes nicely with the method of science endorsed by positive economics. The broad idea is that science explores an ordered realm, independent of our conjectures about it. We capture its workings in statements of laws, describing what always happens in particular initial conditions. There is nothing eternally given or grandly inevitable about these laws – or, rather, even if they were the laws of forces and mechanisms, we could not know it, because our knowledge of matters of fact is only empirical. Experience can reveal what is, was, will be or is always the case but not what must be (or ought to be). So laws are nothing grander than hypotheses which succeed in predicting what experience will find to be the case.

The task of positive economics, as Milton Friedman (1953, pp. 4–7) expressed it in his famous essay, is 'to provide a system of generalisations that can be used to make correct predictions about the consequences of any change in circumstances'. This is to be done by 'the development of a "theory" or "hypothesis" that yields valid and meaningful (i.e. not truistic) predictions about phenomena not yet observed'. The theory is to be a blend of two components, a 'language' and a 'body of substantive hypotheses designed to abstract essential features of a complex reality'. In the former role 'theory has no substantive content; it is a set of tautologies. Its function is to act as a filing system. . . .' In its latter role 'theory is to be judged by its predictive power for the class of phenomena which it is intended to explain'. The essay remains a storm centre even among the orthodox, because of Friedman's contention that, since only the success of prediction matters, the realism of assumptions does not. But he indisputably catches the spirit of a positive approach to scientific method in economics. Positive economics is an empirical science to be judged by its predictions.

These brisk remarks belie the subtleties surrounding positive philosophy of science and we have no space to plunge in. But one matter must be raised for reference later. By every account of positive (or any other) economics the testing of theories is not straightforward. For instance a theory which implies that firms maximize profits is not simply refuted by finding firms which do not. The hypothesis at stake is that *under certain conditions* firms maximize profits and it cannot be refuted unless the conditions hold. Predictions are thus issued, *ceteris paribus* or other things being equal. One particular orthodox use of *ceteris paribus* clauses is to prevent hypotheses about economic behaviour being wrongly refuted by interventions in the economy from the larger society of which it is a part. For example even under general conditions of imperfect competition firms will not behave as the economist predicts, if governments stop them; but that is not to be held against the theory of imperfect competition. Nor will workers price their labour as they would in a competitive market, if there are social norms to prevent it; but the economist is not expected to learn sociology before saying his piece.

That may sound a reasonable enough restriction both on the scope for experience to refute hypotheses and on the scope of economics as an explanation of social life. In all sciences predictions are issued *ceteris paribus*. The law of gravity, for instance, yields the prediction that two bodies will attract each other in inverse proportion to the square of their distance apart, *if* there is no interference by other bodies. Biology predicts the growth of a rabbit population, *provided that* (among other things) landowners do not offer a reward for dead rabbits. Just as the physicist can say what difference an interfering body would make, so too the economist can allow for degrees of market imperfection. Just as the biologist has no duty to allow for landowners, so too the economist need not explain his parameters. So why are the *ceteris paribus* clauses of economics so prone to arouse suspicion?

The most general answer is that, in the eyes of some critics, orthodox theory is so well guarded by its *ceteris paribus* clauses that it is irrefutable. There often seems to be no independent way of testing the theory, so that the failure of prediction would refute it, as distinct from showing merely that 'other things' are 'unequal'.[2] In that case it would fail Popper's (1963) test for distinguishing a science from a pseudo-science – a charge which the orthodox are bound to take very seriously. This is too general a matter for now, however. More specifically, critics, who fly the flag of political economy, complain that other things will *never* be equal for a theory which starts by assuming that economic activity goes on in a social and political vacuum. It is not at all like biologists, rabbits and landowners. Economic events are occurrences in the life of a society and social occurrences are (usually) economic events. When power workers move up or down the wages league, this economic change has political consequences, which change the labour market. When immigration laws are altered, this political fact affects the conduct of bargaining, the level of wages, the price of goods and other matters on the economic agenda. For a complex society the *ceteris paribus* clauses cannot be treated just as a frame.

Were the objection merely that economic events have social and political effects and *vice versa*, it might be enough to retort that academic life is too short to allow for everything. The objection (witness Steedman, 1980) goes deeper, however. It is also that economic events *are* social or political events. The economy includes all production, exchange and distribution of goods and services. Production, exchange and distribution are social activities. They are rule-governed practices, whose rules differ within and between societies. Like all practices, they are regulated and constituted by rules for their proper conduct. To describe them is to specify their governing norms (although these yield neither a full nor a final account, as we shall see). Even religious norms guide the ways in which people treat each other in everyday working life and hence guide the production, exchange and distribution of goods and services. Rabbits can multiply without landowners: people cannot produce, exchange and distribute without a fabric of social rules.

Something more is required of positive economics than a gesture to the boundaries drawn between natural sciences. The same goes for the parallel with the laws of gravity, stated for two bodies, *ceteris paribus*. The analogy here is with orthodox responses to the undoubted fact that preferences change not only because of social or political changes but also because of what happens in the market. It does not worry physicists to think that the behaviour of bodies is determined by the previous state of the system and the laws governing mass in motion. Indeed this is precisely what they do think. But neo-classicists do not believe that economic transactions are a mere consequence of the previous state of the economy and laws of economic motion. Markets can have feedback effects on preferences but they cannot determine them fully. If they did, that would destroy the crucial space kept for individual decision by brutally reversing the order of explanation between individual actions and market states. (That is also a further reason why the dynamics of the wider society can be allowed to shape parameters but must not so dictate choices that economic agents become a mere throughput.) The *ceteris paribus* clauses are not just a convenient, if artificial, way of separating the individual from the system (and the economic from the political or social). They embody the individualism of neo-classical economics and must be upheld by insisting on this individualism.

The crux, then, is the picture of individual decision-makers within a framework of institutions and it is vital that what happens within the frame is the result, for the most part, of calculated choice. Neither market institutions nor the dynamics of the wider society can be the determining factor. What use, critics ask, is an economic theory which starts by assuming that economic activity goes on in a social and political vacuum? The question cannot be parried by a broad appeal to the role of *ceteris parabus* clauses in all sciences. It needs a substantive affirmation of the neo-classical picture. We shall next list three ways of responding to the challenge and then complete our sketch with a reminder of the dissenting claim made by traditional political economy.

The first way of parrying doubts is to reaffirm a pure individualism and show that, despite appearances, neo-classical theory is right about economic activity: that there truly is a realm where individual decisions (and their interplay) explain what happens, with the *ceteris paribus* clauses marking a genuine boundary. The exact placing and policing of the boundary is no doubt to be done in co-operation with other sciences, which lie across it, and they too have their *ceteris paribus* conditions, which economics helps to fill in. If a pure individualist picture of agents is right, then an unrepentant answer is best also; and, even if only partly right, it may still be a good enough answer for the economic activity, which orthodoxy studies.[3]

That reply will not suit institutionalists. The second response also makes the social and political exogenous to a realm of individual decision and interaction but adds that exogenous institutional factors often help to explain much about events inside the realm. The drawing of a boundary is warranted, because some analysis can usefully be done from within; but a fuller story is often needed too, especially to prevent the bias associated with treating an endogenous variable as if it were exogenous.[4]

This is a temporizing response and many institutionalists in fact go on to modify the pure individualist picture. For example Galbraith (1973, pp. 39–40) argues that 'the firm is required . . . to control or seek to control the social environment in which it functions. It must plan not only its own operations: it must also, to the extent possible, plan the behaviour of people and the state as these affect it.' Corporate growth is the response to this imperative. 'Growth both enhances power over prices, costs, consumers, suppliers, the community and the state and also rewards . . . those who bring it about. This growth, with the associated exercise of power, is the primal force by which economic society is altered.' Corporate growth holds the key to understanding economic evolution: the individual is subordinate and the real currency is power, which recognizes no border between the economic, the social and the political. By now, however, the appeal to institutional factors is straining neo-classicism to the limit. If power is the control of individuals by institutions, then there is an urgent need to decompose institutions into the individuals who wield it. Otherwise institutionalism will not serve to buttress and extend orthodoxy but will turn into an awkward fifth column.

The third and most ambitious response is accordingly what we shall dub the new political economy or NPE. It treats the separation of economic and social as an artifice for the ambitious reason that, in truth, human beings are moved by individualistic economic motives in *all* realms of life. For instance people obey the laws of government or the norms of their peer groups because they calculate that to do so will best help to satisfy their own desires. In this spirit 'economic' theories of democracy, voting, gift-giving, friendship and other forms of social exchange have been advanced, with the sources of the utility, which agents maximize, broadened to include power or status. Friedman (1977, p. 460) himself has seen the attractions of exporting economic analysis to the anatomy of social and political behaviour and then reimporting the results to strengthen the orthodox approach. Discussing the future development of economic theory in his Nobel lecture, he suggested that 'it will have to treat at least some political phenomena not as independent variables . . . but as themselves determined by economic events as endogenous variables . . . This stage will, I believe, be greatly influenced . . . by the application of economic analysis to political behaviour, a field in which the pioneering work has been done by Stigler and Becker as well as by Kenneth Arrow, Duncan Black, Anthony Downs, James Buchanan and Gordon Tullock and others.' That is, in effect, to accept the temporizing institutionalist response but then to maintain the integrity of orthodox economics by a take-over of the institutional domain. It is an important and growing tendency, for which we propose the slogan '*social relations are market relations*'.

The three standard responses thus are firstly the unrepentant reassertion of a pure economic (individualist) realm, at least for many economic purposes, secondly a recognition of institutional factors, which may put a query over the individualism, and thirdly an ambitious response to the query from the new political economy, extending economic individualism to the analysis of institutions. All three are in the spirit of the orthodoxy, although the institutionalist one threatens to strain it, and are thus in contrast with the traditional claims made for political economy. Here too the separation of economic and social is seen as an artifice but for a reason which takes the institutionalist response much further. Social and political institutions permeate the economy and affect all transactions between individuals. In the strongest versions this is ultimately because 'in the social production which men carry on they enter into definite relations that are indispensable and independent of their will; these relations of production correspond to a definite stage of development of the material powers of production', as Marx (1913, p. 11) put it. He continued, 'The sum total of these relations of production constitutes the economic structure of society – the real foundation, on which rise legal and political superstructures and to which correspond definite forms of social consciousness.' That is to breach the orthodox boundary both by explaining the market from without and by rejecting the picture of individual decision-makers, even if the ultimate factor is an economic one. But it would be wrong to suggest that traditional political economists (even Marx!) always go so far and we shall defer further discussion to the final part of the essay. For the moment we are content to catch the spirit with the rival, if ambiguous, slogan: '*market relations are social relations*'.

II

These various responses to our question about the boundary are very broad and abstract so far. To bring them to life, we shall next rehearse a puzzle set by the current economic scene. During a recession in a capitalist economy wage levels might naturally be expected to fall dramatically. To be precise, were the labour market perfectly competitive, they would fall to a point where each worker, who would otherwise be unemployed, would just prefer to work, provided that there was an employer, who would just find it profitable to employ him at that wage. The labour market is not, of course, as free as this. But it is still puzzling to find wages as high as they are, when unemployment is rising so notably. Offhand, trades between employers and employed seem not to exhaust the possibilities for mutually beneficial exchange. In this section we shall focus the previous abstract responses in turn and then look for a standpoint for judging among them.

Orthodox explanations of an unrepentant sort usually rely on the growing 'contract' literature. The early contract literature was able to generate stickiness as an optimal response by orthodox agents to real demand variations, when workers were risk averse, employers were risk neutral and there was something like a state-funded unemployment insurance scheme.[5] Later contract theory has focused on the costs of negotiating contracts and the difficulties of writing fully contingent contracts. The idea is that, if it is costly to renegotiate contracts and contracts do not cover every contingency, then 'inappropriate' wages will be observed when an uncovered contingency arises, and wages will appear to be 'sticky'.[6] These explanations, however, seem to us to depend too much on what is external to the analysis. Why is there a state-funded unemployment insurance scheme? Does its operation not interact with the level of unemployment? Why do problems of moral hazard arise in the construction of contingent contracts? What makes the cost of negotiating a contract so high?

Orthodoxy remains quiet on these questions. What distinguishes the institutionalist response is the attempt to answer them. Gordon (1982) is a good example, also showing how the institutionalist explanation typically goes beyond individual preferences. He is concerned with international differences in wage stickiness, which he seeks to explain by history. The historical inheritance is not the same in all countries. This accounts for the different contract negotiating costs and hence explains the varying degrees of wage stickiness. Akerlof (1980) has a different institutional move to transcend individual preferences. He traces stickiness to the social norm of concern for reputation. People do not want just to be rich; they want to be 'rich and famous'. So, although unemployed workers might become 'richer' by bidding down the wage rate to gain employment, they may not do it, if it means breaking a code of behaviour and also makes them 'infamous'.

Any institutionalist response to wage stickiness will make much of the role of trade unions as institutions which influence wage setting. The distinctive contribution of the new political economy is to model unions with preferences which can be mapped as indifference curves in the wage/employment space. Quite conventionally shaped indifference curves can be generated by a variety of political processes within the union – for example, they can be interpreted as the utility function of the typical union member or as the isovote function which the union bureaucrat seeks to maximize, when pursuing the re-election objective – and the analysis proceeds as if we were studying an individual maximizing a mathematically well-behaved utility function.[7] Such well-behaved preferences do not directly cause the wage stickiness in these models. However, it is not hard to imagine political processes that would produce less conventional utility functions, which would contribute more directly to wage stickiness. For example, if career labour markets develop in a firm as a result of specific human capital, then a seniority system can be expected to develop and to identify those who would suffer lay-offs when demand contracts. It is then a matter of simple electoral arithmetic to see that, unless the number of lay-offs is likely to be very large and/or members' preferences are interdependent, a winning coalition of senior members preferring employment reductions to wage cuts can always be put together. In effect, the senior workers will always prefer lay-offs because they are unlikely to be affected, and they will always count for a disproportionate amount in union electoral politics because they show less job turnover and are the more permanent members of the union.[8]

The new political economy stresses the importance of institutions like unions, but interprets their behaviour as a derivative of their members' individualistic preferences and the process through which they are aggregated. In contrast, unions in Marxian political economy are to be understood as institutions which have developed in the specific context of the class struggle under capitalism. Their logic and behaviour depend upon the course of the struggle, and a study of this conflict will prove more revealing than any study which begins with individualistic preferences, Wage setting is yet another arena of the class struggle, with whatever implications that may have for explaining stickiness. Variables, like state-funded insurance schemes, which acted as jokers in the 'contract' literature pack, now become dependent within a wider framework. It is understandable that the costs of negotiating (or renegotiating) contracts will be high, if the process entails reopening a series of essentially irreconcilable conflicts. In general a willingness to explain the individual by the social (thus reversing the neo-classical direction) endogenizes some interesting variables, although that will only make for hot air unless a precise theory of power and social change is forthcoming too.

Marxian political economy also alters the setting of the puzzle about wage stickiness. Orthodox theory postulates an equilibrium value, which is the expected outcome of the pursuit of self-interest in the labour market, and the puzzle arises because it apparently fails to materialize. Marxian theory postulates no such equilibrium value and so no tendency towards it. To that extent wages merely reflect whatever happens to be the current balance of power. Nevertheless unemployment swells the 'reserve army of the unemployed', thus, one might suppose, depressing wage levels. On the other hand institutions like unions help to offset the effects of a growing reserve army on those still employed, with a success which depends partly on human factors like awareness, militancy and skill at organizing.[9] So there is still a puzzle, although now one about power and influence. To make it more tantalizing, the lapidary remarks, quoted earlier, about relations of production as the 'real foundation' contrast with the equally famous words from Marx (1979, p. 103) that, 'Men make their own history, but they do not make it just as they please; they do not make it under circumstances chosen by themselves.' But that takes us into the topics of the next section.

Not all political economists are of Marxian stripe. The slogan was 'market relations are social relations'. It implies that workers and employers do not strike their bargains as the economic individuals of orthodox theory. Bargaining is usually a group or collective activity. Persons taking part in it are usually there as members or representatives of groups. They usually have a role to play and norms to adhere to. They are influenced by the doings of government and by the political and social life of their community. They have ties and aims extending beyond the market. These points take us only as far as institutionalism but they cry out for a further explanation. Some political economists claim to find it in a system or structure of determining forces, others in the essentially social nature of human agents and of the relationships among them. Political economists see institutions as a gateway but they do not agree on the sort of explanation to which the gate leads.

We have glanced at four ways of relating levels of wages to levels of unemployment. The first was orthodoxy reasserted – a thesis that stickiness is either merely apparent (in that, for example, income is being shifted from later periods to earlier) or merely temporary, until market forces work through. Even this response admits to important discontinuities, due to state benefits, union power and so forth, and hence cannot be left at that. The second, institutionalist, move was to bring some political and social institutions within the scope of economics. But we deemed it a temporizing response, because it so plainly raises a query about these institutional factors without answering it. Thirdly, the new political economy gives the robust answer that institutions are sets of actors moved socially and politically by the same economic motives which move agents to maximize utility in the market. This ambitious economic individualism is disputed, fourthly, by any political economy which rallies to the slogan that market relations are social relations. Our own view, looking at present levels of wages in capitalist economies hit by recession, is that the institutionalist step is necessary but not sufficient. If that is granted, at least for purposes of argument, then an advance to some kind of political economy is called for. What kind shall it be?

III

To find out, we shall return to the wider positions, which the responses to wage stickiness illustrated, and then, having come down decisively against NPE, end by identifying the hallmarks of what we regard as merit in a political economy. Orthodoxy and NPE belong to a tradition in social thought older and wider than economics, one which has been often acclaimed and often criticized. From much which might be discussed, we shall pick out the individualism and the instrumental account of social relations and institutions, which goes with it. These distinctive elements are guarded by *ceteris paribus* clauses, which, we shall contend, are doing too much work and hence compromise the explanatory power of the theory. The final crux will be its failure to explain social change.

We left NPE under a banner inscribed 'social relations are market relations'. There need be nothing defensive or *ad hoc* in extending orthodoxy in this way. Although often termed 'rational economic man', the agent portrayed in orthodox economics is not peculiarly 'economic'. He is a broad *homo psychologicus*, a general proposition about people at large. He embodies a psychological account of human nature, which is older than the science of economics and is familiar outside it (for instance, to students of Hobbes's *Leviathan*, Hume's philosophy of action, Bentham's utilitarianism or B. F. Skinner's theory of behaviour). NPE is thus not exploiting a novelty but appealing to a wider habit of social thought, to which the orthodoxy already belongs.

There are two components to this *homo economicus* (or *psychologicus*). One is an instrumental or means/ends definition of rationality, which makes the rationality of choice a matter of how efficient a solution it is to a maximizing problem and is silent about the source and worth of the ends pursued. This is so much in the foreground of the orthodox portrait that it is easy to misstate the other component, motivation. It is easy to assume that microeconomics must take self-interest as the motivating force of economics. As F. Y. Edgeworth (1881, p. 16) put it, 'The first principle of economics is that every agent is actuated solely by self-interest.' Adam Smith (1970, p. 119) gave similar advice – 'It is not from the benevolence of the butcher, the brewer or the baker that we expect our dinner, but from their regard to their own self-interest. We address ourselves not to their humanity but to their self-love, and never talk to them of our own necessities but of their advantages.' That may be good practical sense but it is not definitive. Orthodox economics does not rule out altruism, moral concern or what are sometimes called 'ethical preferences' and indeed NPE often appeals to their existence. But there is still a subtler assumption about motivation, which is philosophical and worth spelling out.

At its most general, the thesis is that action results from desire plus belief, with desire supplying the motor. Belief includes the information needed for rational choice plus the calculations or deliberations which disclose the expected utilities. None of this would produce action, were it not that the agent had 'desires' (or wants or preferences), which the action is aimed to satisfy. This thesis makes economic and social relations instrumental, in the sense that the agent enters into them not for their own sake but to further some desire of his own. The point needs to be handled carefully. It would be too crude to make rational economic man an agent who knows the price of everything and the value of nothing. Nonetheless, even when an agent has a desire to benefit others, it matters that the desire is his own and that he acts on it in order to increase his level of satisfaction.

Here lies the key to institutions in NPE. Since all motivation is of individuals by their own preferences, institutions result from individual decisions and are, so to speak, deposited by the passage of time. Groups and coalitions, too, although conveniently treated as units, are sets of individuals and are moved by the desires of the individuals composing them. These desires, we repeat, need not be self-interested in the sense of 'selfish'. That is a further assumption which NPE often makes, perhaps sometimes for good empirical reasons but not because individualism requires it. Individualism requires only that institutions, groups and coalitions move as individuals combine to move them, each acting on desires of his own. This is enough to make institutional and collective action always instrumental.

Orthodoxy and NPE will stand or fall by the merit of this individualism. Were they committed to the coarser view that self-interest, meaning self-centredness, is the only motivating force, our task would be much easier. We would merely have to prove that norms are not simply tactical devices used by individuals to impose their will on others. To tackle the subtler and more philosophical kind of individualism, we need to go rather deeper into the part played by norms in economic action. We shall do it under three headings, constraint, enablement and commitment. A norm is a constraint, where an agent would prefer to do what he could do in its absence. A norm is an enablement, where an agent prefers to do what he could not do without it. It is a commitment, where an agent upholds it even in the absence of sanctions. Let us see what market individualism says about norms under these headings.

Its first thought is that norms are a constraint on rational choice. This reflects a long-standing trust in the efficiency of free markets, aided by the reflection that norms are pointless, if they command us to do what we want to do, and constraining if they do not. This is only a first thought and will be overtaken in a moment. But it picks up our earlier remark that, for market individualism, relationships are instrumental. If the unit of analysis is a rational individual with given desires or tastes, trying to maximize expected utility, then co-operation will be tactical and its form contractual. We again enter our previous *caveat*: we see no grounds for presuming that people's choices in life are essentially tactical nor that anything is achieved by supposing it 'as if' true for the science of economics.

Norms also enable. They do so unmysteriously, when they give individuals a needed assurance of how their fellows will act. For instance, if a handful of disaffected workers can be dismissed but the bulk of the workforce cannot, then each would rather do what a norm assures him that others will do but cannot risk it without the norm. The general condition is one listed over a century ago by J. S. Mill (1970) among the 'large and conspicuous exceptions' to the 'great principle of political economy that individuals are the best judges of their own interest' and to 'the practical maxim that the business of society can best be performed by private and voluntary agency'. For, he says (1970, V, xi, 12), 'the force of law is often needed not to overrule the judgement of individuals but to give effect to it'. The same applies to other sorts of norms under the same condition that each person needs an assurance that others will do what would be best if (but only if) all do it. It is simply not true that norms are pointless if they bid us do what we already want to do. Whether they are then pointless depends also on what others would do in their absence. Norms can thus help satisfy wants which would otherwise be frustrated.

That much is uncontentious and serves only to correct a false presumption in ways which orthodoxy can accept. However, norms enable in a subtler way. They not only help pre-existent desires to fruition but also create relationships and hence help to shape the identity of human agents. In the picture drawn by NPE a sales director is an individual who happens to be a sales director and a loyal trade unionist, an individual who happens to value fraternal solidarity. For, whatever one's place in the division of labour and whatever norms and relationships go with it, one is at heart a utility-maximizing individual. This is why it is both plausible and peculiar to claim that the orthodoxy holds a key to the understanding of all aspects of social life in all societies. It is plausible, because (even by Marx's account) men make their own history and every choice can be made to fit the model of individuals moved by desire in the light of their beliefs. It is peculiar because it makes all perform-ance of roles and adherence to norms external to the self. This is certainly contentious.

The third heading, commitment, brings out the general peculiar-ity. Commitment to a role, norm or principle gives an agent reasons for action, for which, finally, he has no further reason. The trade unionist committed to the labour movement does not have or need a further calculation to show how utility is maximized by accepting union objectives and disciplines. A coarse version of NPE, relying on self-interest, would have to reject this point altogether and insist that trade unionists were in it for what they could get out of it. In that case we would retort that even economic agents do not live by bread alone (whatever Adam Smith may have thought of bakers!). Some role-playing is tactical and some adherence to norms is for private ends; but we are not ourselves inclined to think it always so. At any rate it cannot be proved so, for the Popperian reason that, if obvious devotion to duty, beyond the call of duty, by principled people is invariably ascribed to self-love, then nothing could count as refuting the hypothesis, which therefore ranks as pseudo-science. Meanwhile, norms will not do their work of enabling and constraining, unless most of those who profess them in public also, for the most part, subscribe to them in private. Otherwise (to cut the story short, where we do not have space to take it seriously) the trade union movement would soon be brought to a halt by the prisoner's dilemma. Our retort to a coarse version of NPE is that men make themselves a history which they value and they do it by means which they think honourable: or, at any rate, that has as good a claim to be a true generalization as anything to the contrary.

A subtler version of NPE, which makes it axiomatic merely that people are moved by their own preferences, can accept that agents do not live by self-interest alone. To incorporate the point, however, it has to treat loyalty (or any other commitment) as a source of utility in itself or as an inelasticity of demand arising from the strength of taste. This, in its subtler way, is just as odd, granted that orthodoxy takes pride in being a descriptive science. It characterizes people as bundles of preferences, whereas the people so described do not see themselves as bundles but as the particular human beings, whose preferences they are. Loyalty is thus, in the eyes of its possessor, not a taste but a commitment which partly defines the self. This, however, is deeper and more philosophical water than we can explore now.[10] NPE will again be tempted to reply that experience confirms its view of the motivation which accounts for institutions and norm-guided behaviour. But that would put it in the uneasy position of arguing for a philosophical view on empirical grounds. So the charge that experience is being laundered with the help of *ceteris paribus* clauses would have added force. Let us call that a stand-off for the moment and turn directly to two deficiencies, as we see them, of dealing with institutions along the lines of market individualism.

The first deficiency of a political economy which relies on the tactical choices made by individuals to explain institutions arises when we consider particular institutions. Joint benefits provide the logic for instrumental co-operation between individuals in NPE; but joint benefits can arise from very varied institutions and NPE gives no reason to expect any particular form. Will self-interested individuals arrive at an industrial, general or craft union as a co-operative solution? Will they choose the institutions of collective bargaining or workers' control? Such questions matter, because the wage structure will be influenced by the precise institutional arrangements.[11] Hence it ought to be a strength of political economy that it has some answers. But, starting from orthodox premisses, we find ourselves unable to say anything, except that all these institutions create joint benefits and are therefore intelligible from an instrumental, individualistic perspective. Yet what distinguishes types of institution in this area is precisely how the joint benefits of collective action are distributed. That calls for an analysis of power in the resolution of conflict and NPE lacks one.[12]

The natural complement to NPE is a pluralist account of power. If power is generated through coalitions of individuals, and shifts as coalitions shift with changing issues, then it is diffused to individuals and varies suitably according to their preferences and skills in building coalitions. Whether this in fact helps is a long story[13] but, *prima facie* at least, there are grounds for doubt. Firstly, a puzzle about the distribution of benefits seems simply to be transferred to one about the distribution of power. Secondly, it is far from plain that power can be analysed without making a distinction between desires and real interests, which is awkward for the kind of individualism espoused by orthodoxy and NPE. Thirdly, the persistence of patterns of power would require a constancy of preferences, which seems likelier to be a consequence of the pattern than a cause of it. Institutions are not simply a passive reflection of patterns of power, but also help in shaping what people do, can do and want to do. Power, in short, is a tricky concept for individualists and they cannot count on being able to do anything with it.

The other deficiency concerns the explanation of institutional change. NPE will have to trace it to changes in preferences and changes in technology. That would be all very well, if NPE could account for either. For the former the snag is still that NPE is premissed on individuals with given tastes. So changes in preferences have to be presented as feedback from previous decisions on pre-existent tastes. Otherwise market events in particular and social events in general might be found to determine tastes, thus reversing the direction of explanation essential to the theory. Yet tastes plainly do change and such changes, for NPE, produce or imply changes in interests (rather than being the effect of them). That leaves a mysterious hole, ready-made for a rival political economy. Changes in technology are less awkward, in so far as they result from the bright ideas of individuals. But that is not their only source and so we wish to put a query over their proper explanation as well.[14]

In illustration, our remarks about wage-levels can be continued. It is widely acknowledged that in several European countries in the late 1960s there was a surge in wages. (A 'surge' here means that wages were much higher than the previous historical relationship between inflationary expectations, unemployment and wage changes would lead one to predict.)[15] Typically orthodox explanations have looked to a shift in the association between the recorded level of unemployment and the degree of excess demand/supply in the labour market. Any particular level of unemployment actually signalled a tighter labour market in the late 1960s than it had done in the years before. This shift occurred because the introduction of earnings-related unemployment benefits encouraged greater 'search' unemployment and increased the incidence of unemployment as disguised leisure. Hence, any particular level of unemployment in the late 1960s contained fewer people who genuinely constituted excess supply than in previous years, and consequently wages rose faster in these circumstances than was expected on the basis of previous experience.[16]

This orthodox account does not explain the crucial element which it isolates, the change in unemployment benefits. NPE is better equipped to include political factors, for instance an electoral majority in favour of higher benefits or an increase in the militancy of trade union members in the context of a bargaining model of wage determination. Again, however, we await an explanation of the preference changes of voters or unionists. This is not just a surly demand that in order to explain something one must first explain everything. It is a complaint about the emptiness of citing a change in what people want as explaining why they act differently from before.[17] In a theory which makes preferences the motor of free action, of course there must have been a change in preferences! The key question, however, is how preferences were moving and it needs a sort of answer which could have been given *ex-ante*, not merely one which reconstructs after the event. For example the British 1979–83 Conservative government was disappointed by the high costs in unemployment, which went with the lowering of the rate of inflation. Advised by their favoured economists, they had been expecting a 'new realism' in wage bargaining. Instead the wage/employment relationship still behaved as it had in the late 1970s, thus keeping unemployment costs up. Why? That is a question about the determinants of preferences and they needed it answered *ex-ante*.

This cannot be done by an economic theory which makes change of preference and social change at large an exogenous matter. Both orthodoxy and NPE do so, thanks to their shared individualism. And, as Jon Elster (1978, p. 90) observes 'the approach to change through exogenous influence is just another case of passing the buck'. Economists cannot hope to influence policy convincingly, if they pass the buck at this point. Furthermore, especially with an account of scientific method which gives pride of place to prediction, failure to predict *ex-ante* is bound to go with failure to explain ex-post. For, with prediction and explanation two sides of the same coin, a generalization can be known to be explanatory after the event, only if it could have been relied on before it. This thought echoes our earlier remarks about methodology and prompts us to take them further now.

If economic science is to pin its faith on prediction, there must be an answer to the charge that its *ceteris paribus* clauses make its hypotheses irrefutable. So far we have confined the charge to the *ceteris paribus* clauses, which protect the core individualism of neo-classical theory, and have given reasons for saying that, judged by the positive rubric, the charge is well founded. But wider issues are at stake, not least the positive rubric itself. Many economic theorists are – or would like to be – Popperians. That should make them ambivalent about the methodology of positive economics. Popper's vintage works insist that the mark of a scientific hypothesis is its being refutable by a test of observation. But, as Popper also points out, testing involves concepts and hence the creative mental activity of arriving at concepts. So we are never the mere pupils of experience and our scientific judgements are never wholly passive.

When this line of thought is combined with Thomas Kuhn's (1970) reflections on paradigms (to say nothing of Feyerabend's (1975) subversive anarchy), positive faith in the power of independent empirical evidence to refute theories is heavily undermined. To hold the line at all, it is widely argued, one must grant an irreducible role to metaphysical commitment in science and then show how that leaves room for, or even strengthens, the idea of objective progress. The most favoured version is Lakatos's (1978) proposal that we think of scientific theories as 'research programmes', containing a meta-physical core and a protective belt of auxiliary hypotheses. (See also Latsis, 1976.) The belt absorbs the impact of contrary experience and to that limited extent theory responds to evidence. But the final question is no longer whether the theory is true but whether the research programme is 'degenerate' or 'progressive'. It is progressing, if it is evolving by throwing up novel predictions in response to unexpected facts, and degenerating, if it absorbs new, unwelcome facts by *ad hoc* adjustment.

Without plunging further in, we can now restate our complaint about neo-classicism in a more useful way. Individualism is the core of a research programme, which is 'degenerating'. When orthodoxy runs into the sorts of trouble we pointed to with wage stickiness,

NPE serves to strengthen the protective belt. But, since preference change and social change at large are exogenous, the belt can only protect by *ad hoc* adjustments. Conversely a research programme for which change was endogenous would have better prospects.

With this in mind, we return to the wage surge of the late 1960s, in order to commend the approach of Phelps Brown (1975, pp. 17–19). Worker attitude and outlook, he argues, are related to actual experience in the labour market, where 'the unprecedented maintenance of a high level of employment' after the Second World War helped to produce a major change.

> Year by year as the 1950s and 1960s went on, the older men, who had grown up in a world where job security took precedence over pay claims, were leaving the labour force, and their place was taken by entrants whose experience was to be of a demand for labour so sustained as to give the individual worker a substantial independence of the employer . . . it may be that the critical mass of the new outlook had been attained in a number of countries by 1968.

Notice how change is built in to the analysis. A tension is identified between worker attitudes and conditions in the labour market. The conditions come to affect the attitudes and the result is change. If that removes the tension, the change is once and for all. But a more complex set of tensions is possible. For instance, if attitudes also affect conditions – in particular if the wage 'responsibility' nurtured by the old outlook helped to maintain high levels of unemployment – then the wage surge will erode the conditions, which produced it, and so prepare the way for further changes in outlook. Phelps Brown thus gives an instructive example of how tensions may fruitfully be built in to the very core of a research programme.[18]

Our own preference is for a political economy with a core tension built in by the proposition that 'men make their own history but . . . they do not make it under circumstances chosen by themselves'. We are hostile both to a pure individualism, for which it is all a matter of men making their own history, and to a pure structuralism for which it is all circumstances not of their own choosing. The latter makes it easy to endogenize change by means of structural tensions,[19] but the former rightly reminds us not to pay too high a price for this advantage. In the rest of the paper we shall suggest how the two can be combined.

To make institutions endogenous is not simply to extend or add a dimension to the individualist neo-classical picture. It involves rethinking the notion of economic agency, so that economic actors can be regarded coherently as (more or less) rational role-players. That this is not simple becomes plain, if we contrast the two obvious ways of doing it. In NPE, as noted, it is done by treating norms as parameters of rational choice, whether because they are external constraints (rather like laws of nature) or because they are internalized and become given features of individuals' preferences. We have stated our objection to the resulting portrait of social actors, who, in our view, define their choices of means in moral terms, and find an identity in the relationships which they value. But that does not incline us to the opposite view that economic action can be explained by understanding only the institutional demands placed on role-players as if people were simply the voice of institutional interests. The playing of institutional roles is a flexible, creative exercise in stewardship, even when the player is neither less than fully committed nor troubled by role conflict. NPE is thus partly right to think of a role as a stock of reasons for action, to be used as a legitimating device in the course of negotiations which call for skill. But it is wrong, we contend, to think of them only in this way and to look for actors' real reasons only in their individual preferences. That misses the way in which human beings are historical persons, how they find themselves in circumstances not of their choosing.

For a promising way to read the tension between history as human handiwork and history as circumstance we advocate a return to the roots of political economy and especially to its concerns with value and change. Any economic theory needs an account of value, considered both broadly as why things are valued and restrictedly as why commodities exchange at particular prices. The account given by orthodoxy and NPE stems from the neo-classical picture of the economy as a set of interactions among rational individuals. Thus a market price reflects the interaction between utility-maximizing individuals and profit-maximizing firms and is a fair measure of social valuation, given the constraints of technology. Indeed there is little place for the very idea of 'social valuation', except as a shorthand for a consensus in valuation among the individuals, who are the units of orthodoxy and NPE. In such theories the consensus is forward-looking and of interest only as a pointer to prices in the near future; and it does not matter how the consensus originated, since the theory is content to leave questions of the past to other social sciences.

This strikes us as a profoundly ahistorical account, which glosses over the crucial fact that actors in markets are bearers of an inheritance of roles and power relations. Their valuations, attempted and achieved, are bound up with this inheritance and with the exercise of power. Exchange value measures social valuation, only in so far as social valuation reflects a balance of power. Equally, if preferences are to be treated as valuations, it is crucial that preferences are not independent of roles and power relations. These points are illustrated by our earlier notes on the labour market, where a neo-classical picture of economic actors did no justice to the institutional context. They are not so much a matter of filling in circumstances not of the actors' choosing but rather of explaining how history is made at all, namely by historically located persons. Political economy has always insisted that the market price of a commodity is a social phenomenon and, we submit, rightly so.

An ahistorical picture of actors also makes for *ad hoc* and *ex post* explanations of change. That is finally why we find the treatment of institutions by orthodoxy and NPE unsatisfactory. If institutions are absorbed merely by extending the individualist analysis of market behaviour to role-playing and the deposits of previous role-playing, then the sources of trouble with prediction are extended too. In contrast, we favour a political economist's view of institutions as a gateway between the rational reconstructions, which neo-classicists do so elegantly, and the real motivating relationships among institutional actors. Once through the gate, it becomes possible to seek the structural tensions, which political economy has always made the key to change.

These have been very preliminary remarks and they leave much unanswered, especially since we are refusing to see history as all circumstance and no choice. Although we do not think it true that 'social relations are market relations', we do not suppose NPE foolish in proposing it, since textbook market relations do embody an idea of choice. Nonetheless we submit that social relations, construed as we suggest, allow for a richer notion of choice. Our conclusion is that wisdom in economics starts with relations of production, which are social relations, thus explaining why markets cannot be studied in isolation. Philosophically this is also our final reason why orthodoxy is forced to overwork its *ceteris paribus* clauses and so fails by its own test of successful prediction. 'Other things' will never be 'equal' while economics abstracts the maximizing decision-maker from the human beings who think of themselves and conduct their affairs in quite different terms. That is a concluding remark in the explanatory mode. But it has a normative implication, which we endorse also. How people think of themselves affects the way they make their own history and economists are powerful guides. If orthodoxy were to succeed in getting us to see ourselves as maximizing individuals, bound only by a cash nexus or other instrumental relationships, and if it can get governments to treat us so, then, perversely, its predictions might fare better. That would be a terrible price for progress in economics. But, we repeat, market relations are social relations – and long may it remain so!

NOTES

1 For a study of the forms of individualism see Lukes (1973a); for a brief sketch, Lukes (1973b).
2 For instance, see Hollis and Nell (1975) especially chapters 1–4. On the related matter of the need to be able to tell a counter-example from an anomaly, see Kuhn (1970).
3 See Becker (1976) for the unrepentant individualist position and Hahn (1982b) for a more circumspect response in this vein.
4 Crotty (1973) provides an early discussion of the specification errors that arise when a government reaction function is ignored and instead government behaviour is treated as exogenous.
5 See Azariadis (1975), Baily (1974) and Gordon (1974).
6 Azariadis (1981), Gordon (1982) and Hall and Lilian (1979) survey and provide examples of the later developments in contract theory.
7 Oswald (1982) is an example which also provides extensive references.
8 This argument (along with many others) can be found in the survey article by Freeman and Medoff (1979).
9 Rowthorn (1980) provides a useful survey of Marx's and Marxist ideas on wages.
10 For further discussion see Sen (1976) and Hollis (1981).
11 For empirical evidence on wage structure, particularly for international comparisons, see Marsden and Saunders (1981).
12 Sen (1983) comments shrewdly on the failure of orthodoxy to discuss problems of conflict resolution.
13 See Lukes (1974).
14 Elster (1983) is a useful review of problems and methods, with instructive examples. See also Marglin (1974).
15 See Perry (1975), Nordhaus, (1972) and Sachs, (1979).
16 This is typical for the UK. For other countries, it is often argued that changes in the age/sex composition of the labour force also increased 'search' employment.
17 Becker and Stigler (1977), recognizing the emptiness, try to find an orthodox way of explaining at least some 'apparent' preference changes. It seems to us, however, that many of the problems simply recur. For example, reliance on costs of information begs the same questions as did reliance on costs of adjustment. Equally to invoke 'addiction' as the

result of individuals' planning to maximize utility with regard to interdependent time periods is to raise more questions than it answers.

18 For more about ideas of tension (or 'contradiction') see Elster (1978)
chapter 5 and Giddens (1979) chapter 4.

19 See, for example, Althusser (1969).

PART I

Approaches to Political Economy

2

The 'Austrian' Perspective

NORMAN P. BARRY

For more than a decade now there has been continuing talk of a 'crisis' in economic theory. Although the 'unity' that once characterized the teaching of economics was perhaps only a veneer that concealed a range of dissenting approaches and methodologies, the subject itself displayed a scientific maturity, with its use of universally applicable theory and sophisticated quantitative techniques, that was the envy of the other social sciences. However, the recent failure of the *strictly* predictive element in economics, especially that concerned with macroeconomics, has led many economists to question the scientific pretensions of their discipline and provoked a somewhat unhealthy period of introspection about its scope and methods. It is in this period of doubt and uncertainty that the 'Austrian' school of political economy, alongside Marxism and neo-Ricardianism, has begun to flourish as a distinctive style of economic reasoning.

Even to professional economists the notion that Austrian economics constitutes a distinct approach may seem strange since its most well-known exponents, Ludwig von Mises and Friedrich von Hayek, are normally seen as somewhat extreme interpreters of the general neo-classical tradition that dates from the 'marginalist revolution' of the 1870s. As we shall see below, this is a mistaken interpretation. But an even bigger error is to identify the Austrian tradition with that of the 'Chicago' school of economics. It is true that both schools espouse a fierce commitment to *laissez-faire* economics, 'monetarism' and political individualism, but the foundations of these principles are so different, and the politics that they generate so dissimilar, that it would be a gross error to present them as economic and ideological twins.

The name 'Austrian economics' now has no geographical connotations. It suggests an intellectual state of mind or particular orientation towards economic and social affairs which derives from the 'older' Austrian school but which is practised now largely by American economists and social theorists. The older Austrian school began with the publication of Carl Menger's (1840–1921) *Principles of Economics* in 1870. Although this, along with the contemporary work of Jevons and Walras, established a *general* theory of price based on subjective evaluation and marginal utility, and thereby overthrew the prevailing cost of production theory of value associated with the classical tradition of Smith, Ricardo and J. S. Mill, a better insight into the distinctive Austrian tradition may be found in Menger's later work, *Problems of Economics and Sociology* (1883). This arose out of the famous *Methodenstreit* (struggle over methods) between the Austrian and later German economists. The latter despised deductive theory and denied the possibility of general laws of human behaviour abstracted from time and place and favoured an historicist and crude empirical approach in which economic science was reduced to a description and cataloguing of particular events. Furthermore, the individualism of Menger was replaced by an organicism and holism in which allegedly observable entities such as the 'national economy' were made the objects of economic science.

Menger's immediate pupils and followers were Friedrich von Wieser (1851–1926) and Eugen Böhm-Bawerk (1851–1914); these two economists extended the concepts of utility and subjective value to the whole of the market economy and developed the marginal productivity theory of factor pricing. Of particular importance is Wieser's notion of opportunity cost, which was defined exclusively in subjectivist terms, and Böhm-Bawerk's theory of capital and interest in which he showed how saving and investment in a capitalist economy generate more 'roundabout' productive techniques, i.e., those that produce a greater supply of consumer goods in the long run. This was of particular importance in the refinement by Hayek of the Austrian theory of capital and the Mises-Hayek theory of the trade cycle.

Furthermore, both Wieser and Böhm-Bawerk made excursions into more general social theory. The latter produced the most devastating criticism of Marxist economics from a subjectivist point of view in his *Karl Marx and the Close of his System* (1896), as well as a more general critique of the economic logic of socialism. The former, surprisingly, was much more sympathetic to interventionism and was by no means convinced that an unhampered market economy would spontaneously maximize the greatest possible level of social welfare (Wieser, 1927).

The 'younger' Austrian school dates from Mises (1881–1973) and Hayek (born 1899). These two writers developed a distinctive Austrian approach to economic and social affairs. The major contributions of the members of the 'older' Austrian school were incorporated into the orthodox neo-classical tradition but Mises and Hayek (especially) were concerned to point out certain crucial differences between their approach and that orthodoxy, especially the 'general equilibrium' concept originated by Walras and developed by Pareto. Mises and Hayek always stressed that, because of the subjective nature of choice, the incessant change that characterizes the social world, the uncertainty that pervades human action and the impossibility of acquiring, centralizing and processing the knowledge (or information) that exists in a dispersed form in an economic system, an 'objective' and predictive 'science of economics', as envisaged by the successors of the Walrasian general equilibrium tradition, was an impossibility. It is these aspects of Austrian economics that have been seized upon, modified and made more sophisticated by contemporary American 'Austrian' economists such as Murray Rothbard and Israel Kirzner. While the contemporary orthodox economist, be he free market or otherwise, is obsessively concerned with objectification and measurement, contemporary Austrian economic theory is distinguished for its attempt to understand the basic features of *human* action and to explain theoretically the inter-relationships between acting men and their institutional environment. Thus, although Austrian economics is associated with political liberalism (and, in some cases, *laissez-faire* anarchism) it is not this that distinguishes it from other systems of thought. What characterizes the tradition is its belief that the existence of purposive and choosing men interacting in a social environment precludes the reduction of economics to the search for observed regularities or the discovery of mechanical laws from which quantitative predictions may be derived.

It follows from this that Austrian economists are deeply concerned with the methodological, epistemological and philosophical aspects of their subject. Of particular importance is their rejection of 'scientism' – Hayek's name for the uncritical adoption of the methods of natural science for the explanation of social phenomena. The unique subject matter of economics, man and his essential characteristics, prevents any behaviourist or mechanical interpretation of events. In Mises's words: 'The characteristic feature of man is precisely that he consciously acts. Man is homo agens, the acting animal' (Mises, 1978, p. 4).

In *The Counter-Revolution of Science*, Hayek argues that the conventional physicalist notion of causality is irrelevant to the social sciences because they deal 'not with the relations between things, but with the relations between men and things or the relations between man and man. They are concerned with man's actions, and their aim is to explain the unintended or undesigned results of the actions of many men' (1955, p. 25). Thus any positivism of the Chicago type in which the 'truth' of a purported economic regularity is established by direct observation, is specifically precluded.

The two key concepts in Austrian economic methodology are *individualism* and *subjectivism*. Methodological individualism holds that the only cognitive propositions in social science are those that can, in principle, be reduced to propositions about individual volitions and actions.[1] The error of methodological *collectivism* is its claim that regularities can be discovered between statistical aggregates: but Austrians maintain that we cannot attribute the properties of action and choice to them since those latter pertain to individuals only. Microeconomics is purely individualistic and for Austrians all economic theory must be derived from this. Hayek has always been highly critical of the notion that macroeconomic variables, such as the general price level, the rate of interest or the level of unemployment have any scientific significance. In the last decade we have witnessed the breakdown of one macroeconomic relationship after another yet as long ago as 1931 Hayek warned against the attempt to 'establish *direct* causal connections between the *total* quantity of money, the *general level* of all prices and, perhaps, also the *total* amount of production. For none of these magnitudes *as such* ever exerts an influence on the decisions of individuals' (1935a, p. 4). Although this was directed against early mechanical 'monetarism', it should be apparent that it has even more relevance to the post-war Keynesian concern with the manipulation of macroeconomic variables.

It should be noted that there is no *logical* connection between methodological individualism and political liberalism. The latter is not an explanatory principle at all but a normative proposition about the form a society ought to take. Although most Austrian economists are aware of this distinction they sometimes write as if a demonstration of the truth of the one entailed the truth of the other: this may partly be a consequence of the fact that they tend to be 'positivists' in regard to ethical values and therefore try to locate their political liberalism within their science of political economy without appeal to moral values.

The other aspect of Austrian methodology is the 'subjectivist' understanding of economic phenomena. Hayek claims that the most significant advances in economic theory have come from the consistent application of the subjectivist method. Nevertheless, there is still considerable confusion over this concept. At the epistemological level it means that our knowledge of social phenomena can only proceed through an understanding of minds: and we can only understand other minds by way of an introspective understanding of our own behaviour. Thus the fact that humans act purposively, that they order their preferences and that their actions accord with the 'law' of diminishing marginal utility are features of social life which it is both impossible and unnecessary to demonstrate 'objectively'. They are simply the 'unalterable axioms from which a deductive economic theory must start' (Mises, 1962, pp. 65–6).[2]

At the more substantive level, however, Austrian subjectivism represents a further extension of the subjective theory of value associated with Menger, Jevons and Walras. Whereas orthodox neo-classical theory restricts subjectivism to the explanation of the formation of prices, for Mises, Hayek and their successors it covers the unpredictability of human action, the uncertainty that necessarily faces each market participant, the dispersed and decentralized nature of economic knowledge and the fact that all market action takes place through time.

The theory of 'subjective cost' may be used to illustrate this point (see Vaughn, 1980). Orthodox neo-classical economists are familiar with the notion of 'opportunity cost' (derived from Wieser): this defines the 'cost' of a course of action in terms of the value of the next best foregone alternative. But in a typical objectivist fashion they try to measure such costs in terms of money outlays. To a thorough-going subjectivist, however, this is highly misleading because cost must be understood in terms of the *utility* foregone and this can only be known by the individuals engaged in an economic process.

This is not merely an esoteric epistemological argument for it has direct economic implications. For example, those welfare economists who, in order to eliminate imperfections of markets, try to replicate a notion of equilibrium, require an objective *measure* of cost. Yet if costs are entirely subjective then the operation of a market *process* is required for them to be revealed. The same argument applies to the supply of public goods and the problem of calculation in a socialist economy (see below).

If the ineradicably subjective nature of choice, ignorance, uncertainty and the time dimension of human action appear as permanent and immutable features of the economic condition, does not this make a genuine science of economics impossible? If economic man is a free and autonomous agent, immune to the promptings of a behaviouristic determinism, does this not remove the basis for any kind of prediction or certainty in the world? What scientific foundation can be given for the Austrians' confident belief in the superiority of markets over planning and capitalism over socialism?

There is indeed a place for economic 'laws' in the framework of Austrian economics. This has two dimensions. First, the familiar 'laws' of economics, diminishing marginal utility, supply and demand, the universality of time preference, and diminishing returns to factors, may be seen as 'necessary truths' which explain the essential structure of the economic world without being able to predict, in an exact or quantitative sense, the movement of any of its constituents. The law of demand tells us that *if* a wanted good is offered at zero price, say, by the state, the demand will go up. But this is not a *predictive* theory since clearly it would not necessarily be falsified if demand did not rise in such circumstances: tastes may simply have changed. In other words the *ceteris paribus* clause can always be invoked to 'save' any economic theory from an embarrassing refutation. It is argued therefore that economic laws are not generalizations from experience but are theorems which enable us to understand the economic world.[3] They obtain only under certain conditions, which may not always be present. Mises, unlike Hayek and other Austrian economists, held that the whole of economic theory could be deduced *a priori* from the concept of human action and it could therefore be neither corroborated nor refuted by experience (1963, pp. 38–9). The category of *action*, like that of causality, is prior to all experience and the theorems that can be deduced from it are used to explain or order what would otherwise be a mass of inchoate data. However, the most illuminating description of the function of the ultimate axioms of economic theory was provided by Lord Robbins in *The Nature and Significance of Economic Science* with his comment that they are the 'necessities to which human action is subject'.

Of perhaps more significance is the second aspect of Austrian economic theory. This is its investigation of those 'aggregate social structures' which are the result of human action but not the results of any specific human design (Hayek, 1967, pp. 96–105). The regularities that social science investigates are those that emerge accidentally or spontaneously (see Barry, 1982) from the actions of individuals who did not intend to generate any aggregate structures.

This continues the theme investigated by Adam Smith and the eighteenth-century anti-rationalists. The point is that those institutions that are the product of design or intention, such as an 'economic plan' or a parliamentary statute, cannot be the subject of a *theoretical* explanation but merely historical description. The actions of individuals that produce these 'conventional' institutions are inherently unpredictable but *markets, money, law* and *language*, which are the accidental products of the interactions of many individuals, can be predicted to emerge if individuals are left to pursue their private interests. There is, of course, a normative pay-off to this argument (although it is clearly not a logical property of it) that the results of those 'natural' processes are likely to be better in a utilitarian sense than those that emerge from the *deliberative* actions of a designing mind. It is the consistent exploration of this theme that has produced the most fruitful results for Austrian political economy. Indeed, Hayek maintains that a predictive science of political economy is only possible for capitalist market systems because only these exhibit regularities which can be investigated theoretically.

The method is sometimes called the 'genetic-causal' method since it necessitates the theoretical tracing back of institutions to their origin; though not in a direct historical sense but in a 'conjectural' sense. The origin of the institution of money can be explained in this way: in an original barter economy some goods are exchangeable for a greater range of goods than others and people will exchange goods for these, even though they do not *immediately* need them, so that they can be used to satisfy their future wants. The far-sighted and self-interested actions of some individuals in this process will accidentally generate an institution, money, which is for the benefit of all (Menger, 1963, p. 154).

Hayek takes this analysis a stage further with his account of the role of knowledge in economic explanation. We have already noted that for Austrians economic knowledge (information about tastes, productive techniques and so on) is subjective and in an important essay published in 1937 Hayek (1948) showed how a predictive economic theory explains how this knowledge is co-ordinated through the market. He makes an explicit distinction between the 'tautologies' contained in the 'pure logic of choice' and empirical science and argues that economics only becomes empirical when it investigates a *tendency* towards equilibrium, or a co-ordination of individual plans in a market process. This 'empiricism' contrasts strongly with Misesian *a priorism*. Mises maintained that the tendency for the market to co-ordinate could be deduced from the concept of man as an enterprising and speculative agent.

It is their analyses of market process, and their critique of static equilibrium, that point up the innovative features of the theories of the 'younger' Austrian school.

EQUILIBRIUM AND MARKET PROCESS

The main objection that Austrian economists have to neo-classical equilibrium theory is that it is used to describe a state of the world that cannot exist, given the uncertainty and ignorance that characterize human action, and given the fact that all economic action takes places through time. In other words, the Walrasian model of an economy is a highly *unrealistic* one since it assumes away the very features of economic life that it is the business of political economy to study. The Walrasian explanation of general equilibrium is a theory of the mutual and instantaneous determination of all variables and for that reason lends itself very easily to mathematical formulation. The Austrian theory, however, is an account of how things come about through time and therefore follows the pattern of 'causal-genetic' explanation mentioned above.

Frank Hahn (1982, p. 125) defines equilibrium nicely as follows:

An equilibrium of the economy is a state in which the independently taken decisions of households and firms are compatible. Thus it is a set of prices such that if they ruled there is a profit maximising choice of firms and a preference maximising choice of households *such that the total demand for any good is equal to the amount of it initially available, plus the amount of it produced.*

In this model, uncertainty, time and ignorance are excluded, all transactors are assumed to be price-takers and 'lightning calculators' of possible outcomes. Such an equilibrium is assumed to be a Pareto-efficient one to the extent that no reallocation of goods can make any one person better off without at the same time making someone worse off.

It is a picture of the economic universe which is profoundly unsatisfactory to Austrian economists. Reflecting as it does a static vision of the exchange process it necessarily represents men as passive reactors to events rather than active creators of them. Furthermore, although the model is often described as one of 'competitive equilibrium', competition, as understood in the layman's sense of 'rivalrous competition', seems to be absent from it. This is because the assumption of perfect knowledge of economic agents means that it describes a state of 'rest', a state which is the *culmination* of a competitive process and not the process itself. The assumption that the observing economist can describe, albeit with great mathematical sophistication, a stable equilibrium is analogous to the proposition that one can 'know' the result of a football match before the game has actually been played. Mises (1963, p. 248) claims that 'such a system is not peopled with living men making choices and liable to error, it is a world of soulless unthinking automatons; it is not a human society it is an ant-hill.'

Nevertheless, it would be mistaken to assume that the concept of equilibrium has no place in Austrian economic thought. Indeed, the idea of 'market process' was not a striking feature of the 'older' Austrian school, the members of which were primarily concerned with laying the foundations of a general subjectivist-marginal utility theory. Mises and Hayek themselves found some use for equilibrium theory. Mises talked of the 'evenly rotating economy', in which the market process had been exhausted and incentive to change removed. But this was no more than an 'imaginary construction', an abstraction from reality which it was necessary to make in order to highlight those equilibrating tendencies which follow from Mises's conception of man.

Hayek's view of equilibrium (see Littlechild, 1982, pp. 87–90) is a little more elaborate and complex. Indeed, his masterpiece of *pure* theory, *The Pure Theory of Capital* (1941), is an exercise in general equilibrium theory in which money and uncertainty are abstracted, and his writings on the trade cycle in the 1930s appear to describe an interlocking system which is almost mechanistically determined.

In all this, however, the Hayekian equilibrium is still some way removed from the notion of a stationary state of neo-classical orthodoxy. What he calls a 'fictitious' equilibrium is not the instantaneous price and quantity adjustment characteristic of the Walrasian model but the result of a learning process in which individual plans become compatible over time. In the Walrasian model of equilibrium, in which prices exactly equate supply and demand in all markets, the possibility of change is theoretically excluded but in the Hayekian approach equilibrium is not used to define a stable state at any point but to explore changes in direction. The ever-increasing elaboration of the theory of the state of equilibrium would be regarded by Hayek as an exercise in the pure logic of choice rather than as a substantive contribution to the study of economic processes (Hayek, 1948, pp. 33–5).

It would follow from this that there is, despite the professed subjectivism of Austrian economics, at least one *objective* statement, i.e., that a market economy if left undisturbed will show a tendency towards equilibrium (though of course, in the real world this will never be reached). Thus there is an *order* in the world, an order that *looks* as if it had been predicted and designed by an omniscient legislator; though clearly no centralized body could have the knowledge to effect such a complex structure. The most pressing question, however, concerns the mechanisms by which this tendency to equilibrium is generated. If the Walrasian model is not an accurate description of reality then what does this reality resemble?

The key concepts here are those of *competition* and *entrepreneurship*, which, as Israel Kirzner (1973) says, are really two sides of the same coin. These mechanisms (along with money and the 'firm') are absent from the stationary equilibrium because they are the motors of *change*. In a series of brilliant essays in the 1940s Hayek defined a competitive process as an *information* system which co-ordinates the dispersed knowledge through the mechanism of prices. Knowledge cannot be centralized but it can be transmitted to actors through 'rivalrous' competition. In the language of cybernetics, the market is a 'negative feed-back mechanism': a rise in price of a commodity is no more than a sign that there are profitable opportunities to be exploited and factors of labour and capital are hence attracted to its production. Thus it follows that the market is not merely an *allocative* device, by which factors are assigned to their most important uses, it is a discovery procedure through which economic agents try out new techniques, experiment with different uses of resources and exploit new opportunities (see Hayek, 1978a).

The other mechanism of the market process is *entrepreneurship*, and again an understanding of this concept is advanced by a comparison between market process and static equilibrium. In a market process the participants are ignorant of many of the facts that govern their economic lives, hence all their actions will be speculative. Since every action takes place through time and nothing is constant in the economic world, speculative entrepreneurial activity is an essential characteristic of human behaviour. This means that error will occur and people will make forecasts about future prices that will turn out to be false. In a market process the entrepreneur is *alert* to price discrepancies and is therefore able to exploit profitable opportunities. The essence of entrepreneurial profit is a difference between prices which has hitherto been unnoticed. In static equilibrium the array of prices is by definition *correct* so that there is no error for the entrepreneur to exploit. Thus entrepreneurial action is essentially *arbitrage*, and each successful act of arbitrage pushes the system towards equilibrium (though, of course, *this* is not the direct intention of each actor).

Kirzner (1973; 1979), building on foundations laid by Mises and Hayek, contrasts entrepreneurial alertness of the human action model with the automatic allocative model of general equilibrium orthodoxy. The entrepreneur is not merely an 'economizer' because the activity of economizing assumes knowledge of appropriate means to be allocated to competing ends. However, it is entrepreneurial activity which makes the co-ordination of knowledge possible. The entrepreneur's role is to respond quickly to market signals and this well illustrates the unpredictability of human affairs. In the 'perfect-competition, general-equilibrium' model, since all adjustment is instantaneous there is no role for the entrepreneur. If the future could be known then adjustment could be replicated in the real world without the need for market process.

It follows from this that entrepreneurship is not a kind of factor of production that is paid an income to secure its services but a category of human action, or mental quality, which all actors possess, though to varying degrees. The successful entrepreneur is not someone who has superior knowledge but rather that person who *perceives* some market imperfection, some disarray in the structure of prices, that can be exploited. Therefore entrepreneurship does not require ownership to exist, though of course the exercise of it may be inhibited by limited access to necessary resources (Kirzner, 1973, p. 20).

According to Austrian theory, competition and entrepreneurship explain how an economy moves through time; how it is that through a process of evolutionary adaptation dispersed knowledge is co-ordinated so that an order is produced. The notions of competition and entrepreneurship, which describe real phenomena, in a sense replace the notion of the Walrasian 'auctioneer' who calls the prices to which market participants adjust in static equilibrium.

The political implication of this economic explanation is that, if misallocations are constantly being corrected through the market process, an economy requires no corrective action on the part of a central authority. This is because it is an epistemological mistake to suppose that any one mind can possess that amount of information that is being incessantly generated in an exchange system.

The problem of knowledge is not a computational problem which could be solved by large computers: the reason is that this knowledge is what is sometimes called (by philosophers) 'tacit' knowledge, i.e., knowledge that cannot be objectified or put into rules or code. It is simply 'know-how' and is possessed by such economic agents as estate agents, middlemen, merchants and traders. It may be profitably contrasted with 'engineering knowledge', which is the ability to combine inputs in as efficient a manner as possible so as to produce outputs. However, an economy (or more strictly, a *catallaxy* or exchange system) is not an organization with a specific purpose but a spontaneous order of individuals with competing and unpredictable ends to whom knowledge is not 'given'. To the extent that Austrian political economy has any 'advice' to offer governments it is that political authorities should not inhibit the correction of misallocations that occurs naturally through the market. This contrasts strongly with the policy implications of the general equilibrium approach. In this timeless view of the economic world, imperfections, for example producer monopoly, are detected by reference to the abstract model of a perfectly competitive market in which no one can influence price. Where a single seller is able to *raise* his price and lower output this is said to represent a 'welfare loss' to society which can be eliminated by appropriate government action. Much attention is directed then to the *measurement* of the extent of monopoly power.

Although there are some differences among Austrian economists on monopoly theory there is common ground in their rejection of the policy implications of general equilibrium theory. Since the market is a process that persists through time the presence of monopoly does not necessitate the absence of competition. A producer monopolist may have acquired his position through superior alertness; furthermore it is illegitimate to compare an actual allocation with an imaginery 'perfectly competitive' solution. It might be the case that without the prospect of monopoly gains a good would not be produced at all, in which case it is quite erroneous to speak of the existence of monopoly entailing an efficiency or welfare loss. Behind all this lies the fundamental Austrian proposition that it is impossible to know what an efficient allocation would be in advance of the operation of a market process itself (see Littlechild, 1981).

It follows then that Austrians do not define monopoly in terms of a single seller in the market since even here there is *potential* competition from new entrants which is a constraint on the power of the producer. The only case where a producer is not subject to the market process is where he is in exclusive control of a set of inputs necessary for the production of outputs. In this view, which is that of Mises and Kirzner, effective barriers to entrepreneurial action could exist in the absence of direct governmental grant of exclusive privilege; this would be the case if a producer secured *sole* ownership of a vital natural resource. Another view, however, associated with Rothbard (1962, p. 592), and which possibly originates with Menger, defines monopoly entirely in terms of some deliberate *political* intervention in the market process. Indeed, examples of exclusive ownership of a resource arising spontaneously are hard to find (O'Driscoll, 1982, p. 209). It is the conferment of a legal privilege on producers that creates monopoly because it removes the constraint of potential competition.

For the Austrians it is clear that those familiar breakdowns and disruptions in the market economy that we experience have *exogenous* causes. If human actions are to be co-ordinated an appropriate institutional framework is required. This will include a predictable legal order, a stable monetary system and the absence of political privileges for particular groups, such as trade unions, which distort the signalling functions of the price system. In many ways Austrian political economy is the study of the interaction between human behaviour and institutions. One problem in establishing Austrian economics on an empirical basis is that the failure of the market to co-ordinate can always be explained away in terms of some institutional impediment to this process. While Hayek maintains that the co-ordinating tendency is in principle falsifiable he never states under what conditions this could be so.

But why should the market co-ordinate? And why should the mere compatibility of actions, which is all that this implies, produce a superior outcome, in a welfare sense, than any known alternatives? It is, of course, logically possible to abandon all talk of 'outcomes' and describe an economy exclusively in terms of processes to which we can attach no teleological significance (Buchanan, 1982b). Yet this seems to me to be not quite the position of Mises and Hayek, who clearly evaluate favourably the capitalist economy in conse-quentialist terms.

Indeed, there are others within the market process tradition who are less sure that the cause of the breakdown of the *catallaxy* is solely institutional and press subjectivism to its limits by suggesting that the confidence Austrians generally have in the equilibrating process of the market may be misplaced. In this view the subjectivist weapon may be too effective: that cutting edge which is used so effectively against general equilibrium theory may well be turned against *catallactic* theory. Those features of change, ignorance and uncertainty that make the replication of equilibrium states in the real world a delusion may well turn out to render the milder proposition that a harmonizing tendency exists itself nugatory. May not the economic world be 'kaleidic', lurching from one disequilibrium to another, rather than smoothly equilibrating?

This is essentially the view of Ludwig Lachmann and G. L. S. Shackle. Both these writers have consistently maintained (see, for example, Lachmann, 1976 and 1977; and Shackle, 1972) that the subjectivity of *expectations* makes the future so uncertain that there is no scientific warrant to suggest that the market shows a tendency to equilibrium – this may therefore only be a chance phenomenon rather than a defining characteristic of a *catallaxy*. Since expectations are no more than guesses about the future we cannot be sure they will be correct: indeed, an expectation that turns out to be successful is already a past event and is therefore irrelevant to the prospects of future successful co-ordination. In a world of such uncertainty can we be sure that profitable opportunities will continue to be exploited in order for the market to be nudged towards equilibrium? Will they even be *known*? Lachmann plays particular attention to 'restless' asset markets which, in comparison to the relative stability of product markets, exhibit no tendency to long-run equilibrium but only 'a succession of market-day equilibria determined by a balance of expectations tilting from one day to the next' (1976, p. 60).

Shackle's not dissimilar critique of the theory of an equilibrating process is generated by an intriguing epistemology and methodology which it is impossible to summarize here. Suffice it to say that Shackle's subjectivism is so radical that it precludes us from making any statement about equilibrium at all. In an instructive phrase he describes the future as 'unknowable but not unimaginable': it consists of expectations, which are a category of the 'imagination', formed by active participants. Thus there are no 'facts' or bits of knowledge waiting to be co-ordinated because the economic world consists entirely of thoughts and speculations. That which can be known in an 'objective' sense belongs to the past: but clearly no regularities in the past can provide even that minimum of stability which market process theory requires. Thus Kirzner's co-ordinating entrepreneur becomes for Shackle a creative and imaginative innovator, the maker of *different* futures rather than the agent of an inexorable equilibrating process. In a world in which there are no limits to the imagination, except presumably Robbins's 'necessities', it is inconceivable that economic 'laws' can describe anything other than temporary rearrangements of the data in an ever-changing process.

It is difficult to refute, philosophically, this beguiling vision of a completely undetermined, almost chaotic, world and easy to be dazzled by the glittering prose in which such unconventional views are expressed. But it is not clear that Shackle's 'kaleidic' picture is destructive of the Austrian position. It is certainly not true that the absence of a demonstrable tendency towards equilibrium necessarily licenses government intervention since there is no reason to suppose that such action will be able to improve upon the (albeit) imperfect processes of the market. Why should government officials be any more 'alert' to profitable opportunities than private transactors? Indeed, the conclusions of 'public choice' theory suggest the opposite: that the vote-maximizing activities of politicians in a democracy are systematically disruptive of the market order. Thus although actions in an unhampered market may merely co-ordinate without necessarily producing some imaginery 'optimum' this may be all we can reasonably expect in a world characterized by ignorance and uncertainty.

DISRUPTIONS TO THE MARKET ORDER

The crucially important Austrian contribution to political economy is the explanation of how the co-ordinating process is disrupted by institutional factors. Although institutional factors such as trade union monopoly power, welfare benefits and subsidized housing are examples of inhibitions to labour markets clearing, the major theoretical interest of twentieth century Austrian economic theory has been in the role that *money* plays as a disco-ordinating factor. Thus even if the political institutional framework were appropriate disturbances will still occur because of the peculiar properties of money – what Hayek calls that 'loose joint' in an otherwise co-ordinating and self-correcting system. Furthermore, it is the irresistable temptation for activist governments to 'play on the monetary instrument' that has been the major cause of repeated disequilibria in market economies in this century. Money has the capacity to liberate us from the constraints and inefficiencies of a barter economy yet also, if mishandled, the ability to institute a form of economic slavery.

The Austrian contribution to monetary theory begins with Mises's *Theory of Money and Credit* (1912). In this Mises incorporated the demand for money into marginal utility theory and produced his famous 'regression theorem', by which he showed that ultimately the value of money must be traced back, hypothetically, to its original *value in use*. Of more immediate significance is his (and later, Hayek's) explanation of the role of money in disequilibria, which is, of course, the normal state of economic affairs for Austrian political economists. It is in this analysis that we can detect the decisive differences between the Austrians and the more familiar 'quantity theory' school associated with Chicago, from Irving Fisher to Milton Friedman (see Barry, 1979, chapter 8; 1981).

The point of departure for Austrian monetary theory, and the theory of industrial fluctuations associated with it, is that in the short run money is not neutral in its effects on the structure of production. This means that increases in the supply of money and credit do not raise prices *uniformly*, as is the case with Friedman's famous 'helicopter' example of monetary injection, but that they have a *relative* price effect. This effect will depend on the point at which the new money enters the economy. In the world of long-run general equilibrium, which is characterized by perfect foresight, money plays no role – except as a *numeraire*. However, in the real world transactors *hold* money because of uncertainty (whereas other goods are simply traded against each other) and it is that which has important consequences for the market economy. Thus Hayek maintains that the crude version of the quantity theory, which precludes relative price changes, applies only to the analysis of comparative statics. Nevertheless, Hayek has stressed that 'it would be one of the worst things which would befall us if the general public were . . . to cease to believe in the elementary propositions of the quantity theory' (Hayek, 1935a, p. 3). Who could deny that this has in fact occurred?

The Austrian monetary theory of the business cycle, developed in the inter-war years by Mises and Hayek, can be discussed within the terms of the methodological framework described earlier. The predictive element in economic science is limited to the prediction of 'orders of events': business cycle theory is concerned with the way in which the capital structure or 'order' of a market economy becomes distorted over time through monetary disturbance. The 'discovery procedures' and information signalling processes of the market fail to bring about the tendency to equilibrium because transactors are misled by faulty price signals generated by the monetary instrument. The Mises-Hayek explanation of the business cycle derives from the Austrian theory of capital (developed originally by Böhm-Bawerk) and the theory of interest associated with the early twentieth century Swedish economist, Knut Wicksell.

In *Prices and Production* (1931 and 1935a), Hayek starts from the assumption of full employment of all resources. Obviously this was a highly unrealistic assumption at the time it was written but Hayek insisted that it was theoretically necessary in order to demonstrate how disco-ordination would occur; he was to start from more realistic assumptions in his 1939 work, *Profits, Interest and Investment*. A business cycle occurs when extra credit emanating from the banking system induces a 'cluster of errors' in the behaviour of entrepreneurs.

Before this can be understood, however, a brief explanation of Austrian capital theory is required. This describes an 'order' of integrated production processes: the capital structure of a market economy is therefore heterogeneous and covers a range of productive activities from those at the 'nearest' stages (making goods for final consumption) through to heavy capital equipment at the furthest stages. Many capital goods are highly specific and therefore cannot easily be shifted from one process to another. Furthermore a capital structure requires that 'complementary' capital goods be available for the integration process to be completed. In the absence of monetary disturbance the amount of capital investment will be determined by the level of voluntary saving by the public. Thus the 'natural' rate of interest, which exactly equates the demand and supply of investible funds, is ultimately determined by the time preferences of individuals. If the structure of production is to be lengthened, i.e., more 'roundabout' methods of production employed, a temporary reduction in consumption is needed (time preferences must be lowered) to make available resources for the completion of the longer processes.

However, credit issued by the (fractional-reserve) banking system lowers the loan or market rate of interest below the natural rate so that entrepreneurs are misled into making long-term investments. These are inherently unstable because they are not the product of voluntary saving but are 'forced savings' made possible only by inflationary money from the banking system. Thus instead of entrepreneurship acting as a motor that produces a beneficial, but unintended, order the presence of misleading price signals means that it generates instability. What Mises called the 'crack-up boom' cannot last because the new structure of production is not financed from an increase in voluntary saving. Since individuals are spending at the same rate as before, higher incomes earned by factors at the longer stages will be spent on consumption goods and resources will tend to be switched back to earlier stages to meet the new demand.

The 'crisis' is precipitated when the loan rate rises towards the natural rate. This will happen as the banks run out of cash (as they must do as long as there is some form of monetary control). Thus ultimately consumers will triumph in the 'battle' for an economy's resources; the malinvestments at the longer stages will have to be liquidated, resulting in a short period of unemployment while the readjustment process takes place. Since the theory holds that the crisis was caused in the first place by inflation it follows that the creation of extra spending power to mop up unemployment can only worsen the maladjustments and inhibit the self-correcting process of the market. What is in fact required is an increase in voluntary saving to make available resources for the completion of all the productive stages. The only way in which the crisis could be generated endogenously would be if the supply of voluntary savings suddenly dried up – an unlikely occurrence.

It is clear that such a theory could have little appeal in the circumstances of the 1930s. Instead of temporary unemployment being confined to the furthest stages of production, all sectors of the economy seemed to be condemned to permanent unemployment and depression with little prospect of an automatic readjustment. Indeed, inflation created by fractional-reserve banking would be unlikely of itself to generate such widespread dislocation. In retrospect contingent factors, such as the return to the Gold Standard in the UK at too high a parity and the collapse of the banking system in the USA, caused by mistaken policies of the Federal Reserve Board, have been identified by market economists as the causes of the extraordinary drop in economic activity at the time. However, such explanations complement rather than displace the Mises-Hayek theory of the business cycle.

Hayek's 1939 version of the theory (see O'Driscoll, 1977) makes different assumptions: for example, full employment of all resources is *not* the initial starting point and the rate of interest is held constant. In *Prices and Production* the crisis is precipitated by a rise in the market rate of interest which prevents longer-term processes being completed but in *Profits, Interest and Investment* it occurs irrespective of changes in the rate of interest. This is because of the operation of the 'Ricardo effect'. Briefly, this states that a rise in the value of the product (a fall in real wages) leads to the substitution of labour for capital. In the course of the trade cycle monetary expansion leads to a rise in the demand for consumer goods but as full employment is reached in these industries any further increase in demand leads to factor substitution. Labour is substituted for capital and the shorter projects attract the less specific capital goods. Longer-term projects cannot attract the capital necessary for their completion so that unemployment results here. In other words, entrepreneurs' expectations are not co-ordinated; they invest in longer projects only to find that there is not sufficient savings to complete the processes.

In both theories, however, the fundamental features of the market as a self-correcting mechanism persist. If the government maintains a strictly *laissez-faire* policy all malinvestments will be liquidated so that artificial and unsustainable extensions of the structure of production are self-reversing. It is important to note that orthodox macroeconomic theories tend to characterize a depression as a period of capital abundance whereas in Austrian theory capital needed to complete the various production processes is *scarce*. This illustrates the microeconomic nature of Austrian trade cycle theory. Unemployment is a consequence of some maladjustment in the structure of the economy and not the result of a fall in *aggregate* demand; therefore it will be eliminated only by allowing the price system to operate throughout.

It is true that Hayek (1939, pp. 63–4) appears to make some concession to macroeconomics when he distinguishes between an ordinary recession and a 'secondary depression' produced by a genuine deflation. In these latter circumstances there might be such a drop in aggregate demand (as occurred in the 1930s) that more expansionary monetary policies could be justified. However, even though Hayek reluctantly agreed to such policies he still maintained that they were the actions of a 'desperado'. Although they might buy some employment in the short run, and here political circumstances might dictate that such action is taken, they will perpetuate the maladjustments in the economy.

Austrian economists always predicted that the attempt to regulate a spontaneous economy and create full employment by manipulating macroeconomic variables would result in both rising inflation and long-term unemployment. The contemporary economic crisis is rather different from that described in the 'classical' trade cycle in

that persistent attempts to mop up unemployment by deficit spending by governments have produced dislocation throughout the whole
economy (Hayek, 1978b). In earlier times, credit created by the
banking system produced unemployment and maladjustments which
were clearly visible in the capital goods industries. Nevertheless, the
cause of the phenomena is the same, the profligacy of the monetary
authorities; and so is the effect of this indiscipline, the maintenance
of capital structures that are inherently unstable. A further compli-
cating feature of the modern world is that the complex structure of
the welfare state (and the vast array of trade union privileges) has
rendered large sections of the labour force relatively immobile so
that attempts to stimulate a depressed economy by monetary expansion cause inflation with little effect on output.

The Austrian solution has always involved the removal of government completely from the monetary sphere. This would entail the
abolition of central banks, which normally validate the inflationary
tendencies inherent in the fractional-reserve system. In a *laissez-faire*
world some version of the Gold Standard would emerge, with the
ultimate sanction of bank failure to guarantee that degree of stability
which an ever-changing economic order permits. It is also argued
(Rothbard, 1962, pp. 670–1) that no increase in the money stock is
ever required since in a world of flexible prices, increasing prosperity
would be associated with a gently falling price level.

After believing for many years in the virtues of fixed exchange
rates (as a surrogate for the Gold Standard) Hayek (1976b) has now
come to believe in a rather dramatic solution to the problem of
getting government out of money – a completely free market in
currency issue. He thinks that if the banks' money, and foreign
currencies, could circulate alongside the government's, natural self-
interest would drive people to hold only sound currencies – good
money would in fact drive out bad.

This is clearly a much more radical proposal than anything associated with the Chicago tradition, and indeed, competition *between*
currencies has not been a feature of Austrian monetary theory. His
rejection of the Friedmanite 'monetary rule' suggestion stems not
merely from his doubt that government can ever be restrained by
such rules but also from a methodological consideration. This is that
since money cannot be objectively measured it will be impossible to
control directly its supply and therefore 'near moneys' will continue
to flourish and have a disruptive effect on the structure of the
economy.

A further (practical) difference is that Hayek favours a rapid reduction in the money supply with very high *temporary* unemployment rather than a gradualist policy. This is because he thinks, oddly, that it will be more acceptable politically and also that it will result in the speedy liquidation of malinvestments, businesses which are only kept in being by the continuing inflation.

THE REFUTATION OF SOCIALISM AND THE DEFENCE OF CAPITALISM

Austrian economists are better known today as advocates of the political economy of capitalism rather than as pure theoretical economists. Indeed, both Mises (1936 and 1972) and Hayek (1960, 1973, 1976a, 1979) turned to political and social philosophy after completing their main work in economics. Yet their defence of the private property market economy owes much to economics and therefore takes a broadly utilitarian or consequentialist form rather than one based on an individualist natural law morality. In this limited sense they are both 'positivist' in that they assume that 'reason' cannot demonstrate the intrinsic superiority of any one set of economic and political values but only inform us of the means for the achievement of values which we (presumably) all share. Hayek's defence of the capitalist order is considerably more subtle than that of Mises but nevertheless purports to rely on 'scientific' rather than ethical arguments.

It is not surprising then that the famous Austrian attack on socialism, which dates from Mises's 1920 article (see Hayek, 1935b) and continued throughout the 1930s, should focus on its alleged 'impossibility' rather than its intrinsic undesirability. By the 'impossibility of socialism' it was not of course meant that a planned economy without markets and private property was literally incapable of generating output but rather that it would be manifestly inefficient in comparison with capitalism in satisfying consumer wants. It must be remembered, too, that at this time socialist theorists were convinced that collectivist methods of production were preferable because they could make Pareto (efficiency) improvements over capitalism and not merely that they maximized social justice or eliminated 'alienation'.

Unfortunately, in the history of economic thought, the nature of the famous 'calculation' debate was misunderstood. The Austrian argument that economic value could not be rationally calculated in the absence of private property, entrepreneurship, 'rivalrous' competition, and money depended very much on the critique of the general equilibrium model of economic society. The original socialist economic models, beginning with Barone's 1908 article, 'The Ministry of Production in the Collectivist State', (see Hayek, 1935b) and continuing with the work of Lange (see Lippincott, 1938) and Lerner (1944) were implicitly general equilibrium models. Because existing markets were characterized by monopoly, the familiar market imperfections and substantial inequality of resource ownership, it was argued that a planner could in effect reproduce the results of a 'perfectly' competitive process. It is to be noted here that in this form socialist planning was thought to be compatible with the satisfaction of consumer tastes and free choice in occupation. There was no suggestion that a major flaw in capitalism was that it manipulated 'wants' in some malign way – which is a predominant theme in contemporary socialist writings.

The most forceful response to the argument that without a market prices and costs could not be calculated, that centralized planners would have no alternative but to command what was to be produced and assign factors to the production process by decree, was contained in the Lange-Lerner model of 'competitive socialism'. It was realized that if the demands of efficiency and consumer choice were to be met some method was required for the calculation of value. In effect, this involved the simulation of a market process in which consumer goods would be priced on the free market and factor prices determined by trial and error and administered by a central planning board. Although there would be no capital market, resources would be efficiently allocated by the planning board functioning as a kind of Walrasian auctioneer. Since the problem was to combine 'given' inputs so as to produce an array of outputs it was held that socialist managers could imitate the role of capitalist entrepreneurs by following certain rules, viz., the instruction to minimize factor costs for a set of given resource prices and to equate marginal cost to price in the product market. In other words, with given knowledge, the economic problem becomes a computational problem to which the unhampered free market provided only an imperfect solution. The property structure of the latter permitted Pareto inefficiencies in the form of excess profits.

In his reply to earlier arguments for the 'competitive solution' (those of F. M. Taylor, W. C. Roper and H. D. Dickinson) in his 'The Present State of the Debate', Hayek *appeared* to concede some of the theoretical ground with his observation that 'it must be admitted that this is not an impossibility in the sense that it is logically contradictory' (1935b, p. 207). However, he seemed to rule it out as 'humanly impracticable'. Many socialists took him to mean that the solution to an almost infinite number of equations which the method required would be beyond human capacity (irrespective of the political problems inherent in entrusting this task to, presumably, an appointed body). Therefore, later socialist equilibrium theorists, notably Lange and Lerner, simply set about devising procedures to make the task more manageable; as well as noting the opportunities opened up by the advent of computers.

However, Hayek was not talking about a 'practical' problem at all but was questioning the applicability of the socialist *theoretical* model (as Mises had done originally in 1920). His claim was that the 'engineering' method implied by socialist economics was appropriate only to an economy with one output and given inputs. But since market economies involve a plurality of ends competing for scarce resources the problem ceases to be an engineering one and becomes a problem of co-ordination. Since knowledge is not 'given' but has to be discovered we require markets: the central planning board can never accumulate the knowledge that is constantly being generated by rivalrous competition.

Furthermore, since the socialist model was, in effect, an experiment in comparative statics it could not theoretically account for change. As we know from the Austrian theory of market process, entrepreneurship is required to cope with the uncertainty and ceaseless change that are characteristic of human organizations. Socialist managers, in this view, cannot be entrepreneurs because the latter are 'speculators' whose actions push the system towards order. Mises argued that a prosperous economic system requires a specialist class (which will be selected out by competition) which excels at the entrepreneurial function, and that this is excluded by bureaucratic socialism. In fact, it was always argued by the Austrians that the absence of private property and the incentive structure of capitalism would, ironically, generate a highly conservative order with managers reacting mechanically to rules and orders. Of fundamental importance is the problem of cost which, for Austrian economists is an entirely subjective matter. From this it follows that it is impossible to objectify costs and embody this information in the form of rules and instructions. Indeed, without the profit motive to impel them socialist managers have every incentive to conceal the true nature of their costs.

The defence of the capitalist order itself is, for Austrians, largely utilitarian. This is especially so in the case of Mises. In his non-

specialist work on political economy he insisted that value judgements not only had no place in economics but were inherently
subjective and beyond rational or scientific demonstration. Thus, to
the obvious question as to how such a fierce proponent of liberal
capitalism could also be an advocate of a *wertfrei* economics the
answer was simple: the political philosophy of liberalism was simply
applied economics. Economics does not pronounce upon the ends
which we pursue, it merely describes those means which are theoretically necessary for their achievement. Mises assumed that those ends
were common to most people and argued that liberal economics
showed the way for their achievement.

Although Mises had no subtly formulated concept of man it is
clear that he regarded men as egoists, ceaselessly striving at want-
satisfaction. For him, to ask questions about the origin and explanation of wants was outside the realm of political economy, which
is solely concerned with the exploration of the implication of men
having wants in a world of necessarily limited resources. Nevertheless, Mises himself was a firm advocate of the consumer society and
contemptuous of 'bourgeois' socialist economists who doubted that
men as consumers represented the ideals of autonomy and
rationality.

Hayek's liberal political economy is much more sophisticated than
Mises's simple utilitarian rationalism. For him the scientific virtue of
liberalism does not lie in the fact that it can be demonstrated by pure
reason, as appears to be the case with Mises. The influence of the
sceptical philosophy of David Hume and Adam Smith has led him to
maintain that our reason is too fragile an instrument to demonstrate
the superiority of any one economic system. Instead he had adopted
an evolutionary philosophy which tries to show how a process of
natural selection of rules and practices produces appropriate social
orders (Hayek, 1960, chapter 2). Since we cannot know all the
consequences of our actions any attempt to plan or improve on
existing practices in a *comprehensive* manner will end in disaster.
Just as a market will contain knowledge which is not available to a
central economic planner a tradition embodies that kind of wisdom
which cannot be stated in formal rules or codes. Thus, although
Hayek has written at great length on the philosophy of liberty his
main justification is not ethical but derives from the instrumental
value it has in promoting progress through evolution.

It is clear that Hayek is a more conservative thinker than Mises
since tradition can clearly speak with an un-liberal voice and Hayek's

anti-rationalism seems to disable him from the appraisal of illiberal evolutionary processes. However, he has managed to accompany this apparent quietism with some extremely radical proposals not only in connection with monetary reform but also for the legal and political structures of western democracies (Hayek 1979). All of these are designed to restore the limited state of classical liberal theory.

Hayek's thought is immensely more wide-ranging than that of Mises or any other Austrian economist, covering as it does law, psychology, the history of ideas and politics. But political economy remains the foundation of his vast and architectonic system of ideas. It constitutes a complete rejection of the prevalent idea that economics is a mechanical discipline or engineering technique that can be made to serve any ends. His claim is that because economics deals with a complex human organism, the behaviour of which is inherently unpredictable in a quantitative sense, the economist must concern himself with other institutions of society if his pronouncements are to have any normative significance.

It is this attitude that coloured Hayek's grim prognosis, first formulated in *The Road to Serfdom* (1944), that even minor interferences with a spontaneous order, such as macroeconomic planning and the collective delivery of welfare services, would produce a tendency to totalitarianism not envisaged by the authors of the schemes. Although this has not yet come about, the theoretical plausibility of the argument has been enhanced by Hayek's incorporation, in his more recent work (see Hayek, 1979), of some of the conclusions of public choice theory. These show how vote-maximizing in a democracy tends to produce policies favourable to group interests rather than the long-run public interest.

It is not difficult to explain the current resurgence of Austrian political economy. The dominance of a purely technical economics has been successfully challenged during the last decade and as a result economists have been more reticent in their claims. The Hayekian stress on the limits of knowledge has perhaps been vindicated more by events than by many genuine intellectual conversions but it has nevertheless brought a tangible shift of opinion. There are gaps, even in so comprehensive a system of thought as Austrian political economy, most notable is the absence of a coherent theory of property rights, but the tradition is a living one anxious to tackle new problems. There is also an almost bewildering variety of policy prescriptions from those who call themselves Austrians, ranging from the *laissez-faire* anarchism of Murray N. Rothbard (1978) to the sceptical conservatism of Hayek, but, then, the tradition was never a monolithic one.

NOTES

1 A distinction should be drawn here between *ontological* individualism and *methodological* individualism. The former asserts the true, but trivial, proposition that ultimate social reality consists solely of acting individuals, whereas the latter maintains that the only genuine scientific explanations of social phenomena are those that are reducible to individualist explanations. These two claims are by no means equivalent, although Austrian economists frequently write as if they were. For example, Chicago macroeconomics, since it deals with aggregates, may be called methodological collectivist yet it clearly does not claim that such aggregates 'act'.

2 In fact, Misesian foundations of economic theory are Kantian, i.e., economic theorems are like mathematical axioms whose truth is independent of all experience. For Hayek, and other Austrians, they are known to be true by introspection, which is a type of experience.

3 It follows from this that Austrians do not accept the logical equivalence of 'explanation' and 'prediction'.

3

The Institutionalist School
of Political Economy

JOHN E. ELLIOTT

Institutionalism has marched to a different drummer from mainline economics in terms of both the scope and content of its subject matter and its methodologies or modes of approaching its substantive concerns. In practical terms, this translates into an insouciant focus on social conflict and institutional change over historical time, in contrast to an emphasis on social balance and equilibrium. Although, as is illustrated vividly by the writings of Thorstein Veblen, typically these two aspects of institutionalist thought, like social practice, are interwoven, it will be convenient for organizational purposes to distinguish them. Thus, after reviewing Veblen's main contributions, this chapter examines two connected and enduring themes in institutionalist thought. First, it gives a comparative review of the institutionalist theory of the evolution of systems of political economy in capitalist development, with focus upon the Veblen-Ayres tradition and contemporary extensions. Here, the emphasis is upon institutionalism's dynamic and evolutionary analysis of technological and institutional change in economic development. Second, it describes the interpenetration of politics and economics in the contemporary political economy, with focus upon the contributions of John R. Commons and J. K. Galbraith. Here, the emphasis is upon the role of political factors in economic life and the conception of the economy as a system of power.

Although references are made throughout to various individuals, in their own right or as representatives of broader themes, essentially we will ignore the intricacies of differentiation among the founding fathers, the late greats, and the contemporary contributors in the institutionalist tradition, and will adopt the technically inaccurate but useful fiction that there exist essential or at least sufficient unity and continuity in their writings to warrant treating them for our present purposes as a group.

THORSTEIN VEBLEN: CONFLICT AND CHANGE IN POLITICAL ECONOMY

Thorstein Veblen, the brilliant though eccentric 'founding father figure' of institutionalism, developed a vision of capitalist evolution trenchant in its criticism and sweeping in its scope. Veblen's incisive analyses and sharp critiques of socio-economic conflict and change provided an alternative to neo-classical economic orthodoxy and a complement to Marxism which has influenced several generations of institutionalists and maintains important insights down to the present day.

Veblen identified technological change as the underlying cause of evolutionary change in economic institutions, and perceived ideas as lagging behind both technological and economic development. Veblen (1899; 1904; 1919; 1921; 1923; 1964; Dowd 1958; 1964) believed that the increasing pace of technological change and improvements in the 'industrial arts' since the mid-nineteenth century had profound institutional consequences. First, advancing technology stimulated the rise of the corporation to a position of economic dominance, notably in the 'key industries' of natural resources, power and transportation. In part, growing corporate ascendance was responsive to increasing economies of large-scale production; in part, it simply reflected the singular commitment of the corporate form of business organization to profit. Second, the growth of the corporation stimulated other important institutional changes, notably the separation of ('absentee') ownership and management, the expanded business role of credit and financial institutions, and the development of labour unions as businesslike attempts to control the supply and remuneration of labour.

The combination of technology, credit, and the corporation generates an interactive proclivity toward depression and monopoly. On the one hand, the high fixed costs associated with large-scale production, coupled with the technology-based tendency toward lower costs, stimulate cut-throat competition and thereby serve as inducement to monopolization. On the other hand, alternating waves of over- and undercapitalization, stimulated by the corporation and the credit system, are the proximate cause of business fluctuations and depressions (which, in turn, also stimulate monopoly). The modern corporate system, with its trusts, holding companies, credit, price rigging, and salesmanship, thus tends to degenerate into a vast arrangement for 'making money' and economic 'sabotage' increasingly alienated from the technological forces largely responsible for its emergence and from the 'underlying population' as well.

In short, late nineteenth-century corporate-monopoly-finance capitalism received low marks in the Veblenian grade book on four main aspects of economic performance: allocation, distribution, stability, and growth. Monopoly systematically restricts output and employment below competitive levels, with resulting monopoly profits, inefficient production and excess capacity. Income and wealth distribution, reflecting monopoly power – to say nothing of chicanery and fraud – become ever more unequal. 'Chronic depression, more or less pronounced, is normal to business under the fully developed regimen of the machine industry' (1923, p. 234). Negotiational relations between big business and organized labour become characterized by a 'competitive use of unemployment, privation, restriction of work and output, strikes, shutdowns and lockouts, espionage, pickets, and similar manoeuvres of mutual derangement, with a large recourse to menacing language and threats of mutual sabotage' (1923, p. 406). The conscientious withdrawal of efficiency (1923, p. 1) for the sake of higher profits promotes long-run economic stagnation and sluggish growth.

These technological and institutional changes in capitalism's structure, and their accompanying consequences for economic behaviour and performance, are interwoven with social conflict. Veblen identified a fundamental dichotomy or antagonism in society, brought to its apogee by late nineteenth-century capitalism. At one level, this conflict is between the 'instinct of workmanship' and the 'predatory instinct'. The first, with such associated traits as 'idle curiosity' and the 'parental bent', represents the propensity to produce, create, and nurture. The second represents the proclivity to exploit and subjugate. At another level, the antagonism is between 'business', or the processes of finance, salesmanship, and profit making, and 'industry', or the processes of technology, work, and production. At still a third level, the dichotomy is one between the 'ceremonies' and rituals of the 'leisure class', including sports, games, and social graces, and the more co-operative and productive activities of the common working person.

These fundamental dichotomies, Veblen observed, are manifested in the class structure and conflicts of capitalist society. Slave and feudal societies were dominated by the predatory instinct. The transition from feudalism into capitalism was characterized by an upsurge in the instinct of workmanship and the industrial arts. As capitalism proceeded in its path of development during the nineteenth century, and such capitalist institutions as market exchange, private property, and the capital-labour relation were extended, 'business', and its predatory and exploitative powers, was strengthened relative to 'industry'. At the same time, the machine process stimulates workmanlike attitudes and habits of thinking among those occupations and groups (engineers, technicians, production supervisors, industrial workers) most directly associated with technology and production. Consequently, by the late nineteenth century, both sides of the Veblenian dichotomy had acquired considerable social power. The instinct of workmanship had come to be embodied in the 'workmen, labourers, operatives, technologists', through whom the 'community's technological proficiency functions directly to an industrial effect' and whose ordinary working lives stimulate a 'technological apprehension of material facts'. The predatory instinct had come to be embodied in the 'owners, investors, masters, employers, undertakers, businessmen', who are primarily concerned with negotiating 'advantageous bargains' and whose training and occupations stimulate 'pecuniary management and insight' (1964, p. 202).

In one sense, the relationship between industry, on the one hand, and business – and its associated absentee owners – on the other, is a symbiotic one. In a modern capitalist democracy, pre-capitalist predatory and exploitative instincts can be effectively implemented, for the system as a whole, only through the productivity of industry. But this symbiosis requires dominion by the absentee owners, through their managerial agents, over production, and the subordination of industry to business. Moreover, this symbiotic dependency is not reciprocal. The 'New Order' of corporate-monopoly capitalism is a 'misfit'. It is characterized by 'irresponsible control' by a 'superannuated general staff of businessmen' using 'old-fashioned strategy toward obsolete ends' (1923, p. 210). In short, business needs industry, but, as evidenced by increasing manifestations of economic derangement, becomes increasingly superfluous to it.

Veblen believed that trends and conflicts in modern industrial capitalism carry within them the potentiality for radical social change. One main alternative scenario, which Veblen hedged with numerous caveats, is the dispossession of the absentee owners and the construction of a new industrial order devoted to maximum production, led by a new technical aristocracy of engineers and production workers, *if* only they would recognize their immense potential power, based on their indispensability and control over technology. Although 'the end is not yet', growing waste and inefficiency, combined with the 'discontent and distrust among the underlying population who suffer the inconvenience of it all', are indicators of the prospective possibility that the 'established order' of business enterprise and vested interests will 'go under in a muddle of shame and confusion because it is no longer a practicable system of industrial management' under twentieth century technology. Moreover, because of 'waste and confusion in the management of industry by the financial agents of the absentee owners', the 'gifted, trained, and experienced technicians who now are in possession of the requisite technological information and experience' and who constitute the indispensable 'General Staff of the industrial system' are becoming increasingly class conscious. A general strike of these technical specialists 'would swiftly bring a collapse of the old order and sweep the timeworn fabric of finance and absentee sabotage into the discard for good and all' (1921, p. 110).

An alternative and, in Veblen's increasingly pessimistic view, more likely scenario is an alliance among vested business interests, government, and the military to keep the technicians and the 'underlying population' in check. Veblen identified several factors conducive to this possibility. First, business enterprise may well turn increasingly to the political system. Government, Veblen argued, is basically supportive of business interests, not only in the crude sense of buying the allegiance of politicians through financing political campaigns, but more prominently through subtle processes of socialization. Because, through education and socialization, the average citizen comes to identify his interests with those of business, legislators, judges, and administrators are almost invariably – regardless of which political party is in office – 'persons of businesslike antecedents, dominated by the logic of ownership, essentially absentee ownership' (1923, p. 405). Because of its numerical inferiority, business enterprise can maintain and extend its dominant position in society only through control over government. Governments exercise 'surveillance and punitive powers'. Government intervention in negotiations between owners and workers 'rebounds to the benefit of the former' (1923, pp. 404–5).

Second, the owning class uses militarism, nationalism, patriotism, and imperialism in pursuit of its interests. Maintaining the economy in a perpetual state of war-preparedness provides lucrative military contracts for business. Imperialist policies yield their major benefits for absentee owners by protecting the dominion of business interests outside the country. Nationalism and patriotism are manipulated by business, through the press and other means of socialization, and by their military and political allies, to foster the illusion of national solidarity. Above all, marshalling nationalist and patriotic sentiment in support of militarism and imperialism produces a 'conservative animus' among the population. The 'disciplinary effects of warlike pursuits' deflect the public's interest in and potential criticism of conduct of the economy to 'nobler, institutionally less hazardous matters. . . . Habituation to a warlike, predatory scheme of life is the strongest disciplinary factor that can be brought to counteract the vulgarization of modern life wrought by peaceful industry and the machine process', to 'rehabilitate the decaying sense of status and differential dignity', and thereby to check social reform pressures (1923, pp. 391–3). Protection of the vested interests and the corporate system by the state, however, has its price. Political and military leadership, reflecting pre-capitalist virtues and values, may well not rest content serving as handmaidens to business enterprise; what begins as business control over the political system can evolve into authoritarian fascistic political control over business as well as society at large.

Third, the underlying population has a tendency toward subservience and emulation of the capitalist and corporate rich, both manifested and reinforced by ostentatious displays of 'conspicuous leisure' and 'conspicuous consumption' by the 'leisure class' (1899). On the one hand, mere possession of wealth or power is insufficient to elicit social esteem. They must be conspicuously displayed, for esteem is extended 'only on evidence'. On the other, a pecuniary culture, where respectability depends on one's relative position in the wealth and income hierarchy, exerts powerful pressure toward emulative consumption. Because others are similarly striving to improve their relative pecuniary standings, endeavours based on such invidious comparisons are likely to generate a treadmill or 'chronic dissatisfaction' coupled with a tendency to sublimate potential criticism of the power structure of the economic system and to substitute self-blame and renewed, but hopeless, pursuit of emulative consumption for radical social change.

THEORY OF INSTITUTIONAL EVOLUTION IN
CAPITALIST DEVELOPMENT

As Wesley Clair Mitchell aptly observed nearly half a century ago (1937, pp. 336–7), if the defining property of institutional economics were merely the study of economic institutions, then Adam Smith and John Stuart Mill must be counted among institutionalism's founders. Institutionalism's *differentia specifica*, he proceeded to suggest, would be focused upon the cumulative process of evolutionary change in economic institutions. Contemporary perspective would probably lead many to amend this view by placing special emphasis upon the development and transformation from the old style political economy embodied in the conception, if not always the practice, of competitive market and essentially *laissez-faire* capitalism to the new style political economy exhibited in one or another variant of contemporary capitalism.

The perhaps obvious but strategic starting point for an analysis of institutional change is an alteration in methodological perspective, namely, the shift into variables of the data compounded in the *ceteris paribus* assumptions of 'orthodox' economic theory. In orthodox price (and national income) theory, the dominant procedure is to construct deductive hypotheses concerning the behaviour of selected economic variables from underlying assumptions. These assumptions, typically pertaining to technology, institutions, and social attitudes and motivations, are perceived of as non- or extra-economic in character. In any event, they are 'given', not in the sense that they do not change or cannot be altered for purposes of intellectual experiment (for example, the substitution of the assumption of oligopoly for pure competition), but in the sense that they are typically regarded as beyond the explanatory scope of economic theory. In institutional theory, by contrast, these kinds of data become variables for which hypotheses are to be constructed.

This perspective immediately raises two procedural problems for economists, one of scope, the other of method. If economic analysis is perceived to include technology, institutions, and social attitudes, at least to the extent that changes in them stimulate and interact with changes in the employment and allocation of resources, and the distribution of, fluctuations in, and growth of income, then clearly the scope of the discipline is broadened, and the boundaries with other disciplines become less precise. As to method, how are economists to construct hypotheses concerning economic behaviour when the assumptions underlying the analysis have been transformed into issues and variables, changes which now themselves require explanatory hypotheses?

Probably the dominant answer to this question within the institutionalist tradition is to focus upon technology as the strategic and decisive dynamic factor in economic development and to attribute technological change in large measure to the entire culture or 'life process' of society. In this view, technology, key to the development process, obeys its own logic. Economic and political institutions (and ideas) serve essentially facilitative, adaptive, obstructive, or destructive roles in economic and social change. The interconnections between technology and institutions are thus perceived to constitute the dynamics of development, the basic logic of which emerges as the prime concern of institutionalist political economy. This basic idea will now be amplified and illustrated by a series of vignettes on the theory of the evolution of politico-economic institutions.

Clarence Ayres: From Absolute Capitalism to Limited Capitalism

In his writings, notably those of the 1940s and early 1950s (1944; 1946; 1952), Ayres continued and elaborated upon the Veblenian themes of the creative impact of technological change upon industrial growth and technology's corrosive effects upon economic and political institutions. His analysis of the prospective shift from the 'money power' system under 'absolute capitalism' to economic planning under 'limited capitalism' exhibits an interesting blend of institutionalist and Keynesian perspectives as well as a valuable exercise in the evolution of systems of political economy.

In *Absentee Ownership*, Veblen had described the view that corporations create capital equipment and tools from accumulated savings which would otherwise have remained idle as part of the 'folklore' of political economy (1923, p. 86). The idea that saving is the proximate cause of investment and thereby technological change and economic growth, Ayres contends, is the reverse of the actual situation. Although saving and 'money capital' (and thereby capitalists and capitalism) no doubt serve a permissive or facilitative role in economic development, it would be more accurate to say that technological improvements, embodied in investment or capital goods, generate the increases in national income which thereby enable saving to rise.

Still, the orthodox analysis of the saving-investment relation has provided a powerful rationale for capitalism and capitalists, a sort of 'divine right of capital' which has helped sustain absolute capitalism and its property and power relations in a manner reminiscent of the role that the concept of the divine right of kings played in helping to sustain absolute monarchy in an earlier era. Increasingly, however, the actual situation has eroded popular belief in this 'legend' and thereby in the moral authority of capitalist institutions. The experiences of the 1920s and 1930s, Ayres suggests, indicate that saving can easily be excessive relative to investment and that the functioning of capital, credit, and bond markets will not automatically equate saving and investment at full employment. This problem does not emanate merely from market imperfections, but is rooted in more fundamental structural and institutional factors. Notable among these, first is a tendency toward insufficient consumption and excessive saving generated by income inequality; second is the rise of the corporation, which has increasingly separated savers from investors at the same time that it has encouraged internal financing of investment.

The solution, identified prospectively by Ayres, and of course retrospectively by others in the post-Second World War period, is a shift to a limited capitalism analogous to limited or constitutional monarchy. The central problem of Ayres's absolute capitalism is its institutional obstruction to sustained economic growth. The central institutional innovation of limited capitalism lies in removing this obstruction through 'planning for stability' (1952, pp. 186ff.). Its essential mechanism would be a redistribution of income (although not of wealth) through a reform of the Social Security system, namely, an extension of 'its benefits to the entire population irrespective of their earnings and even of their other independent income' (1946, p. 100) sufficient to generate a level of mass purchasing power supportive of full employment levels of aggregate demand. Limited capitalism would not require a radical reform of either the market system or of corporate and property power. It would require, however, a strategic institutional change wherein government would compensate for or offset the destabilizing proclivities of the private market economy. In Ayres's view, it would also require a reduction in income inequality as the price for sustaining a prosperous overall economy and thereby prosperity levels of profits and property income as well as the essential institutional features of market capitalism.

John Kenneth Galbraith: From Market Economy to Planned Capitalism, Corporate Model

Many economists in the institutionalist tradition have examined planning as an evolving supplement or substitute for market processes. For Ayres, as already implied, planning 'is itself a manifestation of the technological process'. It is problems resulting from 'institutional obstruction' to technological change that stimulate the emergence of economic planning, and it is institutional innovation to overcome such obstruction (for example, macroeconomic policy to promote stability) that constitutes planning's strategic dimension (1952, p. 192). In a singularly 'modern' essay written in the mid-1930s, to cite a second example, Mitchell attributed the growing departure from *laissez-faire* and the emergence of early varieties of government planning (piecemeal, emergency, and stabilization planning) since the late nineteenth century to an interwoven complex of changes in technology, economic and political organization, and social attitudes. Of special interest is his view that economic progress itself, under capitalist auspices – through growing interdependence, exhaustion of natural resources, increasing incidence of depressions, and growing concentration in income, wealth, and economic power – is conducive to a perceived need for enlarged government control, guidance, and planning in economic life (1937, pp. 103–36).

In his recent works (1971; 1973), Galbraith has identified an evolutionary process of development of economic planning in post-war USA as something approximating a capitalist version of a planned economy. In the Veblen-Ayres tradition, the corporation is perceived as the locus of this trend, and technological change as its underlying dynamic imperative. The most visible and profound evidence of change in twentieth century USA, especially since the beginning of the Second World War, Galbraith asserts, has been 'the application of increasingly intricate and sophisticated technology to the production of things' (1971, p. 1), notably in several hundred large-scale corporations which dominate the 'decisive part' of contemporary industry (1973, p. ix). The consequences of these technological changes – the increasing commitment of time and capital, the greater inflexibility of this commitment, the increased need for specialized manpower and organization – have reduced the reliability of market relations and thereby have made corporate planning 'imperative'. In order to function effectively in the new technological environment, large corporations must be able to anticipate – and control – both consumer demand and their sources of supply, at remunerative prices and costs, as well as the sources of supply of corporate saving for investment. The various strategies for accomplishing this (for example, sales promotion, vertical integration, internal corporate financing) constitute nothing less than the supersession, suspension, or control of the market and its replacement by planning. Corporate planning, in turn, is supplemented and reinforced by appropriate government action, notably the regulation of aggregate demand, the provision of trained manpower through the educational system, the underwriting of new capital and technology, and, to some degree, the promotion of wage-price stability.

In response to his critics, Galbraith readily accedes that this system of political economy 'is not the formal planning of the socialist state. It is a more informal and much less fully developed apparatus. . . . [It] does not have a system of overall coordination; . . . discrepancies in performance exist between different sectors. . . . Nor is the planning complete; market influences are not fully excluded. . . . But it is planning by organizations with the requisite power. . . . [A significant part of the economy] is becoming increasingly subject to the power of the productive apparatus, specifically the great corporation' (cited in Sharpe 1974, pp. 96–100). And it is this kind of emerging planning system, not the impersonal governance of market forces, which is coming increasingly to characterize and control the allocation of resources in contemporary capitalism.

Gunnar Myrdal: From Market Economy to Economic Planning, Contemporary Welfare State Model

For Galbraith, drawing primarily upon US experience, the locus of power and change has been the large-scale corporation. For Gunnar Myrdal, sketching in broad strokes the process of politico-economic change in the rich countries in the Western world over the last half century, the focus is upon the emerging democratic welfare state, that is, a state with fairly clear and developed responsibility for the promotion of such social goals as full employment, equality, economic development, and minimum standards of income, health, education, housing, and so on. As does Galbraith, Myrdal believes planning has become 'a necessity' (1960, p. 62). Planning is distinguished from mere intervention into market relations, however, by identifying it with 'conscious attempts by the government of a country – usually with the participation of other collective bodies – to coordinate public policies more rationally in order to reach more fully and rapidly the desirable ends for future development which are determined by the political process as it evolves' (1960, p. 23). The typical process of development has been that intervention has led to planning in this sense of rationally co-ordinated public policies: when measures turned out to be more than temporary, when policies had important unanticipated secondary or countervailing effects, when different interventions or policies turned out to be inconsistent or raised administrative difficulties.

State interventions into market forces, in turn, have developed by a process of 'cumulative causation'. As Allan Gruchy aptly puts it, 'an original or primary change will cause secondary reactive changes which will reinforce the primary change and cause the social process to move further in the same direction taken by the primary change' (1972, p. 181). For example, modern technology and organization have increased the scale of economic activity and created opportunities for organizational control over markets. This development 'compels the state to large-scale measures of intervention'. Intervention becomes 'necessary' to prevent social disorganization and exploitation (Mydral, 1960, pp. 32–3). But just as private intervention stimulates state intervention, so too does the derivative state intervention encourage further departure from reliance upon market forces. This occurs directly, by developing an institutional and organizational infrastructure (for example, collective bargaining), and indirectly, by tempering the potentially dislocating features of the original changes, thereby permitting their continued growth and extension.

Another 'typical cumulative process of circular causation' (Myrdal, 1960, p. 36) is found in the transformation of social attitudes. Changes in technology and institutions partly explain adaptations of attitudes. But attitudinal changes, especially during periods of domestic or international crisis, have dissolved old taboos (for example, regarding the gold standard, the categorical imperative of the annually balanced budget, the sanctity of private property) and have made people more economically sophisticated and 'rational', thereby contributing to their insistence on expanding private and public control over their economic destinies. Similarly, with the spread of democratic institutions, based on industrialization and urbanization, it became inevitable that larger numbers of people would press for large-scale redistributional reforms, thereby strengthening the basis for fuller participation in the economic and political life of the community by the lower end of the income and power strata.

*Robert Solo: Ideology's Role in the Evolution of US
Political Economy*

Social scientists from Alexis de Tocqueville and Karl Marx to present day writers have observed and commented on differentiating
properties of the US experience, including dimensions of US political economy which distinguish it from the patterns of European
capitalism. Marx, for example, commented that despite robust US
economic development in the nineteenth century, the existence of an
open frontier and public policies conducive to fairly widespread
landholdings and small-scale farming worked to delay the emergence
of a modern industrial capitalist economy, characterized by the
confrontation of a small, property-owning class and a large, prop-
ertyless proletariat. Mydral has recently observed that departures
from *laissez-faire* and movement toward the advanced, participative
welfare state have been slower in the USA than in Europe. 'The
process of national integration' in the USA, he suggests, 'has still a
considerable distance to go before identification, solidarity, and
participation reach the levels common in the other Western countries.,' After rejecting a country's size, relative youth, and degree of
personal mobility as explanations, Myrdal focuses upon cultural
heterogeneity and 'separatistic loyalties' emanating from the diverse
backgrounds of immigrant groups and upon the more legalistic and
bureaucratic structure of social relations in the USA (1960, p. 99).

In a recent work embracing the entire sweep of US history, Robert
Solo (1974; Peterson, 1976) examines the role of ideology as a
strategic explanatory factor in the evolving relations between the
political authority and the market system. *Ideology*, defined as 'any
coherent idea (or set of ideas) as to what ought to be with respect to
some field of choice and action' (Solo, 1974, p. 18), can and does lag
obstructively behind social change. However, because man is a
learning and valuing creature, ideology can also be an autonomous
spearhead or initiator of change. Furthermore, when a former, obstructive ideology dissolves through the corrosive force of the changing pace of events and is transformed into a new ideological perspective, that new perspective itself can become a powerful force for
change (Solo, 1974, p. 8). Thus, political policy '*is an expression of a
prevailing ideology*' and '*policy change reflects ideological change*'
(p. 23). Explanation and prediction of policy changes require identification and prediction of prospective ideological changes. The role
and impact of ideology, Solo avers, vary with different types of

choice processes. Within organizations, for example, ideology has the greatest import in *authoritative decisions*, that is, decisions made by individuals in authority (who are responsible for explaining and justifying those decisions *for* the organization). *Composite choices*, which reflect the diversity of interests and views of the members of the organization (established, for example, by voting) are more likely to represent compromise than ideological clarity. In the US political system, the Supreme Court 'exemplifies authoritative decisions and articulates an ideology. Congress and the President exemplify composite choice, reflecting a balance of pressures'. (Solo, 1974, p. 40).

At the outset of the US political experience, the dominant ideology was a blend of nationalism and property – and market-oriented liberalism. Although a European transplant, the liberal ideology flourished and persisted in American soil for two key reasons: the absence of a feudal and medieval heritage, and the fact that American liberalism was a *pre*-industrialization phenomenon – it was able to take deep roots prior to the disruptive effects of the capitalist industrialization process.

In the first great phase of the evolving US political economy, roughly until the Civil War, the central issue facing the young republic was the locus of political authority, that is, 'whether the political system was to take the form of decentralized authority exercised by quasi-sovereign states or whether power was to be centralized in the federal government' (Solo, 1974, p. 51). The Constitution, far from resolving this issue, had divided authority between the federal government and the states, and among the president, Congress, and the judiciary within the federal government. In this period, the interests of property and wealth reflected in the liberal ideology were best represented by a strong federal government that would provide infrastructure (internal free trade, national banking, security for property and enforcement of contracts) for development of the market system. In this context, the Supreme Court, acting in concert with the prevailing ideology, took the lead in social reform and change to remedy the lag of institutions behind ideology. In a series of landmark decisions (Marbury v. Madison, 1803; McCulloch v. Maryland, 1819), it revolutionized the power structure of the American political system by spearheading the drive to centralize political authority in a strong nation state.

In the second phase of US political economy, from roughly the end of the Civil War to the depression of the 1930s, massive industrialization, and its attendant technological and institutional changes, created problems and perceived needs that the prevailing ideology of *laissez-faire* liberalism was unable to accommodate. Thus, crisis and need called for institutional reforms that conflicted with the dominant ideology. In this context, ideology was an obstructive force, lagging behind new technology and institutions. Congress and the president (agencies of composite choice) led in the thrust for reform, characterized by piecemeal efforts to expand the scope of public action. The Supreme Court (the agency of authoritative decision), firmly reflecting the dominant ideology of *laissez-faire* liberalism, fought against and succeeded in aborting federal efforts to control prices, wages, hours, employment conditions, and production. Throughout this period, ideology played a powerful constraining role. That it was able to do this, 'even in opposition to rational pragmatism and the pressures of interested groups' (Solo, 1974, p. 154), is an indicator of its tremendous power and widespread acceptance. Only the combination of massive depression, war, the internationally derived imperative of economic growth, and the organizational revolution was finally sufficient to cause the process of social change to break loose from the tenacious hold of obstructive ideology exemplified by the functioning of the Supreme Court from roughly 1860 to 1935.

The years since 1935 have been characterized by institutional experimentation and ideological transition, facilitated by the collapse of the Supreme Court's powerful commitment to the traditional liberal ideology. Institutionally, public policy has gone beyond the mere 'housekeeping function' of the pre-New Deal era (maintaining the institutional infrastructure for individual choice and market relations) to the 'offset function' (offsetting poverty, inequality, bargaining disadvantages, insecurity, and, most notably, instability and unemployment). Ideologically, this has been reflected by a 'New Deal Credo', rationalized by Keynesian economics and focusing upon the offset function, and by post-war Supreme Court decisions reflecting the needs of organization and the need to protect the individual in an organizational society. What is needed now, Solo contends, is a movement, institutionally and ideologically, beyond the offset function phase to a new phase of 'systems planning', wherein the public sector initiates, plans, organizes, and manages 'complex activities in pursuit of goals selected through the process of political choice' (Solo, 1974, p. 371) and thus confronts the challenges and opportunities for collective achievement in such areas as race, urban development, inflation, and growth.

THE INTERPENETRATION OF POLITICS AND ECONOMICS

If the evolutionary process of development in politico-economic institutions is the primary theme in the institutionalist approach to political economy, then the *interpenetration* of politics and economics in the institutional structure and behaviour of contemporary society runs a close second. This felicitous expression, apparently coined by J. M. Clark in a seminal paper in the mid-1950s, conveys pointedly the idea that as a result of social change not only have former conceptions of boundaries between politics and economics broken down, but also 'each discipline, and practice, enters inevitably into the field of the other'. On the one hand, within 'official' government, economic processes and interests 'shape political issues and measures': government policy, in turn, 'increasingly shapes the course of economic affairs'. On the other hand, economic and political characteristics are combined in the economic governments or 'nominally private bodies that carry on economic affairs' (Clark, 1957, pp. 226–7; Hamilton, 1957). Consequently, polity has become a process for economizing as well as a system of authority and power, while economy has become a system of power as well as a process for economizing. Some of the major methodological and theoretical implications of the resulting amalgam will now be described briefly by reference to two prominent contributors to the institutional tradition: John R. Commons and Galbraith.

John R. Commons: The Political Economy of Collective Action

For Commons, institutional economics was perceived as virtually synonymous with the political economy of collective action. Collective action, which Commons viewed as expanding and liberating as well as controlling individual action, ranges ubiquitously from unorganized custom to organized private and public 'going concerns'. In contemporary capitalism, the dominant organizational forms of collective action are corporations, labour unions, and political parties. Because collective action has been present in economic thought (although generally ignored or de-emphasized) from the mid-eighteenth century to the present, the intellectual problem is not to substitute a new, institutional economics for mainstream thought, but to create a 'rounded-out Political Economy', so as 'to give collective action, in all its varieties, its due place throughout economic theory' (Commons, 1934, p. 5).

Collective action, as does individual action, begins with scarcity 'as universal for all economic theory' (Commons, 1934, p. 6). But scarcity for Commons goes beyond the biological and psychological dimensions of Malthus and the Austrians, respectively, to the '*proprietary* scarcity' connected with intangible property in contemporary capitalism (that is, to the ownership power to control things, notably to restrict supply), 'enforced by working rules of government and by the collective action of corporations and labour unions' (Commons, 1950, p. 94). Traditional economics, by focusing upon such relatively bloodless and essentially man-to-nature or man-to-himself concepts as utility, commodity, and exchange, in the main was able to slight the institutional dimensions of economic activity. In the traditional view, scarcity leads to individual, economizing choices. In a world of mutual interdependence, choices are co-ordinated through market exchange relations, with static equilibrium and market values as the theoretical results.

By contrast, institutional economics focuses upon man-to-man actions or *transactions*, classified as bargaining (transactors as legal equals), managerial (transactors as individual legal superiors and inferiors, for example, foreman and worker), and rationing (transactors as collective legal superiors and inferiors, for example, a legislature and the citizenry, a labour union and its members). Ownership thus 'becomes the foundation of institutional economics' because ownership interacts with scarcity to create conflicts of interest which are 'predominant in transactions'. But transactors are mutually interdependent as well as conflicting. Because of mutual interdependence, Commons rather optimistically believed, the 'alienation and acquisition, between individuals, of the *rights* of future ownership of physical things' would be 'negotiated between the parties concerned, according to the working rules of society', thus creating not equilibrium or 'harmony', but at least a certain 'security of expectations' or 'order' (Commons, 1934, p. 58).

This negotiational process, in turn, rests upon 'sovereignty', that is, 'the changing process of authorizing, prohibiting, and regulating the use of physical force in human affairs' (Commons, 1934, p. 684). In the USA, the system of courts, ultimately the Supreme Court, serves as the arbiter and determiner of the application of society's negotiational working rules. 'The Court thus becomes an authoritative faculty of Political Economy for the United States' (Commons, 1934, p. 712). Its rulings (and those of the administrative commissions, which have absorbed much of the Court's functions in economic regulation since the mid-1930s), 'correlating law, economics, and ethics', come to represent 'reasonable values'. This is so not because they constitute market equilibria, but because they are based on the distinctly human qualities of 'conflict of interests, mutual dependence, and the rules of order deemed necessary to keep industry agoing with due regard to public and private interests' (Commons, 1934, p. 719). In brief, the mainstream sequence would be:

Scarcity	Economizing Choice	Market Co-ordination	Equilibrium and Market Values

Commons's revised institutionalist sequence would be:

Scarcity	Ownership and Power Conflicts	Negotiation under Sovereignty	Created Order and Reasonable Values

From the perspectives of both the classical theory of democracy and the classical and neo-classical theories of the competitive market, Commons's revised sequence would seem defective as well as vague. On the one hand, it would substitute governance by pressure groups and the negotiations of various private and public governments for genuine, one man, one vote majoritarian democracy (Dahl and Lindblom, 1953, pp. 504–7). On the other hand, it would substitute an elusive bargaining process among restrictionist and monopolizing economic power groups for market choice and co-ordination under a beneficent competitive regime. In Commons's view, both types of criticism miss the point. Drawing upon his own extensive personal experience as well as on intensive study of history, law, and administration, Commons contended that the negotiational, organizational political economy is the way contemporary collective capitalism works. The realistic alternative to organizational pluralism is not the economic individualism of classical theory, he averred, but the monopolizing proclivities of corporate monism. The most likely alternative to national bargaining in political life is not classical democracy, but some variety of totalitarian dictatorship. (Both Soviet-style communism and fascism, he observed, eliminate or emasculate the autonomy of labour unions, corporations, and political parties.) The basic rationale for encouraging and attempting to improve on the emerging and imperfect contemporary collective capitalism stems not from its tendency toward optimality or perfection (classical competition and classical democracy are superior on that score), but from the fact that it appears to be the only workable alternative to politico-economic forms (Soviet communism, fascism) that would destroy liberal and democratic values outright.

Commons was basically optimistic concerning the continued development and strengthening of what he called emerging 'reasonable capitalism' or 'collective democracy', characterized by an 'equilibrium of economic power' among conflicting interests and classes. But that optimism was qualified by recognition of power, yet internal disruption, created by 'banker capitalism' (so-called because of the enhanced role of financial interests in twentieth century corporate activities, notably in mergers and holding companies) and the appeals amid the dangers of the external ideologies and systems of fascism and communism. As to communism, Commons held that 'Marx was even more nearly correct for the United States than he was for Russia or Italy'. Massive industrialization, coupled with the surge to dominance of the large-scale corporation (facilitated by friendly Supreme Court decisions in the late nineteenth century and financial innovations in the twentieth, for example, the holding company), radically reduced the role of small proprietors, who were the 'bulwark of American individualism', and created an industrial labour force of wage and salary workers, 'the foundations of Communism or Fascism'. Small businessmen and farmers are ground 'between the upper and nether millstone of modern technology and business depressions. On the one side big business is absorbing their markets. On the other side wage-earners are demanding higher wages and shorter hours. . . . The conflict is irrepressible.' As private property becomes corporate property, and individualism becomes 'corporationism', as illustrated in the depths of the depressed 1930s, the 'remaining small proportion of farmers become revolutionists by defying the courts and sheriffs in their attempts to foreclose mortgages' (Commons, 1934; pp. 880–1, 885–6).

As to banker capitalism, Commons recognized that conflicts occur between classes or groups as well as between individual transactors, as evidenced by the fact that classes organize and consolidate 'for concerted action according to similarities in economic interests' (Commons, 1934, p. 109).

Power, he emphasized, is fundamentally a 'question of class war, or class struggle, breaking out in strikes, lockouts, and even in military revolutions'. Although these classes are several, rather than one or two, collective bargaining between organized labour and organized capital is the 'major economic issue' to which other organizations and classes (farmers, bankers, merchants, and so forth) must 'conform their policies and methods' (Commons, 1950, pp. 262, 266).

Until the massive depression of the 1930s brought remedial action by government, an altered role for the Supreme Court, and a strengthened position for organized labour relative to capital, there is no doubt that American political as well as economic institutions strongly reflected the dominant position of propertied and financial interests and the large-scale corporations. Indeed, at least up to the depression, both legislatures and 'voluntary private associations of laborers, farmers, small business men, and political parties' were 'getting weaker and weaker in America' (Commons, 1934, p. 898). Still, Commons held, there are fundamental contrasts between American and European capitalism, notably, greater abundance, extension of stock ownership, promotion from within the ranks, and greater tolerance of small business, both because of small business efficiency in some areas and fear of political repercussions to monopoly. These factors, combined with the labour legislation of the New Deal and the resulting improved bargaining position for organized labour, supported Commons's qualified hope that a 'balance of power between self-governing corporations and unions' and a 'constitutional government of balanced equilibrium of propertied and unpropertied classes, capable of holding its own against military despotisms, may be foreseen on the American field' (Commons, 1950, pp. 263, 268).

John Kenneth Galbraith: Power and the Planning System

In Commons's approach to political economy, corporations and labour unions are perceived as private economic governments. Individually, and in negotiation with one another, they comprise legislative, executive, and judicial components; formulate and administer policy; rule vast economic empires; seek legitimation of their rule; demonstrate complex relations between leadership and 'citizens'; exercise moral and economic, if not physical, sanctions; and make treaties and strike pacts with each other. At the same time, government, especially administrative commissions and the Supreme Court, is intimately and inextricably involved in the administration of public economic policy and the economic activities of the 'private' sector generally, notably the adjudication of disputes between the formulation of working rules for corporations and labour unions. The conflicting economic interests of groups and classes constitute the basis and determine the content of public policies, and economic breakdowns and economic class struggles serve as the root causes of wars and revolutions.

As Commons recognized, '*political* economy' is not merely a matter of governance; it is also fundamentally a question of power, of dominance and subservience in the determination and legitimization of goals, rules and policies. From this perspective, politics and economics cannot be distinguished in terms of (overlapping) 'sectors' of national life, 'private' and 'public', but only as alternative approaches to or ways of looking at society; and political economy implies thinking of economic activity as a power system as well as an economizing process.

Among contemporary economists in the institutionalist tradition, Galbraith is perhaps pre-eminent in perceiving and examining the evolving American economy as a political and power system. Schematically, we may identify four major kinds of power relations in Galbraith's writings: (1) those between business, especially large-scale corporate, leadership and the general consuming and working public (and, similarly, between political leadership and the citizenry); (2) the internal power relations within the giant corporations, notably, the shift in power not only from owners to managers, but therein, from managers to the 'technostructure'; (3) the power relations between the 'planning system' and the 'market system'; and (4) the power interactions between business and government, exemplified by the 'symbiosis' between big business and the public bureaucracy (Galbraith, 1971; 1973; Fusfeld, 1972). We have already alluded to the first issue in connection with our earlier discussion of Galbraith's views on the emergence and evolution of corporate planning. In the interest of brevity, we reluctantly refrain from further comment on these matters here and also pass over the much discussed second issue (the shift in intra-corporate power to the technostructure) in order to focus upon the somewhat less familiar remaining two.

Among the remaining issues is the question of power relations between the planning system and the market system. *Power*, Galbraith asserts – defined as 'the ability of an individual or a group to impose its purposes on others' (1973, p. 92) – is a central fact in contemporary political economy, rooted in technology and its correlative, corporate organization (1983a; 1983b). But the comparative growth, size, and consequently power of the relatively more organized versus the relatively less organized parts of the economy (and between larger and smaller organizations) is 'singularly uneven'

(1973, p. 40). Although the national economy is properly perceived as a continuum ranging from the smallest family farm to the largest corporate behemoth, it is analytically useful to distinguish between two broad sectors. The planning system consists of about one thousand Brobdingnagian corporations producing approximately half of all non-government output in manufacturing, power, transportation, finance, and merchandising. The other, the market system, consists of about 12 million smaller firms and farms, in trade, light manufacturing, services, and the arts; it constitutes roughly the 'other half' of the national economy.

In terms of power, there are key differences between these two sectors. Both endeavour to control their economic environment, but by different means and with different degrees of success. In the market system, the enterprise is under the control of an individual (in either the proprietorship or the entrepreneurial corporation). Some degree of control over the economic environment exists in the form of product differentiation and local monopoly. Typically, such control is relatively small and tenuous and often depends on collective action or government assistance (for example, resale price maintenance laws, agricultural price supports, government support for collective bargaining) for its initiation or sustenance. The market system, granting its impurities and imperfections, functions more or less in accord with orthodox theory. By contrast, the control over the economic environment exercised by the giant technology-bred 'mature' corporate organizations in the planning system is both pervasive and powerful. Here, control emanates almost automatically, as a result of large size, supplemented by corporate strategies in such areas as internal financing (to insulate the organization from intrusions of stockholders and creditors), sales promotion, vertical integration, imperialist control over raw materials in Third World countries, multinational operations, and so on. And here, as noted earlier, corporate planning (although by no means the balanced integration of the various corporate plans) has largely superseded the market pricing system as a process for economic co-ordination.

Furthermore, the market system is part of the environment which the planning system seeks to control, while the planning system is part of an environment which is essentially beyond the control of the market system. Large corporations both sell to and buy from smaller firms, but at prices controlled by the giants. Given the uneven distribution of power between the two systems, the terms of trade between them 'will have an insouciant tendency to favor the system that controls its prices and costs and therewith the prices and costs of the other system as well' (Galbraith, 1973, p. 51). In short, inequalities in economic power generate inequalities in income between the two sectors, as the big corporations manipulate prices charged and prices paid to their own advantage. In the absence of 'unimpeded mobility' between the two sectors, these differences in the level and security of income can and will persist.

A second issue pertaining to power raised by Galbraith is that of relations between business and government. Institutionalists, from Veblen to the present, have typically held an ambivalent attitude toward the role of the state and government policy in economic life. On the one hand, many, like Veblen, have taken it as virtually axiomatic that the state heavily reflects the dominant economic and class interests in capitalist society and that government policy, especially prior to the 1930s, essentially favoured capitalist, propertied, and corporate interests. On the other hand, most have viewed the state as partially independent of business interests and thereby capable of at least quasi-independent programmes of action, ranging from deterioration into authoritarian and dictatorial control over business as well as society to, under propitious circumstances such as the New Deal, genuine democratic reforms and policies more broadly reflective of the interests and perceived needs of non-business groups and society at large.

Galbraith's contribution to this ongoing debate has been to distinguish between the methods and character of interaction with the state and influence upon public policy of the entrepreneurial, market-oriented enterprise (either proprietorship or corporation), prominent prior to the Second World War, and the mature corporation of the contemporary planning system. The entrepreneurial enterprise, rooted in the market system, had (and has) essentially a pecuniary relation with government. Under propitious circumstances, especially prior to the 1930s, it bought its favours (tariffs, franchises, mineral rights, tax exemptions) from receptive (and income-maximizing) politicians. Under less propitious circumstances, for example, the New Deal years, these favours would be reduced or (typically temporarily) withdrawn. In any event, it was (and is) not strategically dependent upon the state. The market, not government, was (and is) the main source of its income and wealth; and the temporary interruption of government largesse (assuming, although Galbraith does not make this explicit, the continued existence of market and private property relations) was unpleasant, but not fatal.

By contrast, the mature corporation, rooted in the planning system and ruled, according to Galbraith, by its technostructure, is both dependent upon government and enters into a symbiotic relationship with it. The planning system, 'in fact, is inextricably associated with the state. In notable respects the mature corporation is an arm of the state. And the state, in important matters, is an instrument of the industrial system' (Galbraith, 1971, p. 298). As noted earlier, the giant corporations are dependent upon government, in Galbraith's view, for qualified manpower, education, regulation of aggregate demand, provision of capital, support of technology, and, notably in military production, markets. Consequently, opposition to government's expanded role in the economy (in these areas), so important to the business litany prior to the Second World War, has quietly evaporated in the age of the mature corporation. On the other hand, the mature corporation has come to influence and control public policy in intricate and subtle ways, notably through symbiosis with the public bureaucracies, especially in military production, facilitated by the tendency for many legislators to ally themselves with the bureaucracy and thus, by association, with the planning system. The symbiosis between business and government extends from the public bureaucracy and the regulatory agencies to societal goals. 'The state is strongly concerned with the stability of the economy. And with its expansion or growth. And with education. And with technical and scientific advance. And, most notably, with the national defense. These are the national goals' (Galbraith, 1972, p. 311) *and* those of the giant corporations. 'A final source of political power for the planning system is organized labor' (Galbraith, 1973, p. 161). Labour-capital conflicts in the big corporations have been greatly reduced by the capacity of the corporations to pass on wage increases in the form of price boosts, by the 'psychic identification' of workers in the planning system with the organization, and by the coalescence of corporate goals (for example, big defence budgets, steady employment, high growth rates) with those of organized labour.

INSTITUTIONALISM AND NORMATIVE POLITICAL ECONOMY

Emphasis in this chapter on power relations in political economy and on evolutionary social change has left implicit what many would consider a salient element of institutionalism, namely, its orientation toward policy, planning, and reform, rooted in normative or ethical commitment. Such an orientation, found among many institutionalists, follows readily from focus both on politico-economic power and social change. On the one hand, most institutionalists believe that in

THE INSTITUTIONALIST SCHOOL OF POLITICAL ECONOMY 83

contemporary industrial societies, power is wielded by the few to promote their advantage within the existing status quo. Consequently, a 'value-free' social science and an eschewal of system reform constitutes an implicit acceptance of the status quo and thereby of its institutions and power concentrations (Lynd, 1948, p. 181; Cohen, 1931, p. 348). Conversely, to question the legitimacy of power relations and the institutional status quo suggests the need for explication of social values and of directions for policy and reform. On the other hand, commitment to a perspective of evolutionary social change rather than, say, to an ordered, mechanical view of the social world, reduces faith in universal and unchanging laws of human behaviour, and encourages both focus on policy and institutional change and an active, participatory role by the political economist in planning and reform. (Cochran, 1983; Hamilton, 1953).

Institutionalism as normative and policy-oriented political economy may be illustrated briefly by two major examples. One is the development, most prominently by Adolph Lowe, of methodological design for an explicitly goal-centred and policy-oriented 'political economics'. According to Lowe, mainstream economics exhibits a faith in an orderly world of competitive equilibrium. This faith ultimately rests on the presupposition of a 'universal and uniform behavioral vector' (colourlessly represented by the principle of maximization) yielding an 'immutable law of economic motion' (Lowe, 1980, p. 251). Using a hypothetical-deductive method, traditional economics thus derives from a given, existing state a predicted future state induced by a change in initial conditions. But affluence, monopoly power, technological change, and ecological imbalance have rendered laws of market behaviour otiose. Consequently a new methodology is needed, namely one which attempts to determine the means suitable to attain desired objectives (Lowe, 1965). In this view, goals become the knowns rather than the unknowns of the analysis, which focuses on the technologies, behaviour, and institutions needed for goal achievement rather than on laws of market behaviour.

At first, it might appear that this procedure merely inverts the logic of traditional economic theory. As Tinbergen puts it, the 'task of economic analysis is to consider the data (including the means of economic policy) as given or known, and the economic phenomena and variables (including the aims of economic policy) as unknown. The problem of economic policy considers the aims as given, and the means as unknown or at least partly unknown' (1963, p. 9). According to such defenders of Lowe's 'instrumental' methodology as Heilbroner, however, more is involved than mere logical inversion of a scientific procedure. Although an instrumental or policy analysis depends in part on behavioural generalizations, it does not collapse if these presumed regularities prove unfounded. 'Instead, provided that the target remains the same, it now becomes the task of theory to discover other behavioral routes to the same goal, or to explore specific means of establishing the behavior that is required. Instrumentalism can thus be pragmatic rather than aprioristic with respect to the relevant "laws" of behaviour' (Heilbroner, 1970, p. 19).

To put the matter more broadly, institutionalist analysis is oriented toward problem-solving, based heavily on empirical observation and inductive logic. Deductively formulated generalizations or 'laws' of behaviour are valued essentially as instruments of action and social practice, and derive their interest from their practical relevance (Hill, 1978, pp. 316–17). As Cochran notes (1983, pp. 3–11), this approach is deeply rooted in the institutionalist tradition. Illustrations include: Commons's concept (1961) of ideas as 'guides to action' and science itself 'not as a body of knowledge, but as a process of attaining control'; Ayres's view (1953, p. 285) of institutional change guided by 'organized human intelligence' rather than 'social drift and automatism'; and Dewey's emphasis (1949) on the shift from 'contemplative to operative' knowledge.

A second example of a policy-oriented perspective in institutionalist thought is its espousal of a normative political economy. In part, institutionalist political economy is 'meta-normative', that is, it provides definitions, descriptions, and explanations of policy goals and social values (as distinguished from making judgements concerning their desirability) (Frankena, 1967, p. 230). This, institutionalists suggest, is useful because of the occasionally encountered view that any discussion of social values departs from the ethical neutrality desired in social science. By contrast, institutionalists observe that formulation of objectives, assessment of policies and organizations in terms of degree of correspondence to policy goals, and projection of valuations into future experience by construction of goal-oriented programmes are among the most significant facts of social life and, as such, are essential elements in a meaningful and relevant science of political economy (Elliott, 1980 pp. 5–9). Indeed, because social values condition institutions (and changes in social values elicit alterations in institutions), the analysis of social values is central to the institutionalist paradigm (Bush, 1981–2, pp. 25–6).

Mainstream economists sometimes observe that consideration of social values with a policy-oriented political economy can (or should) be restricted to meta-normative issues. For example, Samuelson (1952, p. 57) has stated that 'any prescribed set of ends is grist for the economist's unpretentious deductive mill . . .' Institutionalists, who generally dissent from this view, contend that whatever the logical possibilities, fact and value, ends and means, and scholarship and advice, in practice, are interwoven. Concerning facts and values, Myrdal states that scientific work presupposes selecting topics and asking questions about them. These 'questions are an expression of our interest in the world, they are at bottom valuations. Valuations are thus necessarily involved already at the stage when we observe facts and carry on theoretical analysis, and not only at the stage when we draw political inferences from facts and valuations' (1954, p. vii). Similarly, economic advisers are seldom in a position to separate normative neatly from non-normative or meta-normative issues. Taking a client's ends as 'given' for purposes of formulating the most efficient means to attain them, for example, 'would mean evasion, because by undertaking his investigation he enters their service' (Johr and Singer, 1949, p. 35). It is also contended by institutionalists that separation of means from ends is artificial and discordant with the logic of inquiry itself. In a dynamic and continuous means-ends process, a former end (what John Dewey called end-in-view) in turn may become a means for pursuit of yet another end. Thus, there is no 'given' or 'final end': 'Nothing happens which is final in the sense that it is not part of an ongoing stream of events' (Dewey, 1939, p. 43). Moreoever, because of the dynamic means-ends continuum, it is unduly restrictive as well as impracticable for social inquiry to be limited to analysis of the efficiency of means in pursuit of ends. Instead, the function of human intelligence is 'to project new and/or complex ends – to free experience from routine and from caprice', to 'liberate and liberalize action' rather than merely using thought 'to accomplish purposes already given in the existent state of society . . .' (Dewey, 1928, p. 219; cited in Cochran, 1983, p. 3).

Beyond examination of meta-normative issues and denial of a practicable dichotomy between fact and value, institutionalists embrace an explicitly normative political economy, that is, an attempt to evaluate social values. This expressly normative perspective is strongly rooted in institutionalist thought, notably in the Veblen-Ayres tradition and that tradition's contemporary successors. Normative evaluation is implicit in the basic Veblen dichotomy between 'business' (and its predatory and destructive propensities) and 'industry' (and its creative and constructive properties). Dewey's view of a means-ends continuum (as distinguished from a given or final end) also contains important normative implications. For Dewey, ends-in-view are evaluated in terms of their serviceability or efficiency in problem-solving. This suggests that normative propositions, like explanatory theories, 'are a form of empirical knowledge . . . and must be justified as well as confirmed by reference to experience' (Lewis, 1947, p. 365), that is, that tests for values are based on an open-ended 'process of inquiry itself' (Bush, 1981-2, p. 22). It also implies that sustenance of the processes of inquiry is good, whereas its obstruction, by impairing comprehension of the consequences of actions and thereby efficiency in problem-solving, is bad (Tool, 1977, pp. 830-1). Dewey supplemented this instrumentalist argument with a liberal democratic perspective. According to Dewey, the 'full development of individuals in their distinctive individuality' and a sharing by 'every individual' in the rights and duties pertaining to 'control of social affairs' is essential to social co-operation and enrichment and thereby the 'common welfare'. As a corollary, the 'walls of privilege and monopolistic possession', and restrictions on the opportunity of 'each individual for full development' based on 'status, wealth, birth, and sex, etc.' should be 'eliminated' (Dewey and Tufts, 1922, pp. 387-8; cited in Tool, 1977, p. 831).

Ayres elaborated and refined the Veblen dichotomy, integrated it with Dewey's instrumentalist philosophy, and applied it as an explicit normative criterion. On the one hand, he posited a 'technological continuum' essentially similar to Dewey's means-ends continuum of inquiry, which serves as the 'locus of truth and value' and thus as the basis for 'objectively' defining and understanding social values (Ayres, 1943, p. 477; cited in Tool, 1977, p. 834). On the other, he distinguished (1944) between technological and instrumental activities, which, being based on tool-using capabilities and inquiry, further the 'life processes' of the culture, and 'ceremonial' and invidious behaviour, which, being based on status, power, hierarchy, and so on, inhibit and obstruct change.

Contemporary institutionalists in the Veblen-Ayres tradition (Culbertson, 1978: Hill, 1978) continue the process of blending normative evaluation with logical and empirical analysis. Marc Tool (1977; 1979), drawing on the largely oral tradition of J. Fagg Foster (1981, pp. 899-905), a student of Ayres, has both integrated and extended previous institutionalist normative political economy by presenting the following 'social value criterion': 'The continuity of human life and the noninvidious re-creation of community through the instrumental use of knowledge' (Tool, 1979, p. 574). This criterion contains four salient parts: (1) the continuance of human life, at least in terms of physical survival, at best in terms of a 'reverence' for life and a 'deference to human potential and developmental capabilities' (1979, p. 294), is prerequisite for all other human pursuits, including social thought; (2) the expression 'noninvidious' reflects the Veblen-Ayres critique of judgemental comparisons based on race, sex, wealth, ownership, and so on; (3) the criterion incorporates Dewey's notion of efficiency in use of knowledge in problem-solving; (4) reference to 'community' indicates, as in Dewey's earlier analysis, that human life occurs only in society and culture.

Institutionalists of the Commons-Galbraith variety have been no less committed to normative political economy than those claiming intellectual lineage from Veblen, Dewey, and Ayres, although the former have been less inclined to develop formal statements concerning criteria for assessing social values. Commons's concept of 'reasonable value', for example, as illustrated by public utility regulation and promotion of economic stability, is based on construction of a workable and ethical 'consensus of opinion' of those participating in transactions (1961, p. 743). Galbraith's notion of social imbalance (1957, pp. 251–69), described as an 'opulent' supply of privately produced commodities and 'niggardly' provision of public services, is clearly value-impregnated, both in the sense of a value judgement or criterion for evaluation ('social balance') and interpretive application of that criterion to particular instances (for example, 'over-investment in things' and 'under-investment in people'). Institutionalists – Galbraith is a prominent example – are often criticized by their mainstream colleagues for just this tendency. The institutionalist response has generally been that mainstream economics also contains its value assumptions and judgements (for example, the premisses underlying the notion of Pareto optimality and its applications), but that these presuppositions are typically tacit or at least insufficiently exposed to systematic examination and assessment (Tool, 1980).

CONCLUDING REMARKS

The primary focus in this article has been expositional and illustrative rather than evaluational and comprehensive. Some brief comments of critical assessment thus may be in order. First, institutionalist political economy from Veblen to Galbraith does seem to demon-strate at least the unity and continuity implied by the expression 'useful fiction' used at the outset of the article to justify treating contributors in the institutionalist tradition as a group. As we ex-amine the views of such economists as Veblen, Commons, Ayres, Galbraith, and Myrdal, it would be misleading as well as ungenerous to deny that, despite individual differences on specific matters, somehow the whole of institutionalist political economy *is* greater than the sum of its individual parts.

Second, it is important to emphasize that the institutionalist approach to political economy, with its focus upon the interblended evolutionary development of technology, institutions, ideology, and economic behaviour, group and power conflict, and the inter-penetration of politics and economics, does not primarily (although it certainly does in parts) offer different answers to the traditional questions of orthodox, economizing-oriented economic theory. In-stead, it asks and endeavours to answer no less important but typical-ly different – and larger – questions, notably those pertaining to issues such as discussed herein. In so far as this is true, institutionalist political economy is essentially complementary to standard econo-mic theory, even when economists of institutionalist persuasion offer their neo-neoclassical and neo-Keynesian colleagues few compli-ments (and vice versa). Assertions of superiority in debates between institutionalists and their critics – illustrated, for example, by Robert Solow's majestically disdainful concluding comment in his inter-change with Galbraith (Solow, 1967, 'Après moi, la sociologie') – often seem to be more reflective of alternative methodological and philosophical perspectives concerning questions to be asked than of the validity of answers to given questions.

Third, ironically, compared to such analysts of institutional evolu-tion as Marx and Joseph Schumpeter, a case may be made for the proposition that many American institutionalists have been *insuf-ficiently* institutional, that they have spread their analytical nets too narrowly rather than too broadly. Although his judgement would probably be tempered somewhat today, notably as regards Gal-braith, the main thrust of R. A. Gordon's assessment of the early 1960s retains much merit. Marx and Schumpeter, Gordon observed, 'took the entire story of capitalist evolution and possible decline' as their province. American institutionalists have not gone this far with their institutionalism. Typically, their analyses have been framed 'within a limited time perspective and with reference chiefly to American conditions. They have therefore not produced the comprehensive, evolutionary, and institutionally oriented theory that they sought. Their perspective in time and space was more limited than they realized. . . . They thought very largely in terms of American economic and social conditions during a few decades. And, in a sense, they did not ask big enough questions, did not equip themselves with the tools to answer systematically the questions that they did ask' (Gordon, in Dorfman, 1963, p. 146).

Last, and related to the third point, institutionalist political economy, from its own perspective, might well benefit from closer links with other dissenting or unorthodox approaches (quite apart from maintaining interchange with the general body of economic analysis). With the notable exception of Veblen, institutionalists have kept Marx (and thereby possible insights from Marxian analysis) at arm's length. Despite the obvious parallels between his analysis of capitalist development and that of institutionalism, Schumpeter typically fares no better at the hands of institutionalists. His name appears only once, for example, in Gruchy's comprehensive volumes on institutionalism, in a footnote reference to Mitchell's cycle theory (Gruchy, 1972, p. 44; 1947).

More recently, one wonders about the potential benefits of attempting to connect institutionalist analyses with the unorthodox studies of such British neo-Keynesians as Joan Robinson. Her dissent from the post-Keynesian orthodoxy (somewhat impudently but pointedly labelled 'bastard Keynesianism') – including her focus on income distribution and its relations to consumption and investment, her denial of a marginal product of labour or of capital, her rejection of the concept of equilibrium and substitution of a non-mechanistic process of historical dynamics, and, especially, her insistence upon saving as investment-determined rather than the other way around – are remarkably similar to views expressed by Ayres, among others (Kregel, 1973). But, then, if economists in the institutionalist tradition were to establish closer connecting linkages with Schumpeter, Marxian studies, and such contemporary economists as Michael Kalecki, Robinson, and Piero Sraffa, the resulting interaction could well approach what a resurrected Veblen might call a Grand Union of dissenting perspectives; and one wonders whether *that* might not be more than the economics profession, if not Western society, could reasonably absorb, to use Veblen's apt expression, 'just yet' (Veblen, 1921, p. 169).

4

Modern Marxian Political Economy

ARUN BOSE

Marxian political economy is an essential part of a Marxian paradigm of social revolution. A brief acquaintance with this paradigm must be the starting point of any introduction to Marxian political economy.

In 1844–6, Karl Marx, when discussing the prospect for a communist revolution in Germany, declared that the 'material force' represented by the state apparatus could only be overthrown by material force, but that 'a general theory of the world', a world-view, social theory or social paradigm, 'also becomes a material force once it has gripped the masses'.[1] This can be accomplished, he argued, by forging suitable 'weapons of criticism' to be used for 'ruthless criticism of all that exists'.[2] These 'weapons of criticism' can then be exchanged for 'criticism with weapons' to initiate 'a political revolution with a social soul',[3] i.e. a political revolution which implements radically new social aims, instead of ensuring that 'the more things change the more they remain the same', or that 'things are changed so that they will not change'.[4] For, in the final analysis, 'not criticism but revolution is the driving force of history'.[5]

Since this time, Marx's own social theory has become a material force to be reckoned with in some countries, and it has inspired several political revolutions, more successful than abortive, in the twentieth century. These successful political revolutions have initiated social revolutions whose mutations and convulsions[6] remain some of the most arresting events of the century. This remains true, even though and precisely *because* how and how far the secular social aims of these revolutions will be fulfilled will almost certainly remain undecided until the end of the century and well into the next.[7]

As stated above, Marxian political economy is an essential part of this Marxian world view or paradigm which has become so influential in the twentieth century in moving the masses into political and social action. Its main ideas, elaborated and perhaps sometimes over-elaborated, still very much 'hang together' as expounded in a massive scholarly work consisting of *Capital* (three volumes), *Theories of Surplus Value* (subtitled, appropriately, volume 4 of *Capital*), as well as the fragments – *Contribution to a Critique of Political Economy, The Economic and Philosophical Manuscripts* (1844), *Grundrisse, Results of the Immediate Process of Production* and *Critique of the Gotha Programme.* On a very different wavelength, much better adapted to the beginner, the same basic ideas, still very much hanging together, are put across in the concise and compact popular expositions – *The Communist Manifesto, Wage Labour and Capital, Lecture on Free Trade* and *The Eighteenth Brumaire of Louis Bonaparte.* Together, these texts of Marx on his own version of political economy help us to understand better modern capitalism – which he criticized – as well as 'socialism as the first stage of communism', which has been established in some countries on the basis of his ideas.

Marxian political economy has, however, had only a slight influence on economic theory as taught in most countries, a theory which has been increasingly 'de-politicized' over the past century. On modern 'radical political economy' which has been taking shape over the last 20 years or so, Marx has had an acknowledged pervasive influence.[8] Amongst the possible reasons for reluctance to accept Marxian political economy is the repetitive style used in Marx's scholarly texts where the same point is made again and again, though from many different angles and at many different levels of analysis. This is in striking contrast to the crisp assertiveness of his popular tracts on the same subject. Both put off modern readers. Marx's research level works on political economy are 'too difficult' but his popular tracts are 'too easy'. For this there is a reason (even if this is no excuse) which must be considered by anybody who wants to make a serious effort to come to grips with Marxian political economy.

CAPITALIST MYSTIFICATION

When Marx began to work out his social theories in the 1840s he was already committed to the notion that processes which promote (or retard) a social revolution are more akin to dialectical, reciprocally interacting biochemical processes than mechanical, mono-causal physical processes. He conjectured that, at any time and in any country, there was a precise *mode of social production* (or the 'economic basis' or the 'economic structure'), to which corresponded the 'superstructure' or the *civil society* appropriate to it. The reciprocal interaction of elements of the social mode of production (the social productive forces, such as machinery, railways and steam ships, and the social production relations, including rights to own, manage and control productive assets) and the elements of the superstructure 'acting through the state' (i.e. 'all the theoretical products and forms of consciousness, religion, philosophy, morality, etc., of these various sides on one another depicted in its totality') co-determine ('is the basis of') all history.[9]

Three points should be noted about this conjecture. First, it is emphatically not a sophisticated way of making the banal statement that in social life everything depends on everything else. On the contrary, it suggests that, in any one country at any one time, some specific elements belonging to both levels – the economic basis and the civil society – interact to promote historical change, and that these can be clearly identified. Thus, Marx and Engels identified the major preconditions of revolutionary changes in England in the seventeenth and eighteenth centuries specifically as (1) the Tudor monarchy, which drove the vagrants emerging from a disintegrating feudal society into a 'free' labour market by penal legislation;[10] (2) internal free competition won by the revolution of 1640–88; (3) an expanding world market outgrowing supply by existing productive forces in England; (4) development of theoretical Newtonian mechanics and its popularization in the eighteenth century;[11] (5) the use of the steam engine for driving machinery in factory, mine, railway and in steam navigation.[12] Of these, (1), (2) and (4) belong to the 'civil society'; (3) and (5) belong to the economic basis or mode of production. The rise of the 'steam mill', for example, was, according to Marx, aided by such developments as the formation of the free labour market on one side and also by, for instance, the decline of classical studies and the rise of scientific studies (including theoretical Newtonian mechanics) in the universities, the establishment of the Royal Society, etc.

Third, the English example drives home the point that Marx attached *equal* importance to specific elements at the different levels of the base and superstructure as co-determinants of the historical process; *which* particular elements at each level played the role of co-determinants differed from case to case and from time to time. If a contrary impression, that 'the economic is in some sense the ultimate point in the chain of causes' (Weber),[13] is sometimes given by Marx (notably in his Preface to *Contribution to the Critique of Political Economy*),[14] this need not be taken too seriously. Not only do we have before us what Marx had to say about the English revolution but we also know of the Russian revolution, which his ideas inspired, and which certainly has been co-determined by both political and economic factors on any interpretation available.[15] Marx also conjectured at this stage that a crucial role would be played in this co-determination through reciprocal interaction by political and economic factors of processes of social change in modern capitalist society, by class formation, class conflict and by domination of class hegemony.[16]

In the next few years, Marx turned to a close study of the literature of political economy which, dating it from the first publication of Quesnay's physiocratic *tableau économique* in 1785, was the youngest branch of social studies but already half a century old. Regarding classical political economy as the ideological product of rising capitalism *par excellence*, believing also that 'reason has always existed, though not always in a reasonable form' and that a critic can therefore 'start from any form of theoretical and practical consciousness' to 'develop the true reality', Marx hoped to find the concept of class, of exploitation, on which he already insisted the concept of class must be based,[17] the analysis of social class formation,[18] and the role of class conflict all clarified or laid bare in the literature of political economy.

His extensive researches, however, left him increasingly dissatisfied. He found that political economists were crippled by imprecise and ambiguous words and concepts. Probing more deeply he came to the conclusion that there was a 'religion of everyday (economic) life' under capitalism which concealed, camouflaged and 'mystified' economic relations.[19] Classical political economy was unable to penetrate this mystification by theoretical analysis. Thus, Marx's verdict on classical political economy was similar to the verdict of the twentieth century analytical philosophers such as Wittgenstein (1922; 1953) or Winch (1958), about the 'word traps' and 'thought traps' which hinder cognition of the real world by *any* philosophical theoretical system. Of course, Wittgenstein came ultimately to the conservative conclusion that man, trapped like a fly inside a fly-bottle, should be reconciled to his fate and leave 'everything as it is'.[20] Winch (1958) on the other hand draws comfort from the thought that social action, unlike technocratic activity, is completely spontaneous and needs no social theory to guide it. Marx, by contrast, tried hard to work out a 'de-mystifying' and logically consistent political economy of capitalism in which concepts approach reality 'asymptotically'.[21]

Commitment to this asymptotic approach to comprehending realities with the aid of theory partly explains Marx's 'hit-and-run' attempts to de-mystify capitalist economic realities, as mentioned above. As we shall shortly see, some of his 'hits' were failures although others did ensure that definite progress was made in explaining realities. First, however, we must run through as quickly as possible some of the major 'word traps' and 'thought traps' which, according to Marx, crippled pre-Marxian political economy.

Marx found that the word 'class' *was* used in classical political economy – rather more persistently by Quesnay the physiocrat, only casually by Adam Smith and less casually by Ricardo – but the meaning was ambiguous in the writings of all three. Quesnay, for instance, identified the triad of three classes – landowners (*classe des propriétaires* or *classe souveraine* or *class distributive*), farmers (*classe productive*) and 'all citizens occupied with other services and other labours than those of agriculture' (*classe sterile*). Here was a schema of a class-divided society without any clear conception of exploitation of one class by another, which was what Marx was looking for.[22] In this scheme the nearest approach to a concept of exploitation Marx could find was in the physiocratic analysis of the appropriation of the surplus product of agricultural land in the form of rent claimed by the landowners. Both the wages of the workmen in industry and of 'capitalists', understood to mean suppliers of tools and raw materials to workmen, are regarded as 'wages' in some form (minimum subsistence wages for workmen and 'higher wages' for capitalists).[23] On the other hand, in the writings of Turgot, regarded by Marx as representing the physiocratic system in its 'fully developed form', the class of landowners who are *also* capitalists appear as the 'true' capitalists at the apex of the economic system.[24] For Turgot, the agricultural landowners are the *salariants* (i.e. payers of wages) not only to farmers or members of the *classe productive* but also to labourers, manufacturers and artisans in all branches of industry (*stipendiés*).[25] These ambiguities made Marx interpret physiocracy as 'a bourgeois reproduction of the feudal system' in which 'fedualism is made bourgeois, [and] bourgeois society is given a feudal semblance'.[26]

Further studies made Marx come to the somewhat regretful conclusion that interest in class analysis flickered brightly but briefly with the physiocrats, and only the dying embers were left after them.

Adam Smith, their contemporary, like Cantillon, a notable precursor, spoke of 'orders', a concept even more amorphous and imprecise than the Quesnay-Turgot 'classes'. The dying embers were to be seen in the works of Ricardo who did emphasize that the struggle between the 'three great classes' of landlords, 'owners of the stock of capital necessary for cultivation of land' and 'labourers by whose industry it is cultivated' for the distributive shares of the 'produce of the earth' was 'the principal problem of Political Economy'.[27] Ricardo also consistently opposed the rent-receiving landlords' claim on 'unearned' income or revenue which he feared would increase in the course of capitalist development, He also referred once in a while to 'capitalists' but not as exploiters of labour.[28]

However, in a gradual change of vision of the economic process that followed, the physiocrat 'triad of three classes' was metamorphosed into what Marx criticized as the 'trinity formula' of three factors – capital, land and labour.[29] There was a fading out of the paradigm of what Schumpeter (1954) called 'red-blooded' (p. 551), animated and conscious contending classes, geared to notions of exploitation of one class (or a coalition of classes led by the most exploited class) by another class (or a class coalition under the leadership of the socially-dominant class). What emerged was the paradigm of inert, *co-operating* factors 'combined in producing organisms' (p. 555). Actually, the vision formalized in the trinity formula was long in the making as the analytical tools of political economy were being fashioned, and its key concepts worked out, through trial and error. Long before Quesnay (1694–1774), Hobbes (1588–1679) had worked out a theory of the capitalist state on the basis of the aphorism that 'men naturally love Liberty and (also) Dominion over others'. He had also declared that 'desire for Power' is man's main 'Passion' and that wealth or 'Riches' is power, so that a 'war of all against all' must be restrained by an awe-inspiring, visible, social coercive power.[30] Observing all this, Marx also noted that 'for Hobbes . . . Labour is the source of all wealth',[31] but that with Hobbes this conception remained 'more or less sterile'.[32] However, picking up this clue, Hobbes's contemporary Locke (1632–1704) – who argued rhetorically that labour accounted for 'ninety-nine hundredths' of all wealth[33] – and still more Petty (1623–87)[34] introduced the 'factor approach' in the analysis of the nature and sources of wealth. Accordingly, the theme of wealth – its sources and implications – was the common starting point of European post-medieval anti-clerical political theory of the state and of classical political economy.

Of course, this ongoing trend towards working out a factor

approach in analysing economic relations under capitalism encountered many obstacles of a technical nature which made its proponents twist, turn and run into inconsistencies. Thus Petty, ruminating on the 'source(s) of exchange-value or wealth' had more than one answer to the question, What are the sources of wealth? As sorted out by Marx,[35] with Schumpter more or less concurring,[36] Petty gave two inconsistent answers to the question, viz., (1) 'labour which determines exchange-value is the particular kind of concrete labour by which gold and silver (i.e. the money commodity) is extracted', and also (2) exchange-values (whether ships or garments) are 'creatures of lands and men's labours'. According to answer (1), labour of the producer of the money commodity is the source of all exchange-value, i.e. this *concrete* labour is the only factor. According to (2) labour in general (Marx's *abstract* labour) and land are the *two* sources of exchange-value or the two factors of production. Among the physiocrats, whether there was a theory of 'land as the (only) productive factor' struggling to get out of Quesnay's writings is debatable.[37] Marx's suggestion that Turgot was in two minds as to whether land made a 'pure gift' of surplus to cultivating husbandmen or whether husbandmen's labour was the source of all value must nevertheless be taken seriously.[38] In other words, the ambiguous 'class analysis' of the physiocrats was also getting cross-connected with an ambiguous analysis of the economic process in terms of 'factors'.

The intrusion of the factor approach is also strongly in evidence in Smith and Ricardo. To take Ricardo first, three points should be noted. First, consistent with his opposition to landlords, he denies that land plays a role as a factor in the production process. The denial takes the form of the well-known technical proposition that only 'corn and cattle [that] yield no rent . . . regulate the value of all other corn and cattle',[39] implying that rent-yielding scarce land is not a factor of production. Second, capital according to Ricardo 'is that part of the wealth . . . employed in production [which] consists of food, clothing, tools, raw materials, machinery, etc. necessary to give effect to labour'.[40] Implicit here is the adoption by Ricardo of a two factor approach, i.e. the acceptance of the idea that quantities of capital and quantities of labour are the two factors (not land and labour as with Turgot). Third, but inconsistent with his own version of the two factor approach, Ricardo must be credited with having an *idée fixe* that labour is the *only* factor, that 'labour realised in commodities regulates their exchange-value . . ., that all things become more or less valuable in proportion as more or less labour was

bestowed on their production'.[41] Granting that this principle is modified by the 'employment of machinery and other fixed and durable
capital', he still insisted that 'any other cause, but that of the quantity
of labour required for production was comparatively of very slight
effect'.[42] Indeed, Ricardo thought the effect was so slight as to be
ignorable altogether in his chapters on the role of machinery and of
foreign trade. In the former case he assumed that machines are
produced by labour alone, without the use of tools, raw materials
and other machines, so that they represent, or are 'resolved into',
labour plus food and clothing (themselves produced by labour
alone). In the ultimate analysis, machines are nothing but 'embodied
labour' quantities.[43] In the chapter on foreign trade, in his well-
known numerical example illustrating the doctrine of comparative
advantage as the basis of international trade, Ricardo assumed
straight away that cloth and wine were produced in both England
and Portugal by labour alone.[44] The foregoing textual evidence
ought to convince the reader that Ricardo was 'the head of the
school which determines value by labour-time'.[45] Interpretations
which deny this must be considered to be false. According to these
forced interpretations, Ricardo was interested only in justifying the
use of labour-time as an invariant *numeraire* or measure of value,
income or wealth, and not in justifying the notion that labour is the
only cause or source of value or wealth. The truth is that he was
interested in both, even though his interpreters might be interested
in either one, the other or neither.

Adam Smith, on the other hand, opened his *Inquiry into the
Nature and Causes of the Wealth of Nations*, with the sentence: 'The
annual labour of every nation is the fund which originally supplies it
with all the necessaries and conveniences of life which it annually
consumes. . . .' Smith, in other words, begins with his commitment
to the view that 'labour is the only original source of wealth' and that
labour is the only factor. However, on elaborating his views, he
changed his mind abruptly to say that 'wages, profit and rent, are
three original sources of all revenue as well as of all exchangeable
value'.[46] This statement implies several things, one of which is the
adoption by Smith of the method of analysing the capitalist production in terms of the 'trinity formula', i.e. in terms of the three factors,
labour, capital and land, co-operating for mutual benefit and being
'rewarded' by wages, profit and rent. The finishing touches to this
formula were put in by later, and lesser, authors, principally Say and
John Stuart Mill.[47] Say even made a point of raising strong objections to Smith's occasional concession to the view that 'all values

produced represent pre-exerted human labour or industry, either recent or remote . . . in other words, that wealth is nothing more than labour accumulated'. He insisted that 'industry [a well-known euphemism for labour often used in French writings of the period] capital or land . . . all three concur in the creation of value'.[48] Better known now and more highly regarded, later writers such as Jevons, Leon Walras (whose major works were published when Marx was still alive but which were ignored by Marx) and Böhm-Bawerk all took this trinity formula for granted in working out their more sophisticated theories.

This unexpected *dénouement* was most disconcerting for Marx. Political economy and its sequel had ended up by systematizing the paradigm of the 'bourgeois religion of everyday life' instead of de-mystifying capitalist realities! Instead of replacing this bourgeois religion, classical political economy had been overpowered by it. Social classes comprising animated and multi-dimensional 'whole' human beings were now mis-perceived as anaemic, abstract factors, one-dimensional economic men engaged in 'ghost walks'.[49] Clash of interest (sometimes latent, sometimes active) between non--co-operative exploiter and exploited classes is replaced by a continuous sequence of co-operative games played by the factors in this banal, superficial picture of 'economic forces' (now divorced from 'political forces') at work in capitalist society. The process of mystifying capitalist economic relations had been consumated. Those who were expected to 'de-mystify' had themselves turned into 'mystifiers' *par excellence*!

In the early 1860s, Marx seems to have come finally to the conclusion that the root cause of this first-rate intellectual disaster which had overtaken political economy (now termed 'economics') lay in a *mystique* about the nature of capital which was the centrepiece of the trinity formula. According to this thought trap for the unwary, capital is believed to be a mere thing, or collection of things, an innocuous factor. 'On the contrary!' Marx protested in his *Theories of Surplus Value* (1861–2) and in *Capital*, volume 3 (1959), and went on to expound that which amounts to the central formula of Marxian political economy, to be contraposed to the trinity formula: 'Capital is not a thing, but an all-pervasive social power, on the basis of which industrial capitalists, heading the exploiter classes, exploit the exploited classes, potentially headed by the industrial workers.'[50]

Marx conjectured that this formula could be proved to be logically valid, and empirically verified, for the world capitalist system and each national economy integrated within it as it had emerged in the late nineteenth century. If proved and verified in this way political economy would be put truly on the rails of 'class analysis' and the foundations could be laid for a re-integration of economic with political analysis in a radically new political economy. By making economic exploitation interdependent with political oppression by a coercive social power the formula brings political analysis into the heart of economic analysis.

DEMYSTIFYING CAPITAL

Sensing that to prove his central counter formula and in order to make it operationally meaningful he had to reconstruct the foundations of political economy, Marx experimented for nearly 20 years with two distinct and mutually exclusive analytical approaches.[51] The first of these used the Hobbes-Locke-Ricardo notion that 'labour is the only source of value'. This labour value approach is the basis of the 'old' Marxian political economy. The second approach was firmly anchored to the fundamental idea that 'capital is not a thing but a coercive social power' (and a *negation* of the notion that labour is the only source of value). This 'capital theory' approach is the basis of a 'new' modern Marxian political economy.

There is no doubt that both Marx himself and generations of adherents and opponents of his views (the critical as well as the uncritical ones) have taken the first approach seriously. Indeed, for nearly 100 years, only the first approach received recognition as Marxian political economy and the second has begun to receive some attention only in the past decade. However, it is also on record, although rarely noted and then only to be explained away until recently,[52] that Marx himself had doubts and misgivings about this labour value approach, from the beginning to the end of his career as a political economist. A few years before his death in 1883 (in 1875 to be precise), he finally called for its rejection for mystically and 'falsely ascribing *supernatural creative power* to labour'.[53] In other words, Marx renounced the labour value approach because it was based on a *mystique* about labour which was as unacceptable to him as the *mystique* about capital inherent in the trinity formula. Both were tenets belonging to the 'bourgeois religion of everyday life'.[54]

This renunciation *could* have caused a fatal miscarriage of the entire theoretical system of Marxian political economy as Böhm-Bawerk (the first influential critic of Marx's ideas) had wrongly thought *was* caused by the difficulties Marx faced with the artificial problem of the transformation of labour values into prices of production.[55] No such problem existed, however, for a variety of reasons. One is that, at a time when 'bourgeois political economy' was shrinking to purely technical 'economics', the Marxian stress on reciprocal 'dialectical' interactions between economic and political factors in a 'social formation' rather than an 'economy', and the Marxian analysis in terms of social classes, continued to have an appeal.[56] Another reason is that the applied theories of Marxian political economy (e.g. the development of capitalism in Russia, the differentiation of the peasantry in Germany and Russia, the Marxian theory of 'state capitalism' and 'civil society' with reference to Germany, Russia, the USA and Italy)[57] inspired a great deal of research and controversy. All this had no necessary connection with the doctrine that labour is the only source of value. Indeed, much of this literature was based on a rejection of this doctrine restated in an inverted form and based, instead, on the assertion that 'value does not originate in investment in labour-power alone'.[58]

The most important reason – with the benefit of hindsight it can now be seen clearly – is that Marx had left the most important clues for a reconstruction of Marxian political economy based on the capital theory approach. In recent years it has been possible to reconstruct a sturdy analytical structure. The remainder of this section summarizes the story of Marx's experiments with the labour value approach and the capital theory approach, whose highlights are not sufficiently well-known.

Marx tried seriously to make precise the inchoate notion that 'labour is the only source of value', a view found in Hobbes, Locke, Ricardo, etc., to rescue political economy from the trap of the trinity formula.[59] At one place he said: 'value is only another expression for labour'.[60] At another he wrote: 'labour . . . [is] the *living source* of value.'[61] In a third context he said that labour 'is the common social substance of all commodities'.[62] Fourth, 'all commodities are but definite measures of congealed labour-time.'[63] Fifth, 'a commodity has value because it is the crystallization of social labour.'[64] In a sixth context, he quoted approvingly the Ricardian socialist Hodgskin: 'labour [is] . . . the creator of all wealth.'[65] Finally, he also says that 'labour is the yeast thrown into capital which starts [it] fermenting'[66] to 'produce surplus value for the capitalist'[67] of which the substance is 'surplus labour'.[68]

Right from the start, however, when he put his iron in the fire, so to speak, Marx was assailed by doubts and misgivings. He finally gave up the experiment for the following main reasons.

(1) Schumpeter (like Humpty-Dumpty in Lewis Carroll's *Through the Looking Glass*) insisted that 'on principle, we may call things what we please' (even, it would appear, call the moon a piece of green cheese if we choose to do so). As 'there is no logical rule to prevent us from *defining* labour embodied as exchange value', Marx was quite within his rights to do so (1954, p. 598). But though Marx did say 'value is only another expression for labour' at one place he did not back it up by claiming any royal prerogative to make words mean whatever he chose them to mean. For, if he were to do so, he could hardly object, as he did, to a Turgot-like assertion that 'value is only another expression for *agricultural* labour', or a Torrens-like assertion that 'value is an expression for capital'.[69] Committed as he was to the methodological principle that 'concepts [must] approach reality asymptotically', and being engaged in an attempt to de-mystify the nature of commodities by making the Hegelian essence 'appear' by analysis,[70] Marx obviously could not afford to 'solve' the problem by means of definitions.

(2) Consistent with his methodological principle, Marx realized quite early what is almost self-evident – labour would be the only source of value if, and only if, it were true that all commodities, from cheese and chalk to steel and coal, were produced by raw materials, tools, machines, etc., which were themselves produced by labour alone or 'unassisted labour'. As this would seem to imply, at the limit, food grains being produced without seed and raw materials being produced without tools, would historical data for any human society justify such an assumption? In *Capital*, volume 1, Marx was in two minds about the answer to this question. At one place he says No – 'As the earth is his [the labourer's] original larder, so too it is his original tool-house. . . . No sooner does labour undergo the least development, than it requires specially prepared instruments. Thus in the oldest caves we find stone implements and weapons. . . .'[71] This opinion is somewhat qualified a few pages later where Marx says: 'in the beginning, the only participants in the labour-process were man and earth' and 'even now we still employ . . . many means of production provided directly by nature, that do not represent any combination of natural substance with human labour'.[72] In *Capital*, volume 2, the answer is an unqualified and categorical No. Referring to Adam Smith, he asserts that Smith simply cannot demonstrate that 'the entire price of [all] commodities . . . resolves into the means of production . . . which are themselves produced by . . . mere in-

vestment of capital in labour-power'. Smith's example of collectors of Scotch pebbles on the sea-shore is not proof, because even they employ means of production, 'such as baskets, sacks and other containers for carrying pebbles'.[73]

(3) If all commodities cannot be resolved into commodities produced by labour alone then it follows that the value of all commodities cannot be resolved into wages, profit and rent without a physical remainder or 'commodity residue'. This is exactly what Marx says in *Capital*, volume 3, rejecting the contrary view as an 'erroneous dogma' which is 'as false as the axiom [i.e. that all commodities are ultimately produced by labour alone] on which it is based'.

(4) If, going backwards from commodities to 'class revenues', the value of all commodities cannot be resolved into wages, profits and rent (because the axiom 'all goods are produced by labour alone' is false) then it is still more true (as Marx states in *Capital*, volume 1) that, going forward from class revenues to exchange values, the 'capital of society' cannot be 'laid out exclusively in the payment of wages', nor can 'the whole of that part of the surplus product which is converted into capital [be] consumed by the working class'. This is as it is expounded in a 'doctrine of Adam Smith' which 'serves the interests of the capitalist class'.[74]

This completes our list of reasons behind Marx's renunciation of the doctrine that labour is the only source of value expressed in *Capital*. The foregoing makes it clear that Marx's strictures in *Critique of the Gotha Programme* (1875), referred to at the beginning of this section, were no casual outburst. The final rejection of the labour value approach was a well thought out rejection. This rejection cannot be wished away by quibbles about Marx rejecting the notion of labour as the only source of use-values but *not* the notion of its being the only source of exchange-values (as claimed by Medio, 1972, p. 315). Marx (rightly) had a multi-dimensional definition of capitalist society, one dimension of which was that it is the society in which 'wealth . . . presents itself as an immense accumulation of commodities' which are 'the material depositories of exchange value'.[75]

From around 1928, Marx's 'second iron in the fire', the capital theory approach, began to receive serious attention. It was finally tempered and its findings delivered to the public in 1960 (Sraffa, 1960). These findings made available fully worked out models of the capitalist economy (reminiscent of the physiocratic *tableau économi-*

que and Marx's reproduction schemes in *Capital*, volume 2) and explicitly dispensed with the factor approach,[76] whether 'trinitarian' or 'unitarian' (the latter being represented by the labour value approach of Marx and Ricardo). Piero Sraffa, the author of these new models which resembled Leontief's input-output tables only superficially, used them to demonstrate the complete dispensibility,[77] as well as the impossibility, of using 'any notion of capital as a measureable quantity independent of distribution and prices',[78] (i.e. any notion of capital as a factor on either familiar Walrasian or 'Austrian' assumptions) in analysing the working of the model of the capitalist economy. He also acknowledged explicitly that he had worked out his new paradigm on the basis of a key analytical clue provided by Marx in his reference to a 'maximum (possible) rate of profit' corresponding to a bare subsistence wage for labour. It is also implied in Marx's emphatic rejection (noted earlier) of Adam Smith's doctrine that the value or price of every commodity 'resolves itself entirely', either immediately or ultimately, into wage, profit and rent, and of the notion of the existence of 'ultimate' commodities produced by pure labour without means of production into which all commodities can be 'resolved'.[79] The author of these 'commodity production models' (as they may be called) also acknowledges Marx as the source of the classification of commodities into 'basic' and 'non-basic', and the conceptual plan of treating worn-out machines as a joint product along with the main product (e.g. worn-out weaving machines emerging as a joint product with woollens). These ideas were first adopted by the physiocrats and Torrens respectively, although Marx was the last to make use of them before they fell into oblivion.[80] Other clues supplied by Marx have been detected and made use of by *inter alia* Bose (1980a) when discussing the theory of land rent earned by owners of scarce land treated as a 'non-basic', and the case of the 'wine ripening in cellars' to which Marx paid some attention with the help of commodity production models (pp. 105–7).

Modern commodity production theory, however, while eschewing the factor approach and hammering home the idea that capital is not a factor, does not explicitly spell out an alternative theory of social classes based on the notion of capital as a coercive power. Nevertheless, an opening in that direction is made. This opening can be utilized to prove the logical validity of that which lies at the core of the 'central formula' of Marxian class analysis – 'capital is not a thing, but a coercive social power on the basis of which industrial capitalists exploit industrial workers' (a simplified form of the formula stated earlier). This formula can be shown to be logically valid by adopting as reasonable two axioms about capitalist society. These are, first, that in a capitalist society capitalists alone have the social coercive power to decide what, how and for whom to produce and whether, indeed, to produce at all, and, second, that to accumulate and expand the coercive social power of capital is the *raison d'être* of capitalist activity.[81]

Further steps are needed if the Marxian central formula in its fully-expanded form is to be shown to be valid. In its expanded form, the formula speaks of a coalition of exploited classes potentially headed by the industrial workers. This requires an amplified theory of social classes in a capitalist society, including an understanding of the precise nature of relations between capitalists and capitalist landlords (or a hybrid class of capitalists turned landlords), or landlords turned capitalists on the one side and of labourers and the 'subaltern' peasant classes on the other, of the dialectics of the formation of class coalitions and their internal relations, and so on.[82]

In the past decade the required additional steps have, in fact, been taken, partly by adapting and extending commodity production models (which have proved to be remarkably versatile), and partly by borrowing ideas and analytical devices from the modern mathematical theories of games and collective choice. These have been used to understand a wide range of 'revolutionary', as well as 'non-revolutionary' problems of both capitalist and socialist societies, which have come into existence in the twentieth century, in terms of the central formula of Marxian class analysis. Studies in this area, published or in preparation, in recent years cover such themes as:

(1) Mutation of capitalist societies (emergence of capitalist colonialism, imperialism and neo-imperialism) arising out of the long-run tendencies towards 'under-accumulation', 'demand/supply disproportionality' or 'a declining average rate of capital accumulation'. (All capitalist and socialist societies are treated as constantly 'evolving', both institutionally and economically).

(2) Mutation of capitalism and socialism in politically de-colonized and (in the case of socialist societies) economically de-colonized former semi-colonies (with special attention being paid to state capitalism with large state-owned sectors e.g. India and resource rich former semi-colonies).

(3) Rationale of private and state monopolies and monopolistic competition with unequal profit rates, analysed with adapted commodity production models of the capitalist economy.

(4) A restatement of the Marxian theory of international trade on the basis of the capital theory approach, and Marx's *Lecture on Free Trade* (including a critique of the theory of unequal exchange of labour between rich and poor capitalist countries on the labour value approach, relying instead on a theory of unequal terms of trade).

(5) Agrarian reform, international trade and development of capitalist countries.

(6) Conditions of revolutionary breakdown of a capitalist society (including an analysis of factors preventing such a breakdown).

(7) Alternative strategies of transition to socialism (including a critique of the familiar Barone-Lange-Lerner 'economic models of socialism' and based on an alternative to such a rationalization of socialist price-fixing).

(8) Outlines of a 'political economy of socialism', with special attention being paid to the role of the market mechanism, to problems of bureaucratic waste, to the problems of 'democratic centralism', of 'parasitism', alienation and inegalitarianism under socialism.

(9) The question of 'change of colour', or the breakdown of a socialist society.

(10) The specific features of the political economy of countries of the Indo-West Asian region.

(11) The modes of production, the state and civil societies of colonial and modern India, with special reference to state capitalism in tandem with a multiplicity of class differentiated civil societies corresponding to a single state capitalist apparatus.[83]

CONCLUDING REMARKS

A theory must look 'right' not only in the 'small' but in the 'large'. In a painting, not only the trees but also the woods must impress. That 'capital is a coercive social power' is the key idea of the modern Marxian political economy whose emergence has been traced in this essay. The opinion that this *is* the key idea of Marxian political economy and, moreover, that it is valid seems to be gaining ground even among those who do not see eye to eye with the details of the reconstruction of Marxian political economy as here attempted. Thus, a writer who probably adheres to the labour value approach and makes the unacceptable statement that there is freedom in the market place under capitalism does nevertheless say that 'authoritarianism in the workplace' is 'an essential characteristic of capitalist society'.[84] Another writer, who has elaborated a Sraffa-based critique of Marx rather than an integration of Marx and Sraffa on the basis of the capital theory approach common to both, agrees that 'Marx's emphasis on the labour process, of coercion therein' remains untouched by his critique.[85]

However, against this key idea of capital as a coercive social power, three crucial 'fundamentalist' (rather than fundamental) objections have been raised, in oral and published comments, to which some attention must be paid.

The first is the objection that the 'capital' concept is in any sense hopelessly elusive. The concept of capital in economic theory is rather like a circular building which looks circular by straight photography but which can be made to look flat by trick photography (Das Gupta, 1982, p. 112). To this there is, of course, an easy reply – a circular building does not *become* flat just because a trick photographer wants to entertain us by making it appear so. Whether a building is circular or flat, or whether capital is a thing or a coercive social power, can be verified objectively by means other than trickery.

The second objection maintains that to say that capital is a coercive power is to introduce a *political* concept. By making power its central concept modern Marxian political economy is forfeiting the right to be taken seriously by economists. On the sophisticated level of modern analytical philosophy, this objection can hardly be sustained. After all, the literature on Gödel's theorem makes us aware that 'mapping' techniques have helped to solve some of the problems of Euclidian geometry by transferring them to the domain of other geometries or to algebra (Nagel and Newman, 1968). In economic theory too there has been a lot of such transference to solve problems, e.g. from marginal calculus to geometry and back again, and from both to linear algebra. What, therefore, is wrong with going from the strait-jacket of economic theory on the basis of the factor approach to the larger and more expansive domain of political economy and a 'class' approach? Besides, Gödel's theorem does say that any proof of the formal system, L, must use methods and notions not contained within L itself (Newman, 1965). So why should we be forbidden to go beyond economics proper to politics in order to solve economic problems (and vice versa), and to integrate economics and politics into an analytical political economy?

The third objection is not methodological as the others but is based on doubts about the realism of a paradigm whose key idea is that capital is a coercive social power. It asks, Can capital really be coercive in the twentieth century, in the workplace, in the market place or in society in general? Perhaps it *was* so in the mid-nineteenth century when Marx was writing, but is it so nowadays?[86] Or, maybe capitalism was never coercive at all, unlike pre-capitalist feudalism which certainly was? Here, when we are debating what the wood looks like, the reader must judge for himself. In consideriang the matter, however, a distinction should be made between the exercise of the coercive social power of capital, in the sense of a capitalist social dictatorship *only*, or in the double sense of a social combined with a political dictatorship. The former involves the denial of access to the alienable assets of society to non-capitalists. These assets are managed exclusively by capitalists who always manage more than they own, either in the expanding state-owned sector or in the private sector, as an increasing volume of the savings of workers and the non-capitalist 'intermediate strata' are invested. The latter double sense involves both such social dictatorship by capitalists as well as political dictatorship by capitalists, which suppresses dissent in thought, word and deed, against capitalist social dictatorship.

Capitalist social dictatorship was established everywhere by an act of political dictatorship e.g. by Cromwell in England (and Ireland), by George Washington during the American War of Independence, by Robespierre and Bonaparte in France. Whenever the capitalist social dictatorship was threatened by a 'political revolution with a social soul', or was felt by the political 'general staff' of the capitalist class to be so threatened, a political dictatorship has emerged to protect it, successfully or otherwise. This, barring differences of degree and detail, has been the story of country after country both in the nineteenth and the twentieth centuries. In between, of course, in 'normal times', the political dictatorship has been diluted to the point of being extinguished *internally* in the advanced 'stable' capitalist societies. The capitalist social dictatorship has shown a 'soft' democratic face internally (though usually a 'hard' dictatorial face externally, whenever there was a real or imagined threat to the capitalist system internationally) so that physical and outright political coercion is replaced by ideological brain-washing or 'hegemonism' over the apparatus of civil society (Gramsci, 1975, pp. 210–78).

Nevertheless, the twentieth century has also seen the emergence of a socialist 'counter-dictatorship' (to prohibit private ownership and management of the means of production), backed by a political dictatorship in several countries which have been frozen and 'mystified' by a 'socialist religion of everyday life' in obeisance to Marx. Modern Marxian political economy, which de-mystifies capitalism ruthlessly, can hardly afford to ignore the problem posed by the socialist social and political dictatorships.

If we take seriously the Hobbesian aphorism that 'men naturally love Liberty and Dominion over others', and whether or not we limit its applicability to the 'bourgeois man' *a` la* Marx, few except Marxist 'social astrologers' will be sure that, as we approach the end of the twentieth century, the socialist 'social dictatorship' will ever pass away. Neither can they be sure that the state will 'wither away' or that the market mechanism or 'commodity relations' can ever be abolished (although, of course, they can and must be subordinated and only utilized under socialism to attain social goals set outside the market). Yet there is no doubt that the forms of socialist social dictatorship have been evolving (naturally by fits and starts rather than smoothly) and the political dictatorship protecting the socialist social dictatorship has proved highly unstable in every socialist country almost without exception, even if each reformation has produced a new version of the socialist political dictatorship.

In viewing these matters, students of modern Marxian political economy can take their cue from Marx's half-serious, half-ironical, but unqualified, commitment to democracy as 'the essence . . . the reference point (or "truth") of all state constitutions . . . [it] is the self-determination of the people'. This he contrasted to the 'despotic state' where 'the political state is nothing but the caprice of a single individual'.[87] Marx also made another complementary statement, somewhat oracular, equally unqualified, but without irony, that 'the mortal danger for every being lies in losing itself', hence 'lack of freedom is the real mortal danger for mankind'.[88] When these forgotten Marxian statements begin to be remembered, and their implications are discussed seriously rather than cynically, modern Marxian political economy will perhaps be absolved of blame for any 'inconsistency' in its attitudes to capitalist and socialist coercion. It may then begin to matter more than the old Marxian political economy.

RECENT TRENDS – A CRITICAL POSTSCRIPT

As I was writing this chapter in the middle of 1983, I was unaware that the 'new' Marxian political economy, based on a rejection of the notion that labour was the only source of value, was gaining some ground, at the expense of the 'old' Marxian political economy anchored to that notion. Some of these gains were to be expected. Walsh and Gram (1980) had earlier already gone some way towards a rejection of labour values and had worked out a Sraffa-based reconstruction of Marxian political economy in which *no use* of labour values is, quite explicitly, made. In a recent survey article (Gram and Walsh, 1983), they seem to have endorsed proofs of 'impossibility theorems' published by the present writer (Bose, 1980a, pp. 24–37, 63), relating to the non-existence of labour values under capitalist conditions.

Somewhat unexpectedly there were two other developments. First, it was not long ago that Mark Blaug castigated both Marx and Sraffa, showing a weakness for Ricardian 'empirical labour values' geared to the notion of labour as the single factor, on the grounds that 'labour costs dominate costs in almost all industries'.[89] However, later he launched a rather fierce flank attack on Marxian labour values, denying the possibility of 'reducing skilled labour to unskilled labour', as a step towards reducing values to embodied labour time. What is more, Blaug admits that there is some merit in Sraffa, acknowledging that 'there simply is no labour reduction problem in Sraffa'. He concludes that 'Marxists have been so busy solving analytical brain-teasers (like the labour reduction problem) that they have sorely neglected the task of studying how capitalist economies actually work'.[90] Blaug thus withdraws his earlier endorsement of Ricardian empirical labour values, and this is a welcome development.

Second, Michael Howard, in an earlier piece written jointly with J. E. King (Howard and King, 1976) which had contained flashes of clarity and confusion in almost equal measure, had put up a diehard conservative defence of labour values. It was claimed, wrongly, that Sraffa had shown that the Marxian transformation problem (labour values into production prices) could be reformulated so as to provide a complete solution, thereby implying that labour values exist in the first place. But now Howard, this time in collaboration with Ian Bradley (Bradley and Howard, 1982a) makes a 'U-turn' by admitting, correctly, that 'the concept of labour values plays *no role* in the construction of (Sraffa's) theory' and 'as a consequence, Sraffa's work is free of the limitations associated with the use of the concept' (p. 31, emphasis added).

As belief in labour values as products of what Marx called the 'supernatural creative power of labour' (n. 53 above) is deep-rooted, countervailing activity by both conservative and innovative defenders of labour values has continued at a brisk pace. Thus Howard's former collaborator, the anti-neoclassical and anti-Sraffa conservative Marxist J. E. King has recently advanced the desperately causistical argument that, if labour values are unobservable abstractions then so are prices. This is somewhat disparagingly referred to as the 'Straffa-Samuelson theory' (King, 1982, pp. 172, 175–6). On the other hand, the anti-neoclassical, but pro-Sraffa, conservative Marxist G. C. Harcourt sticks essentially to the Howard/King 1976 position, misinterpreting Sraffa to justify Ricardo-Marx labour values (Harcourt, 1982, pp. 255–63).[91] Meanwhile, the innovative pro-Sraffa Ian Steedman had earlier stressed that labour values are unnecessary to Marx-Sraffa systems (Steedman, 1977). Even so, he has now moved backwards to justify Ricardian labour values by a misinterpretation of Sraffa's 'reduction to dated labour' procedure (Steedman, 1982, pp. 128–9, 138–9). He goes further back from there to justify Ricardian notions that values are resolvable into wages and profits, thus adopting the two-factor approach which, as we have seen, was sometimes adopted by Ricardo himself.

These controversies about labour values reveal an interesting feature. Those who discuss Marx increasingly line up for or against Sraffa. There has been some laboured and carping criticism – you invent problems which can be solved by Sraffa's methods but do not try to do so, or you pick on small errors committed by Sraffa without correcting them within his system, even when this is possible (for example, Bradley and Howard, 1982b, pp. 243–50). At the same time, those who are lining up for Sraffa have taken steps to see that his analytics are extended in scope, adapted, sized-up and corrected to serve as the analytical core of a new Marxian political economy. The interesting thing about these corrections is that they are carried out well within the bounds of Sraffa's theory, using tools fashioned by Sraffa himself and by invoking methodological principles laid down by him.

The main corrections so far are of errors in Sraffa's essentially Ricardian land rent model (Sraffa, 1960, pp. 74–8), a model economically irrelevant to the modern world and mathematically faulty.[92] A corrected Sraffian land rent model is essential to complete the basic structure of an economic model without labour values. It is also needed to head off the most sophisticated challenge so far to the second *differential specifica* of the new Marxian political economy viz. the proposition that capital is not a thing but a coercive, exploitative social power. This is a challenge from a modern neo-physiocratic 'land theory of value' which accepts the physiocratic 'vision' – that land's return is the only true surplus and that both farm and manufacturing labour are 'sterile' – as essentially correct. This necessitates the imposition of the arbitrary assumption of strictly 'subsistence wages' for labourers by *fiat*, and the theory thus reverts to the original version of the 'one factor' theory discussed earlier, corrected for logical loose ends and ambiguities. This modern land theory of value has been taking shape since 1959 and is now available in a fully developed form (Samuelson, 1959, pp. 1–35 and 1982, pp. 48–52).

The assumptions and findings of this theory of land-rent, such as the finding that private landowners are the only exploiters, are in stark contrast to the Marx-Sraffa theory of rent in which land which is not productive is a non-basic commodity and is therefore not an ultimate source of surplus, either in agriculture or in anywhere else. The source of surplus in agriculture is labour, seed corn and other basic inputs, such as fertiliser. Land rent is a share of the surplus produced by labour and inputs of basic commodities in all the basic producing sectors of the economy. It is appropriated from profit-extracting capitalists by capitalist landowners. Instead of a subsistence wage, a variable wage is the crucial assumption made in this theory, and this accounts for the difference in the 'vision' and the results. In short, the logical structure of the corrected Marx-Sraffa theory of rent is *prima facie* as complete as that of the corrected physiocratic theory of rent, and therefore has a fighting chance against it.

All in all, recent trends in controversies over Marxian political economy noted in this Postscript suggest that a logically robust and technically versatile Sraffa-based political economy is making progress, attracting both adherents and attention from opponents.

NOTES

1 Marx (1844b, 1975) p. 182.
2 Marx (1844a, 1975) p. 142. The full quotation reads: '. . . ruthless both in the sense of not being afraid of the results it arrives at and in the sense of being just as little afraid of conflict with the powers that be'.
3 Marx (1844c, 1975) p. 206.
4 Giuseppe di Lampedusa, *The Leopard* (1958, 1974) pp. 28, 36 ff.
5 Marx and Engel (1845–6, 1976) p. 61. '. . . not criticism but revolution is the driving force of history, also of religion, of philosophy, and all other kinds of theory'.
6 Involving the peasants (in the Soviet Union, the European people's democracies and China), the workers (in Czechoslovakia and Poland),

inter-communist civil war in Kampuchea, and inter-communist international war in Indo-China.

7 See the comment by Leszek Kolakowski (1977) pp. 16–7.
8 For such an acknowledgement, see Assar Lindbeck (1977) p. 3.
9 Marx and Engels (1945–6, 1976) p. 61.
10 Marx (1964) p. 111.
11 Marx and Engels (1945–6, 1976) p. 81.
12 Engels (1844, 1975) pp. 479–805; Marx and Engels (1848, 1950) p. 37.
13 Madan (1979) p. 64, quoting Marx Weber, *Economy and Society: an outline*, ed. G. Roth and C. Whittich (1968) p. lviii.
14 Marx (1859, 1970) pp. 20–1.
15 Including a recent interpretation which says that the Russian socialist revolution (and, by implication, the Chinese, Cuban or Vietnamese socialist revolution also) is a misnomer for delayed bourgeois revolution which has established socialized capitalism.
16 Marx (1844b, 1975) pp. 184–7.
17 Marx (1844c, 1975) p. 141.
18 Marx (1844b, 1975) pp. 184–7.
19 Marx (1894, 1959) p. 809.
20 See Edgley (1983) p. 274.
21 See Engels (1895): 'the concept of a thing and its reality run side by side like two asymptotes . . .'
22 Of the many interpretations of physiocractic doctrines, those given by Marx (1861–3, 1954) pp. 44–59, and by Schumpeter (1954) pp. 239–41 are sufficient for our present purpose.
23 Marx (1861–3, 1954) p. 47.
24 Ibid., pp. 49–50.
25 Ibid., pp. 55–7.
26 Ibid., p. 50.
27 Ricardo, (1817, 1951) pp. 5–7.
28 See Ricardo (1817, 1951) pp. 105–6 for his advocacy of the abolition of the English poor laws, where it is made clear that he did not believe capitalist exploitation was responsible for poverty.
29 Marx (1894, 1959) chapter xlviii, p. 794.
30 Hobbes (1651, 1974) pp. 139, 189, 223, 296.
31 Marx (1861–3, 1954) p. 354. He obviously refers to Hobbes's statement: 'Plenty dependeth . . . merely on the labour and industry of men' (Hobbes, 1651, 1974, p. 295).
32 Marx (1859, 1970) p. 53.
33 See Marx (1861–3, 1954) p. 355.
34 See Marx (1859, 1970) pp. 52–3; Marx (1861–3, 1954) p. 351; also Schumpeter (1954) pp. 213–14 for a similar verdict.
35 Marx (1859, 1970) pp. 52–3; Marx, 1861–3, 1954, pp. 350–1.
36 Schumpeter (1954) pp. 213–14.
37 Dumont (1980) gives this interpretation on p. 277.

38 Marx (1861–3, 1954) pp. 54–6.
39 Ricardo (1951) p. 70, where he insists that '*some* corn and *some* cattle that yield no rent' can always be found.
40 Ricardo (1817, 1951) p. 95.
41 Ibid., p. 13.
42 Ibid., pp. 30–8; Ricardo (1951) p. 59.
43 Ibid., pp. 388–9.
44 Ibid., pp. 134–5.
45 Marx (1846–7, n.d.) p. 107.
46 Smith (1776, 1937) vol. 1, p. 46.
47 Schumpeter (1954) p. 555.
48 Say (1803, 1949) pp. 298–9.
49 See the surrealistic imagery employed by Marx in Marx (1894, 1959) pp. 794, 809–10 *passim*.
50 Marx (1861–3, 1954) p. 91: 'Capital is productive of value *only as a relation*, in so far as it is a coercive force on wage-labour, compelling it to perform surplus labour . . .' [my italics]. Marx (1894, 1959) p. 794: '. . . capital is not a thing, but rather a definite social production relation, belonging to a definite historical formation of society, which is manifested in a thing and lends this thing a specific social character. . . . 'Ibid., p. 801: 'capital is a perennial pumping machine of surplus labour for the capitalist'.
51 Alexander (1975); Bose (1980a), preface.
52 For example, by Dobb (1968) p. 55; Medio (1972) p. 315; Elson (1979) p. 114.
53 Italics in original. See Bose (1980a) pp. 186–98 for extracts from Marx and comments.
54 Actually, in *Results of the Immediate Process of Production* (Marx, 1863–6, 1976, pp. 1083–4), Marx had noted that writers from Locke to Ricardo had defended the capitalist mode of production by claiming that private capitalist property is 'founded on labour' (i.e. the capitalist's own) when, in reality, it is founded on 'expropriation of immediate producers'. In *Critique of the Gotha Programme* (1875, 1949) he criticized it as a 'bourgeois idea' (see Bose, 1980a, p. 198 for extract).
55 Marx's error in 'solving' the transformation problem was a small error within the larger error of the labour value approach. Böhm–Bawerk (1896, 1975) made a mountain out of this small error, side-tracking attention from the larger error, and the need to correct it.
56 Thus Lenin denied that Marx had a theory of 'economic materialism'. See Lenin (1894, 1960) p. 157.
57 On these issues, see Lenin (1899, 1956); Engels (1874, 1950); Lenin, (1894, 1960); Gramsci (1975) pp. 206–316.
58 But also in investment in raw materials, machinery, etc. (i.e. 'constant capital'). See Lenin (1899, 1956), chapter 1.
59 See Bose (1980a) pp. 184–98 for detailed references from Marx.

60 Marx (1847, 1950) p. 72.
61 Marx (1857, 1973) p. 296.
62 Marx (1865, 1950) p. 378.
63 Marx (1859, 1970) p. 30.
64 Marx (1865, 1950) p. 378.
65 Marx (1867, 1958) p. 537.
66 Marx (1857, 1973) p. 298.
67 Marx (1861–3, 1954) p. 148.
68 Marx (1894, 1959) p. 147.
69 See Marx (1867, 1958) p. 184.
70 So that it is no use trying to legitimize Marxian concepts by throwing dark hints about Marx's 'Hegelian problematic', as Veblen (1906) did a long time ago. A 'problematic' cannot be just anything we choose it to be.
71 Marx (1867, 1958), p. 179.
72 Ibid., p. 183.
73 Smith (1776, 1937) vol. 1, p. 44; Marx (1893, 1957) pp. 373–4.
74 Marx (1867, 1958) pp. 590–1.
75 Ibid., pp. 35–6.
76 Sraffa (1960) p. 93.
77 Ibid., p. 9.
78 Ibid., p. 38.
79 Ibid., p. 94.
80 Ibid., pp. 93–4.
81 Bose (1890a) pp. 73, 78. If the reader has a taste for an axiomatic approach he may consult Bose, 1980a, chapters 8–10, for a proof of the so-called 'Fundamental Marxian Theorem' of capitalist exploitation in terms of the axioms just noted.
82 Marx (1894, 1959) pp. 329, 743, 754–5; Bose (1980b).
83 For 1, 2, 6, 7, 8, see Bose (1975); for 9, 10, see Bose (1977); for 3, 5, 8, see Bose (1980a); for 5, see Bose (1980b).
84 Space limitations preclude discussion here except to state that, in the Marxian capital theory approach, no distinction can be made between non-coercive capital in the market place and coercive capital in the work-place. The quotation comes from Roosevelt and Hymer (1972) p. 131.
85 Steedman (1977) p. 206. Steedman drops 'labour values' only because they are 'redundant' (p. 202).
86 See Deane (1978) p. 140 for this vague but highly popular opinion.
87 Marx (1843, 1975) pp. 30–2.
88 Marx (1842, 1975) p. 164.
89 Blaug (1978) p. 118. This is a mistake. Unless wage-goods, like all other goods, are ultimately produced by labour alone, 'wage-dominated costs' are not equivalent to labour costs or embodied labour time.
90 (Blaug 1978) pp. 195 and 199. Actually there *is* a reduction problem in Staffa; he also assumed the 'reduction in difference in quality to differences in quantity of labour of uniform quality' (1960, p. 10). The assumption can be eliminated with some adaption of the Sraffa system.

91 An apparent 'proof' of this misinterpretation by Harcourt and others is given in Steedman (1982), pp. 128–9. An optical illusion which vitiates the proof is spotted in Bose (1980a) pp. 40–1.

92 A model corrected using Sraffa's own device of basic equations is presented and explained in Bose (1980a) pp. 111–21. Its implications are explored in Bose (1980b).

5

Public Choice, Markets and Utilitarianism*

ALAN P. HAMLIN

Some ambiguity surrounds the interpretation of the phrase 'Public Choice'. Sometimes it is used to describe a subject area within political economy, whilst on other occasions it identifies a particular methodological approach to the study of political economy in general. The former usage relates to the economic investigation of collective or group behaviour, whilst the latter is based on a substantial critique of the inherited, neo-classical economic orthodoxy. When public choice is defined as 'the economics of politics' it is all too easy to overlook the fact that it is the methodological approach to economics which truly distinguishes the public choice school, rather than the application of the reformulated economic analysis to the subject matter of politics.

Public choice analysts have extended the range of their studies to include, for example, the operation of alternative electoral systems, the power of the bureaucracy, and the structure of the law.[1] Several surveys are available[2] and I shall not attempt to review this large and rapidly growing literature; rather I intend to identify and develop the methodological position which transforms public choice from a subject area into a school of thought. The three main methodological planks making up the public choice platform are individualism, subjectivism, and contractarianism. Each of these aspects will be discussed in more detail below although I shall concentrate particular attention on contractarianism as this is, perhaps, the most unfamiliar of the three to economists. The overall aims of this chapter

*I am happy to acknowledge the benefits of many stimulating discussions with John Aldrich, Geoffrey Brennan, Jim Buchanan, Alan Ingham, Gordon Tullock, Alistair Ulph and Jack Wiseman.

are to develop and clarify ideas in such a way as to point out the relationship between the public choice perspective and mainstream, neo-classical economic analysis, and, equally importantly, to isolate those ideas which provide public choice with its distinctive position relative to other schools of political economy.

The public choice perspective is often characterized as being essentially pro-market, and it is certainly the case that the market plays a very significant role in public choice analysis. However, the precise meaning of 'the market' in this context is rather subtle. Mainstream, textbook economics typically considers the market to be a very special institution, and is primarily concerned with the properties of market equilibria rather than the market process itself. By contrast, the public choice school define markets more broadly as a set of institutions which share a common constitutional (i.e. contractarian) property; they are then concerned with the origin and operation of markets rather than the outcomes they produce. This contrast in the treatment of markets is explored more fully below as a means of viewing the contractarian basis of the public choice perspective.

The acceptance of contractarianism automatically implies the rejection of utilitarianism, and later sections develop some of the major issues involved in the debate between utilitarianism and a variety of contractarian positions. It will be argued that the particular form of contractarianism embodied in the methodology of public choice differs crucially from that of Rawls (1971), and represents a position which accommodates many of the criticisms advanced against utilitarianism.

Before concentrating on the contractarian element of public choice, I provide a brief discussion of the inter-relationships between the major themes of public choice analysis and the methodological precepts of individualism and subjectivism.

METHODOLOGY AND THEMES

The starting point of the public choice approach is the position of methodological individualism[3] in which individuals are taken to be the sole source of valuation and of economic and political activity. To the methodological individualist institutions simply provide the superstructure or environment within which individual actions are translated into final outcomes. The central point here is that whilst attention is focused on individuals as the source of decision-making it is recognized that the institutional and procedural environment will, in general, influence actual outcomes, and that this influence may itself feed back to affect the incentives, and hence the actions, of the individuals within the institution.

This basic insight, that institutional structure may drive a wedge between individual actions and ultimate choices, is fundamental to the public choice approach. Indeed, one of the major themes within the public choice literature is that of the comparative study of alternative structures of decision-making and their impacts upon both final outcomes and the behaviour of the particpating individuals.[4]

An analogy which is frequently used within the public choice literature compares institutionalized decision-making procedures with the rules of games. In terms of this analogy, the first thematic concern of public choice scholars has been the analysis of games in terms of the tactical options open to the various players and the expected outcomes associated with those tactics. A second theme is concerned with the choice amongst games and is therefore constitutional, rather than merely institutional in its perspective.[5] This branch of the public choice literature investigates a conceptualized individualistic constitutional calculus in which an individual is faced with a choice amongst alternative constitutions in the context of considerable uncertainty. This uncertainty concerns, *inter alia*, the individual's own position in post-constitutional society. In terms of the game analogy this choice is equivalent to selecting which card game to play before you know which cards you will hold.

This conception of the choice amongst constitutions clearly belongs to the contractarian tradition of political philosophy which has returned to the forefront of debate since the publication of Rawls's major work (Rawls, 1971). We will return to the links between the Rawlsian and public choice analyses below, but for the moment it is sufficient to note that both attempt to derive an authoritative constitution from the agreement of individuals.

Several further themes are present within the public choice literature. The particular institutional structure of the market has always occupied a very special place in public choice writings; indeed one definition of the domain of public choice as a sub-discipline is the study of non-market decision-making (Mueller, 1979, p. 1). However, the precise role and significance of the market in public choice is far from simple, and it is one of the tasks of this chapter to clarify and critically discuss this aspects of the public choice approach. However, whatever the details of the argument concerning the importance of markets it is clear that the voluntary nature of market transactions will be of importance in any individualistic evaluation of institutions. This voluntarism is a particular case of the unanimity criterion which forms yet another theme within public choice deriving from the work of Wicksell. I have discussed Wicksellian individualism as embodied in the unanimity principle elsewhere (Hamlin, 1983), and I will not reproduce that argument here beyond noting that one of the conclusions reached was that the Wicksellian unanimity rule could not, of itself, provide a justification for free market institutions.

A second methodological tenet to be noted as playing an important role within the public choice analysis is subjectivism.[6] At the individualistic level, subjectivism stresses the inscrutability of individual choice which depends upon the personal evaluation of opportunity cost, and the interpretation of uncertainty as 'the unknowable' rather than the merely 'probabilistic'. These characteristics of the discussion are pervasive in that it is a subjectivist approach to uncertainty which informs the analyses of institutional performance and constitutional choice, and it is the subjectively evaluated choices of individuals which play a vital role in the argument concerning the central importance of the market.

At the social level, subjectivism denies the relevance of any well-defined social welfare function as a basis for evaluating alternative policies or institutional reforms and is, therefore, fundamentally opposed to the mainstream, utilitarian tradition within economics. Indeed, as I have already noted, the public choice school is contractarian in its underlying philosophy and stresses agreement amongst individuals rather than the maximization of utility (or anything else) as the basis of economic or political activity.

Of course the methodological tenets of contractarianism, individualism and subjectivism, combined with the themes of comparative institutional analysis, the choice of constitutions, the importance of market processes and the unanimity principle, can not fully define the broad and rapidly growing sub-discipline of public choice. Another author would, I am sure, choose other themes and positions as more characteristic of the school. Such diversity of opinion is entirely proper, but surely most would agree that the public choice school is, for better or worse, distinct in both its methodology and its typical subject matter from other schools of political economy. Perhaps the closest relative is the institutionalist school[7] which also recognizes the importance of economic, social and political institutions, but the public choice approach goes far beyond this recognition in analysing the origins of such institutions within a cogent, if controversial, methodological framework in an attempt to provide a novel perspective on the emergence of a society in its full economic and political complexity.

MARKETS AS INSTITUTIONS

The 'traditional' and 'public choice' views of the significance of the market as an institution are summarized and contrasted by Buchanan (1964), who writes in answer to the question, How should the economist conceive of the market organization?, that the mainstream economist 'will look on market order as a *means* of accomplishing the basic economic functions that must be carried out in any society. . . . In this conception, the "market", as a mechanism, is appropriately compared with "government", as an alternative mechanism for accomplishing similar tasks' (p. 219), whereas public choice theorists and Buchanan himself would argue that 'the "market" or market organisations is not a *means* toward the accomplishment of anything. It is, instead, the institutional embodiment of the voluntary exchange processes that are entered into by individuals in their several capacities' (p. 219).

This view is expanded to leave the reader in no doubt that the 'market' is here being viewed as those institutions which arise out of individualistic agreement, whether those institutions are private or collective in nature and regardless of the outcomes of those institutions. In offering this broad definition of the market, Buchanan also suggests that economists (and public choice theorists) should be concerned only with this class of institution. Indeed, economics is defined as the study of the institutions and social relations which arise out of voluntary agreement, in contrast to politics which is defined as the study of social relations based on coercion (Buchanan, 1964, pp. 220-1).

The distinction between the narrow and broad conceptions of the market raises several questions concerning the relationship between these notions. Unfortunately, it also opens the way to much linguistic confusion, as exemplified by the superficially contradictory definitions of public choice offered by Mueller, who utilizes the traditional market concept in describing public choice as the study of non-market decision-making, and Buchanan, who makes use of the broader market concept in asserting that it is the market process itself which is the proper subject for public choice theorists. In order to avoid these ambiguities I shall use the terms 'micro-market' and 'meta-market' for the traditional and public choice concepts respectively.

One line of argument begins by considering the distinction between the micro-market and collective decision-making procedures in terms of the implied inter-relationships amongst individuals.[8] In the idealized micro-market, each individual carries full responsibility for making an effective choice and bears the direct consequences of his/her own action. Furthermore, in the limit where the micro-market is made up of many individuals, no particular individual exercises any control over any other individual although, of course, each individual is affected by the choices of all other individuals in aggregate.

By contrast, in the case of the idealized collective choice where each individual has an equal vote in determining an outcome which will apply equally to all, the typical individual is not responsible for making an effective choice and neither does he/she bear the consequences of his/her own actions. Whilst the individual may be responsible for casting a vote, he/she does so in the knowledge that there is only a remote chance that this vote will be decisive; and by definition the consequences borne by any individual will be independent of the way in which that individual voted. It is this basic lack of personal, individualistic responsibility which both erodes the incentive to participate effectively (e.g. by collecting relevant information etc.) and makes it plausible to suggest that a fully enfranchised individual may reasonably regard democratic decisions as being imposed by an impersonal 'them'.

The micro-market is thus characterized as an institution which acts to co-ordinate individual choices without unduly restricting each individual's independence of action. It is as if each individual operates at arm's length from the institution. In the voting model the degree of co-ordination may be increased to the point where outcomes are equally applicable to all but the individual loses his/her independence of action and becomes an integral part of the institution. It is worth noting, in passing, that in small number cases the two institutions tend towards each other since the micro-market loses the property of anonymity whilst, in the voting model the probability of being decisive increases so that each individual becomes increasingly responsible for the ultimate choice.

Having sketched the distinction between the micro-market as an institution and the general class of vote based collective choice procedures, it is appropriate to clarify the status and purpose of this distinction. It is clear that the distinction is *not* intended as a basis for

arguing that the micro-market produces relatively desirable outcomes. Rather, it is the basis for the argument that the micro-market
will tend to be chosen by individuals in the meta-market context
since it provides an institutional structure which ensures individuals
the maximum attainable degree of independence. This argument, in
outline, is simply that since the individual faced with the meta-
market choice amongst institutions is also confronted with uncertainty as to his/her own position under the chosen institution, he/she
will tend to choose that institutional arrangement which will allow
the greatest scope for the pursuit of whatever ends the individual
may ultimately have. Thus, the preferred institution will be one
which allows for variety and individual flexibility, and these are
precisely the qualities which characterize the micro-market.

Under this line of argument, the special position of the micro-
market in public choice analysis can be seen to be based not on any
claim that the micro-market is in some particular sense 'good' or
'optimal', but rather on the claim that it is the institutional structure
which will tend to be chosen by individuals at the meta-market or
constitutional level of choice.

In the preceding paragraphs I have argued that the meta-market
individual will *tend* to choose the micro-market institution; that this
is a tendency rather than an iron rule is important. If the preservation of individualistic independence was the sole or overriding objective of the meta-market individual then, of course, such independence as is guaranteed by the micro-market would always be chosen,
just as Rawls argues that the specification of his original position
produces a firm lexicographical preference for liberty over equality
which itself consists of the lexicographical maximin principle.
However, this is not the nature of the subjectivist, public choice
position.[9] At the meta-market level individuals are unable to predict
the circumstances in which the chosen institutions are to operate (i.e.
the future is 'unknowable' rather than merely uncertain); furthermore, the details of individual's preferences cannot be known. It
follows immediately that we cannot predict what agreement (if any)
the individuals will come to. This argument then acts as a subjectivist
criticism of *any* contractarian position which seeks to identify particular social institutional arrangements, or particular social end-
states as being *the* specific option chosen above all others. Indeed,
for the subjective individualist the only information of relevance is
that all meta-market individuals definitely share an interest in individuality, and it is this common feature which produces the tendency
to favour micro-market institutions.

Once the presumption in favour of micro-markets is established, the question arises of how, in practical circumstances, one may justify non-micro-market institutions in any particular case. Once again, the relevant criterion is that of meta-market agreement. Whilst the typical, traditional economist would concern himself with the alternative resource allocations expected to be generated under the alternative institutions, using a hypothetical compensation test to search for a potential Pareto improvement which would demonstrate the 'superiority' of one institution over the other, the public choice theorist would be more likely to phrase the question in terms of a conceptual choice as between institutions to be made by an individual ignorant of his own eventual position.

The concentration of attention on the evaluation of institutions under uncertainty (in its subjectivist interpretation) ensures that public choice theorists cannot be solely concerned with the expected outcomes associated with alternative institutions. A significant aspect of constitutional choice or reform must lie in the direct evaluation of the alternative decision-making processes themselves. Here again there is a distinction between the public choice tradition and Rawlsian contractarianism which is concerned only with the end-state allocation of primary goods (including liberty) regardless of the decision processes or institutions utilized within the society.[10]

The public choice attitude to markets is often crudely summarized into a slogan – 'let markets work' or 'give markets a chance' – which is normally taken to be a plea for a reduction in the level of governmental regulation or intervention. Of course, such pleas are commonly found in the public choice literature (and elsewhere), but my argument here has been that such pleas do not accurately characterize the fundamental public choice approval of markets. I have suggested that a more appropriate, though less resounding, slogan might be 'let institutions be freely chosen', indicating that the 'market' which is of crucial importance in the public choice perspective is the meta-market. Only when support for the micro-market can be derived from meta-market choices does approval extend to the micro-market, and exactly the same degree of approval must be extended to *any* institutional structure chosen at the meta-market level. This lack of automatic support for private rather than public decision-making is expressed by Buchanan, 'People may . . . decide to do things collectively. Or they may not. The analysis, as such, is neutral in respect to the proper private sector-public sector mix' (1964, pp. 221–2).

In summary then, whilst the traditional economist considers micro-markets in a forward looking sense and seeks to evaluate them by reference to their outcomes or consequences, the economist of the public choice school adopts a more backward looking stance which evaluates micro-markets in terms of the origin of the institution in the meta-market. The force and appeal of the public choice viewpoint is, therefore, intimately tied up with the justification of the particular conception of the contractarian position which, as we have seen, differs in several detailed respects from that of Rawls whilst clearly retaining the essential emphasis on the ethical authority of agreement at the meta-market or constitutional level. In constrast, the ethical principle underlying the traditional economist's view of the micro-market as a means to an end is clearly that of utilitarianism. The next two sections of this chapter are, therefore, devoted to discussing in more detail these alternative ethical positions as they relate to the evaluation of economic reform of either institutions or policies.

UTILITARIANISM

As an ethical principle capable of judging between alternative economic policies or institutions,[11] utilitarianism can be decomposed into three basic parts. Following Sen and Williams (1982) we may name these parts, welfarism, sum-ranking, and consequentialism. Welfarism (Sen, 1979b) is the view that individual welfare levels or utilities are the only legitimate *basis* for the assignment of an aggregate value to a social state. Welfarism is, therefore, responsible for reducing the stock of ethically relevant information contained in any social state to a vector of utility levels with one element for each individual.

The sum-ranking component of utilitarianism asserts that the appropriate *method* for establishing the value to be assigned to a social state given the relevant information contained in the utility vector, is simply to add up the elements. Thus 'sum-ranking merges the utility bits together as one total lump, losing in the process both the identity of the individuals as well as their separateness. The distributional characteristics of the utility vector are all consequently lost. By now persons as persons have dropped fully out of the assessment of states of affairs' (Sen and Williams, 1982, p. 5).

Finally, consequentialism provides the prescriptive element of utilitarianism which asserts the choices regarding social policies, institutions and actions are to be made solely by reference to the value assigned to the social state which arises as a consequence.

In recent years a number of economists have joined with philosophers in discussing a number of outstanding questions which are thrown up by the widespread use of utilitarianism as the basis of welfare economics. Indeed, whilst it is still clearly the case that 'the economic theory of public policy is relentlessly utilitarian' (Hahn, 1982, p. 187) it is possible to point to a growing dissatisfaction with the evaluative structure imposed by utilitarianism. Such dissatisfaction is clearly recorded by many of the contributors in Sen and Williams's recent volume,[12] although several of the authors attempt to incorporate their criticisms in an expanded definition of utilitarianism which sometimes threatens to render the theory unrecognizable.

Amongst the criticisms aimed at utilitarianism by economists, perhaps the most powerful are concerned with individualism, welfarism, and the utilitarian treatment of uncertainty. The tension between individualism and utilitarianism is clear-cut and has already been noted in the discussion of the sum-ranking component of utilitarianism. Any attempt to reintroduce into the ethical calculus some concern for individuals as individuals must clearly breach the sum-ranking condition.[13] As Hammond has noted in a slightly different context: 'Individuals are no more than the pieces in a utilitarian game, to be manipulated for utilitarian ends, though with their best interests in mind' (Hammond, 1982, p. 101).

We may summarize the remaining two lines of critical argument by reference to two hypothetical cases which have been discussed in the literature. The first case concerns welfarism and is reproduced from Sen (1979a). The table shows the utility level of each of two individuals (1, 2) in each of three social states (x, y, z).

Case 1 Welfarism

Social State	x	y	z
1's Utility	4	7	7
2's Utility	10	8	8

Welfarism implies that states y and z *must* be valued equally since, in utility terms, they are identical. Whilst welfarism does not, by itself, tell us whether y is superior to x, it does tell us that *if* y is superior to x then z must also be superior to x. Sen's demonstration of the limitations of welfarism then consists of supplying further information about the social states:

In x person 1 is hungry while 2 is eating a great deal. In y person 2 has been made to surrender a part of his food supply to 1. . . . Consider now z. Here person 1 is still as hungry as in x, and person 2 is also eating just as much. However, person 1, who is a sadist, is now permitted to torture 2, who – alas – is not a masochist. (Sen, 1979a, pp. 547–8)

To the welfarist, this information must be irrelevant – the *only* ethically interesting facts are the individual utility levels however they have come about. So that if we wish to take the additional information into account in judging between the social states – perhaps by asserting a moral distinction between torture and food redistribution as alternative means of producing utility changes – we must be in breach of welfarism.

Our second case derives from Diamond (1967).[14] A policy (A, B) must be chosen before the uncertainty concerning which social state (x, y) will occur is resolved. The various possible utility consequences for the two individuals $(1, 2)$ are shown on the table.

Case 2   Uncertainty

Policy:	A		B	
Social State:	x	y	x	y
1's Utility	1	0	1	0
2's Utility	1	0	0	1

From a utilitarian perspective the choice amongst policies is a matter of indifference since each policy generates an identical ex-post utility level, regardless of the social state which actually occurs. However, Diamond argues that policy B is to be strictly preferred since it offers both individuals 'a fair shake' in the sense that their ex-ante, expected utilities will be equal.

That Diamond's claim is anti-utilitarian is clear, but precisely which component of utilitarianism is under criticism is somewhat less clear. One interpretation would suggest that sum-ranking is the target since it is the *distribution* of expected utilities entry into the ethical calculus which is stressed. On the other hand Broome (1983b) has argued that Diamond's argument is based on the intrinsic valuation of fairness in the process which generates the utility outcomes over and above the valuation of the utility generated. This then is a clear breach of welfarism and parallels our earlier case. Indeed, Diamond distinguishes between individual and social choice by noting that 'it seems reasonable for the individual to be concerned solely with final outcomes while society is also interested in the process of choice' (Diamond, 1967, p. 766) which would seem to lend some support to the anti-welfarist view. However, the passage could also support an anti-consequentialist interpretation since it suggests that 'final outcomes', whether valued solely in terms of welfare or not, are not to be viewed as the only criterion underlying the choice of policy.

Whichever of these interpretations is accepted in respect of Diamond's original argument it is clear that the introduction of uncertainty opens up a variety of lines of criticism of utilitarianism. For our present purposes it is appropriate to leave on one side the whole question of the distribution of (expected) utility and concentrate on one or two issues raised by the simple distinction between utility and expected utility, between ex-post and ex-ante conceptions of welfare.

The first issue concerns the identification of the relevant notion of hypothetical compensation. The central technique of contemporary cost-benefit analysis is the identification and estimation of ex-ante compensation, which may be defined as the monetary value of an individual's change in expected utility. The alternative, ex-post concept of compensation seeks to identity the eventual monetary value of an individual's change in actual utility. Much of the debate concerning the relative merits of the two approaches has been carried on in the context of the valuation of human life.[15] However, Ulph (1982) provides the following simple example of the substantive difference between the two approaches which avoids some of the contentious issues arising in the value of life controversy. Consider a world made up of five identical individuals, each with an endowment of 25 units of financial wealth and a house. A project is under consideration which would raise, with certainty, each individual's wealth to 36 units, but would also destroy one house. It is not known whose house will be destroyed but all agree that each house is equally at risk. Suppose that each individual's utility function is given by:

$$U(h, w) = (1 + 15\,h)^{1/4}w^{1/2}$$

where w is financial wealth, $h = 1$ if the individual has a house and $h = 0$ if his house is destroyed. Without the project, each individual has a utility level of 10. Under the proposed project, expected utility[16] for each individual is 10.8 so that the project would be approved by the standard, ex-ante, cost-benefit criterion as being a

Pareto improvement. Yet, ex-post, the compensation required by the individual whose house is actually destroyed[17] is 64 financial units whilst the total monetary gain to the four remaining individuals is only 44 units. Clearly, the 'loser' could not be compensated by the 'gainers' so that the project fails an ex-post compensation test.

In this example it is the ex-ante compensation test which accords with the utilitarian prescription since aggregate utility is increased under the project from 50 to 54. This result in part reflects the fact that all individuals share identical beliefs concerning the outcome of the project which match precisely the actual outcome. This then brings us to our second issue, since if individuals differ in their subjective views concerning possible outcomes and/or the probabilities attached to them, or if all individuals agree but are in fact mistaken, then a further wedge is driven between ex-ante and ex-post conceptions of welfare.

For example, if three of the individuals in the previous example mistakenly (but genuinely) each believe that the probability of their own home being destroyed is 0.4, then the project would no longer pass an ex-ante compensation test. In this modified case the ex-ante and ex-post compensation tests would reach the same conclusion, but neither would yield the utilitarian prescription. The point here is simply that the correspondence between the ex-ante compensation test and the utilitarian criterion depends, *inter alia*, on all individuals expectations being fully informed and rational. Only when everyone agrees on the future and will be proved right by events can utilitarianism in its strongest form be operationalized. As a response to the challenges of uncertainty, this can hardly be viewed as satisfactory.

It is this inability of utilitarianism to cope with the difficulties of variations in individual expectations and the resultant mistakes which arise in situations of genuine uncertainty which leads many economists to shore up utilitarianism with the requirement that the individualistic preferences and expectations which form the bedrock of the doctrine should not be merely the actual or manifest preferences and expectations but must rather be 'perfectly prudent' and derived from 'a full understanding'.[18] Of course, the difficulty here is the impossibility of distinguishing, ex-ante, between a 'perfectly prudent' view and a merely 'actual' one. In the modified example of the house-destroying project, for example, who could know, *a priori*, whether 0.4 or 0.2 was the prudent expectation? Note in particular that this example was designed so that the majority are, ex-post, wrong.

At the heart of much of this critical debate on utilitarianism and its role in economics is the existence of two alternative views on the appropriate definition of 'utility'. Thus far we have implicitly accepted the traditional view of 'utility' as an independently measurable quantity reflecting an individual's valuation of his/her position. Indeed, the numerical cases laid out above would make no sense unless this definition is accepted. However, many contemporary economists define 'utility' purely in terms of choice.[19] That which is preferred is simply defined as that which is chosen. As Sen and Williams observe, this definitional stance 'would seem to remove the content from the notion of valuing . . . Basing choice on valuation is cogent in a way that basing valuation on choice is not' (Sen and Williams, 1982, p. 13).

Whilst we shall return to consider the potential merits of focusing ethical attention on choices rather than independently defined values in the next section, it is sufficient for our present purposes to note that a choice-based definition of 'utility' must be inconsistent, in general, with utilitarianism as we have defined it.

Our brief consideration of a variety of points and cases has done little more than scratch the surface of the contemporary debate on the economic relevance of utilitarianism. However, it has served to point out that each of the identified components of utilitarianism – welfarism, sum-ranking, and consequentialism – is currently subject to reappraisal and criticism by economists. Many economists attempt to expand the doctrine of utilitarianism to accommodate particular difficulties; but this process of piecemeal modification of an ethical theory often results in a hybrid which carries little intuitive conviction and is utilitarian in name only.

Whilst it is certainly still true to say that the basic structure and broad perspective of contemporary mainstream economics is 'relentlessly' utilitarian, it is equally true that wherever economists come up against the tenets of utilitarianism in particular cases, it is increasingly the case that it is utilitarianism that is modified or rejected.

PUBLIC CHOICE, CONTRACTARIANISM AND UTILITARIANISM

Having identified the three component elements of utilitarianism, it is worthwhile to use these concepts as a checklist to underline the differences between utilitarianism and contractarianism and, in particular, the two versions of contractarianism identified as the Rawlsian position and the public choice position.[20] The Rawlsian ethical criterion is clearly consequentialist in that it is the final distribution of primary goods in all possible future states of the world which provides the motivation for ethical prescription. However, the role of the mult-dimensional set of 'primary goods' as the *basis* for the evaluation of any particular social state makes it equally clear that the Rawlsian approach is not welfarist, even though a large number of economists utilize a utility-based version of Rawls's difference principle. On the matter of sum-ranking, the lexicographical difference principle obviously replaces the simple summing of individualistic values. Thus the Rawlsian position may be summarized as consequentialist, non- welfarist and anti-sum-ranking.

Our earlier discussion of the subjectivist public choice view of the meta-market or contractarian level of analysis allows us to conclude immediately that all three aspects of utilitarianism are rejected. The analysis is not welfarist even though individuals are assumed to be utility maximizers, since it recognizes the possibility of (for example) individual rights being valued intrinsically rather than solely by reference to their ability to generate utility. It is not sum-ranking since it denies the existence of any relevant ex-ante social welfare function – a denial which includes the Benthamite sum of utilities function. Finally, it goes one step further from utilitarianism than Rawls by rejecting consequentialism and allowing actions to be judged, in whole or in part, by considerations other than their outcomes.

The basic intuition underlying any contractarian position concerns the binding nature of the commitment and obligation which are generated by the act of agreement. To revert to the game analogy employed earlier, a referee's power in enforcing the rules of a game derives from the player's prior agreement on those rules and the referee's authority under them. Take away the initial agreement and neither the game nor the referee's authority has any independent existence.

In the simple circumstances of interpersonal exchange, the notion of contractual obligation and authority is both intuitively appealing and uncontroversial. A central question in discussing any contractarianist view of constitutional choice and its ethical standing is, therefore, whether the intuitive appeal attaching to the authority of prior agreement can be retained in moving from the level of direct interpersonal trade (the micro-market) to the constitutional plane (the meta-market).

In addressing this question it will be useful to distinguish between three categories of contractarianism. The first, which I shall term 'naive' contractarianism, supposes that the social contract (whatever its content) is a historical fact – that society actually emerged by means of a process of agreement amongst the then extant individuals. This naive position is clearly insupportable and is included here primarily to indicate that contractarianism need *not* contain such a simplistic view of the historical development of society. It is also informative to rehearse the reasons underlying the insupportability of the naive view.

There are essentially two distinct lines of argument either of which is sufficient in itself to refute naive contractarianism. On the one hand, it may be argued that a study of history simply contradicts the hypothesis of contractual agreement as a major engine of social development. This is an essentially empirical argument. On the other hand, it may be argued that even if such agreements between individuals did occur from time to time in the past, they could have no authority over present day individuals. Just as an individual is not bound by a current agreement between other individuals, so he/she cannot be argued to be under any obligation to an agreement reached by arbitrary historical figures. This second argument has no empirical content but nevertheless undermines the authority of any naive contractarian position.

The second category of contractarianism may be termed 'hypothetical' contractarianism and is based on the construction of an imaginary group of individuals set in unreal circumstances. An argument then deduces the principles or constitution which such a group would be expected to agree. These principles are then held up as yardsticks by which to judge actual societies, and as targets to be aimed at when considering reform. Clearly, the basic argument in any such theory is that individuals will accept the authority of a particular constitutional principle if they accept that the principle is one which they would agree to if they were placed in an appropriately specified 'original position'. The Rawlsian theory of justice is an example of hypothetical contractarianism in the Kantian tradition.

> . . . the undertakings referred to are purely hypothetical: a contract view holds that certain principles would be accepted in a well-defined initial situation. The merit of the contract terminology is that it conveys the idea that principles of justice may be conceived as principles that would be chosen by rational individuals, and that in this way conceptions of justice may be explained and justified. (Rawls, 1971, p. 16)

This type of argument depends upon an indirect or second order form of consensus. Individuals do not agree directly on the constitutional principles to be adopted; rather they agree on an appropriate definition of an original position, and on the principles which they would agree if placed in that position.

In criticizing this category of contractarianism we may again identify an essentially empirical critique and a second, more abstract line of argument. The empirical objection relates to the likelihood of all individuals agreeing to a particular conception of the original position and to the particular principles that may be expected to flow from it. As Rawls (1971, p. 15) notes, his characterization of the initial position on the one hand, and of the principles of justice on the other, are separable in such a way that one can accept either without being committed to the other. Under these circumstances it is perhaps rather hopeful to believe that agreement on the twin pillars of the theory, which has proved so contentious amongst social philosophers, will be sufficiently widespread to form the basis for the justification of reform.[21]

A more abstract criticism of hypothetical contractarianism in general and the Rawlsian analysis in particular has been put by Honderich (1976) in a manner which parallels the argument put in respect of naive contractarianism above. Even if it were accepted that particular principles would derive from the original position, Honderich argues that such principles would have no special claim to authority since even 'if we grant, as we are urged, that "we" *would* agree to the principles *if* we were as the people in the Original Position are. *We* are different, have never been there, and have made no agreement.' (Honderich, 1976, p. 75 – original emphasis.)[22]

This argument amounts to the claim that the only agreements which have a claim to authority over us are those agreements in which we actually participate. It translates the old slogan 'no taxation without representation' to read 'no authority without participation'.

If naive contractarianism is concerned with justifying the present by legitimizing history, and hypothetical contractarianism is concerned with evaluating the present by constructing an ethical yardstick applicable to all societies, the third category of contractarianism – which I shall term 'prospective' contractarianism – is concerned with the process by which the future should evolve out of the present.

Under this interpretation, the starting point for the discussion of institutional and constitutional reform is not some historical or hypothetical 'original position', it is simply the present society – whatever its imperfections. Agreement is then seen as the process which can produce change which carries with it both obligation and

authority. Of course, it is recognized that a full unanimity requirement for any change automatically builds in a presumption in favour
of the status quo (Buchanan and Tullock, 1862; Hamlin, 1983).
Whilst some see this as a crucial failing, others see it as reflecting the
normally slow evolutionary pace which we observe in most societies.[23]

Given this starting point, the appropriate analytic technique is that
of bargaining, with each individual agent attempting to 'sell' his/her
agreement in return for his/her own conception of good reform.
Here one may object that conflicting self-interests will make the
bargaining solution arbitrary at best and non-existent at worst. Without some analogue of the 'original position' acting to bring together
the perceived self-interests of the bargaining agents, this view of
contractarianism might be accused of bringing the subject matter of
the meta-market down to the mechanics of the micro-market. The
necessary analogue is provided by emphasizing that, in undertaking
institutional and constitutional reform, the agents are consciously
participating in a long-run debate – they are effectively choosing a
framework which they expect to survive, in at least its general
principles, for a considerable time.[24] The time dimensions associated
with constitutional decision-making bring uncertainty and the expectations of the bargaining agents firmly to centre stage. Under a
subjectivist interpretation of uncertainty it is therefore the 'unkno-
wability' of the future rather than some artificially produced 'veil of
ignorance' which ensures that pure short-run (i.e. micro-market)
self-interest does not dominate the bargaining process, whilst simultaneously ensuring that some distinction between individuals is retained so that bargaining is a meaningful concept.

This prospective variant of contractarianism overcomes both the
empirical and the abstract lines of criticism which have been discussed. The empirical critique is simply irrelevant since prospective
contractarianism has no necessary empirical content; rather it is an
ethical prescription deriving from normative individualism (Hamlin,
1983). The abstract criticism is met since individuals are actually
involved in the constitutional process so that the basis for authority is
provided.

It is clear from this discussion of the prospective contractarian
position that the public choice analysis can be considered to fall
under this heading. This categorization is not to deny that public
choice theorists have devoted considerable attention to investigating
hypothetical constitutional agreements in order to form some view
concerning what might be agreed in any actual constitutional contract (e.g. Brennan and Buchanan, 1980). However, these consid-

erations on the substance of what might be agreed must be seen as tentative explorations which are subordinate to the central thesis that institutional agreement – regardless of the precise details of what is agreed – is the appropriate benchmark.

Our characterization of the public choice analysis as an example of prospective contractarianism may now be utilized in returning to examine in more detail the contrast between the utilitarian and public choice schools with which we began this section. In the previous section I argued that much of the current criticism aimed at each of the three component elements of utilitarianism could be traced to the two alternative concepts of utility used within economics. It was also suggested that the purely choice based concept of utility is essentially incoherent in a utilitarian context. What we have in prospective contractarianism is, then, the alternative approach to this impasse between choice and utilitarianism. Rather than attempting to revive utilitarianism by use of a new, but incoherent, concept of utility, public choice theorists adopt the more radical line of abandoning the utilitarian framework and, hence, the need for any objective definition of utility, in favour of an undiluted attention to the process of choice itself.

This central distinction can be illustrated by returning to the example of the house-destroying project discussed above. Recall that in the original example the individuals were taken to choose the project unanimously even though, ex-post, the 'loser' could not be fully compensated by the 'gainers'. Clearly, the prospective contractarian would have no hesitation in endorsing the ex-ante decision here and, as we have seen, this prescription accords with utilitarianism. In the modified example where the individuals are acting under different subjective beliefs, the prospective contractarian would still insist on the appropriateness of the ex-ante, choice-based criterion even though it no longer accords with utilitarianism. In this case the public choice analyst would have no hesitation in describing the wedge between the chosen course of action and the eventually realized outcome as an example of the type of 'mistake' which can only be identified with hindsight and which is inevitable in any situation of genuine uncertainty. Such mistakes may, of course, be important ex-post, and may influence further choices (e.g., to compensate those who suffer as a result of past 'mistakes', etc.), but since it is definitional that such mistakes cannot be foreseen, they are argued by prospective contractarians to be irrelevant to the ethical evaluation of alternative courses of action at the ex-ante stage.

In essence, the public choice approach can be reconstructed out of the critique of utilitarianism summarized above. The prospective contractarianism positions embraced by the public choice analysts accept the various lines of criticism aimed at utilitarianism and build on them to formulate an alternative, individualistic basis for the economic analysis of organized society. The framework, by its very nature, fits well with the ordinalist, choice-based analysis of the individual decision-maker in the micro-market and provides a counterpart to this analysis at the meta-market level. Of course, the basic framework must remain controversial, and much detailed analysis concerning the constitutional calculus of the individual remains to be done;[25] nevertheless it is possible to regard the growing public choice tradition as a reaction against the limitations of the utilitarian doctrine which extends both the provenance and the domain of economic analysis.

CONCLUDING COMMENTS AND A FURTHER DEBATE

The public choice literature contains a wide variety of substantive issues and a number of detailed points of view. In my attempt to distil some of the essential features out of this literature I have consciously (and, I am sure, unconsciously) simplified or omitted many interesting lines of argument. I have chosen to emphasize the methodological basis of public choice with its component parts of methodological individualism, subjectivism and prospective contractarianism, since it is in this area that the nature of the radical departure from orthodox, utilitarian economic analysis is most clearly identified. Once the basic shift in what Buchanan refers to as 'mind-set' is recognized, many of the detailed, substantive arguments fall more easily into a proper perspective.

Throughout this chapter I have sought to establish and develop the distinctive public choice position relative to both the mainstream economic tradition and the Rawlsian contractarian stance. It is therefore appropriate to end by briefly considering the public choice analysis alongside a further approach to political economy which is also critical of the mainstream economic analysis.

In their critique of neo-classical economics, Hollis and Nell (1975) identify the three key aspects of neo-classical orthodoxy as being methodological individualism, utilitarianism and positivist empiricism. In rejecting each of these elements in turn they argue in favour of classical Marxian analysis. Despite the apparently wide difference in the conclusion, there are considerable similarities between the

Hollis-Nell critique of economic orthodoxy and that of the public choice school. Indeed, the only major difference between the two critiques lies in the interpretation and evaluation of methodological individualism. The Hollis-Nell attack on individualism argues that:

> Once it is granted that social organisation creates wants, it becomes absurd to aim ideally at organising society so that it serves the performed presocial wants of the atoms. Individuals do not exist, as what they are, apart from the jobs they do and the services and commodities they produce. Their wants grow out of their daily lives which in turn rest on the work by means of which the system is reproduced and there is no such thing as abstract choice. (Hollis and Nell, 1975, p. 265)

This line of argument based on the notion that preference is not a basic or primitive concept but one which may be adapted or shaped by social circumstances, is also put by Elster (1982), although in this case it is interpreted as an argument against utilitarianism rather than against individualism. Indeed, Elster's interpretation is specifically anti-welfarist and anti-consequentialist, forming a 'polemic against end-state principles in ethical theories' (Elster, 1982, p. 238) which seems to be entirely consistent with an individualistic, prospective contractarian view.

The Hollis-Nell anti-individualistic interpretation of this line of argument seems to be based on the idea that methodological individualism must assert that each individual is fully self-contained and complete. Whilst this may be an acceptable caricature of *homo economicus* in an egoist, positivist world, it is not a recognizable description of the subjectivist individualism underlying public choice. Rather, the distinctive element of methodological individualism in this context is that individuals are not only the sole class of active agents in society, but they are also the only potential source of values. These values may differ as between individuals and over time as individuals interact and make mistakes but, nevertheless, they are the only values to be had and hence must be the values which, in one way or another, shape society.

Notice that this methodological individualism does not in any way rule out socialist (or Marxian) outcomes. It merely argues that if such outcomes are to be valued – and chosen – they must be valued by individuals. The *bête noire* of the public choice analyst is not any *particular* form of social arrangement, but *any* form which is imposed upon the members of society.

The possibility of an essentially contractarian analysis which under slightly varying specifications can produce alternative chosen outcomes ranging from the private exchange economy through a society reflecting Rawlsian principles of justice to socialist and communist societies, has been investigated in a recent series of publications.[26] Whilst this work is beyond the scope of the present work, it is clear that it falls into the category of hypothetical contractarianism discussed above and must, therefore, be viewed as a series of experiments as to what might be chosen in a constitutional contract rather than a statement of what should be chosen.

It is unlikely that methodological debates in the field of political economy can ever be decisively concluded. Recent controversies regarding the basic structure of the discipline can be welcomed as evidence that a varied and lively discipline is once again emerging from the orthodoxy of the past. It is in this context that the public choice perspective is establishing itself as a cogent approach to the problems of political economics which is capable of generating an alternative analysis and fresh insights.

NOTES

1 For examples of public choice applications in these areas see Tullock (1965, 1967, 1971) Downs (1967); Niskanen (1971, 1975); Breton (1974).

2 For surveys of public choice see Buchanan (1975a); Mueller (1976, 1979).

3 For more extensive discussions of methodological individualism and its role in public choice see Downs (1957); Buchanan and Tullock (1962); Buchanan (1975b); Hamlin (1983).

4 This theme in public choice is normally traced to Black (1948a, 1948b, 1958).

5 The *locus classicus* for this branch of the public choice literature is Buchanan and Tullock (1962). For discussion and extension of their analysis see, for example, Rae (1969, 1975); Brennan and Buchanan (1980); Kafoglis and Cebula (1981); Hamlin (1984).

6 For discussion of subjectivism and its implications see Shackle (1972); Buchanan and Thirlby (1973); Loasby (1976); Wiseman (1980).

7 See chapter 3 of this volume.

8 For this argument in more detail see Buchanan (1954, 1982a).

9 For a subjectivist discussion of why the maximin difference principle may *tend* to be chosen see Buchanan and Faith (1980).

10 For a more detailed discussion of procedural and end-state evaluations see Hamlin (1983, 1984).

11 This simply distinguishes between classical or aggregative utilitarianism – which is our subject here – and utilitarianism as a theory of personal morality.

12 Sen and Williams (1982); in addition to the editor's introduction see particularly the articles by Hahn, Mirrlees, Hammond and Elster.

13 Introducing concern for the distribution of utility is a small step towards recognizing individuality, but even this breaches sum-ranking. For a defence of sum-ranking see Harsanyi (1976).

14 See also Broome (1983b); Hammond (1981, 1982), Ulph (1982).

15 See Broome (1978); Ulph (1982) and references therein.

16 Expected utility $= 0.2 \{U(0,36)\} + 0.8\{U(1,36)\} = 10.8$

17 Compensation, C is given by: $U(0,36 + C) = U(1,25)$.

18 Harsanyi (1976); Mirrlees (1982); discussed in the introduction of Sen and Williams (1982). On a related point of the problems of 'adaptive' or manipulated preferences see Elster (1982).

19 For example, Harsanyi (1976); Mirrlees (1982); for a discussion see Broome (1983a).

20 For a comparison between utilitarianism and yet another variant of contractarianism see Scanlon (1982) who also presents an argument as to why we should not expect utilitarian principles to emerge from contractarian agreement.

21 This is not to deny the validity of Rawls's work as an explanation of the ways in which justice can be conceived. The point is the more practical one relating to the theory as a basis for the evaluation of actual societies.

22 Honderich also argues that the concept of agreement is redundant in Rawls since all individuals are identical in the original position (Rawls, 1971, p. 139). For an interpretation of Rawls in which individuals differ, and where the concept of agreement is more substantial see Buchanan and Faith (1980).

23 Rapid, revolutionary change does of course occur, but may be explained under this theory in terms of a build-up of pressure caused by the successive imposition of non-agreed reforms.

24 Of course it may not, since the essence of the prospective view is that reform can be a continuous process; nevertheless, each generation can be expected to act as if they were choosing a constitution once and for all.

25 For a recent attempt at providing a taxonomy of the options confronting the individual see Hamlin (1984).

26 See particularly Howe and Roemer (1981); Roemer (1982a, 1982b).

PART II

Themes in Political Economy

6

Modelling Politico-Economic Relationships

BRUNO S. FREY

There are innumerable relationships between the political and economic sectors of society. In order to advance our knowledge it is necessary to simplify these interactions by concentrating on particular aspects. The choice of the model, and therewith the abstractions, have to be guided by the goal of the research.

From many perspectives, government stands at the centre of interaction of economic and political forces. From observation it is immediately apparent that government actually has a great and sometimes dominating influence on the course of the economy, and that in turn government depends on economic factors. Thus, for many purposes it is fitting to model politico-economic relationships by considering government as an *endogenous* part of a social system composed of political and economic sectors. Such a view has dramatic consequences for economics, which so far has been accustomed to take government as an institution outside the system considered. Based on this exogenous view, government could be attributed the task of steering the economy to the 'common good'. The traditional theory of economic policy thus assumes that government maximizes a social welfare function within the opportunities provided by the economic system. This view is explicitly found in the quantitative theory of economic policy as championed by Tinbergen (1956) and Theil (1968), as well as in the more modern versions applied to dynamic problems, i.e. the normative theory of economic growth, in Shell (1967), and the theory of optimal control, in Chow (1973) and Pindyck (1973). Exactly the same approach is used in the recently developed theory of optimal taxation, in Diamond and Mirrlees (1971) and *Journal of Public Economics*

(1976) where the social efficiency losses due to the distortive effect of taxation are minimized. If, however, government is *not* taken to be independent of the economy, but rather as an endogenous part of the politico-economic system, such a welfare maximizing view is no longer logically possible. The change in perspective from an exogenous to an endogenous view thus requires a new theory of economic policy. It is easy to see that the change in perspective also has an impact on *positive* economics. For example, government being endogenous, it may play an active role in creating and amplifying business cycles. In the extreme, it may be considered as one of the major producers of instabilities in the economic system ('political business cycle').

The form of the relationship between the economy and government depends on the particular political and economic institutions existing. Government behaves differently according to the economic and political environment in which it is placed. As a consequence, there are many types of government behaviour observable. We will show below how various *types* of government behaviour are associated with particular politico-economic institutions.

Government behaviour which is at the centre of most politico-economic models can be analysed with the help of various methodologies. No effort is made here to survey these theoretical approaches. Rather, one particular approach, the economic theory of politics, is used here. This theory applies modern economic theory, and in particular the economic model of behaviour (see Becker, 1976), to political processes. In the USA, the approach is commonly known as Public Choice. (For surveys see, for example, Frey, 1978, Mueller, 1979, Whynes and Bowles, 1981, and Hamlin in this book.) The workings of this theory are exemplified below for the case of governments acting within the institutional conditions of representative governments in highly industrialized countries. It is shown how the theoretical models can be empirically tested with the help of econometric methods, leading to *'politometrics'*. The quantitative analysis of the economic model of government is contrasted to a competing approach by ex-post forecasts extending beyond the estimation period. The consequences of politico-economic modelling for positive analysis and policy-making are pointed out, and the last section of the chapter offers some concluding remarks.

TYPES OF GOVERNMENT BEHAVIOUR

A basic assumption in the economic theory of politics is that the politicians forming the government pursue their own goals. They gain utility from putting their ideological conceptions into reality, but they are also strongly interested in staying in power. Survival is a necessary requirement for being able to influence the course of events effectively. It is therefore reasonable to assume that politicians and government are ready (temporarily) to give up their ideologically motivated pursuits when it turns out to be necessary to guarantee survival in office. A very general model of government is thus based on the maximization of utility (composed of the particular ideology of the government), subject to a survival constraint. This general model yields widely different kinds of behaviour according to the politico-economic system considered. This means that the impulses of economic conditions on the political sector, and of the political decisions of the economy, may assume a great variety of forms. Six different forms of institutional conditions and corresponding types of government behaviour are distinguished here, extending from extremely democratic to authoritarian conditions.

Direct democracy

In this institutional set-up, the citizens take the political decisions in an assembly. A government barely exists, its only function is to do exactly what the citizens decide; the politicians have no discretionary power. If there is only one issue – usually the amount of public service as measured by expenditure – on which to take a decision, if individual preferences are single peaked (i.e. for each individual there exists a preferred amount of public services, and the level of satisfaction is decreasing with increasing distance in both directions from this position) and if everybody has perfect information and participates in the vote, the decision-making based on simple majority voting produces the outcome which is preferred by the *median voter*. The median voter model has been applied particularly to democratic decisions concerning public school expenditures in US communes (e.g. Borcherding and Deacon, 1972; Bergstrom and Goodman, 1973; Lovell, 1978) and to all kinds of public expenditures in Swiss communes (Pommerehne, 1978; Pommerehne and Schneider, 1978), and the corresponding income and tax price elasticities have been empirically determined.

The median voter model of direct democracy constitutes a clear advance over the earlier estimates (see, for example, Fabricant, 1952, and Sharkansky, 1967) which simply assumed that the demand for publicly provided goods followed the same rules as the supply of goods provided by the market. In addition to explicitly acknowledging the *political* framework of public provision, the median voter model also takes into account that the informed voters know that they have to 'pay' for the goods via an increase in taxes ('tax price').

The assumptions on which the median voter model is based exist only under quite restricted conditions. As soon as there are multi-dimensional issues, the necessary conditions for the existence and stability of an equilibrium whose properties are used for the econometric tests are unlikely to be met even with any reasonable approximation in reality (see, for example, Hinich, 1977). A careful critical examination of the data, methods and application of the median voter model even under favourable institutional conditions (Romer and Rosenthal, 1979) concludes that there is in general rather limited support of this approach.

Semi-direct democracy

In this institutional set-up, there exists both a government and parliament, but the voters have the possibility to influence the political outcome by advancing initiatives and by voting in referenda. A classical case of semi-direct polity is Switzerland. A politico-economic model working on the assumption that the government maximizes its utility subject to the survival constraints has been constructed for that country (Schneider, Pommerehne and Frey, 1981). The Swiss government being composed of all the large parties represented in government, its utility is taken to be best served by minimizing conflict, i.e. by granting as many demands as possible coming from the strong interest groups and from public bureaucracy, while the consumer-tax payers have to pay the bill. This usually means that public expenditures are augmented. This policy is, however, subject to the survival constraint, which in this case means that a sufficient share of referenda is decided in the way proposed by the government. When the economic conditions are good and in particular when the rate of inflation is low, citizens will be more inclined to decide in favour of the government's wishes in a referenda irrespective of its specific content. When economic conditions are bad, the voters tend to blame government and are more ready to reject the propositions advanced by the government.

If the citizens reject too many propositions, the government has to make an effort to win the support of the citizens again, which is done by reorienting the policies undertaken in the direction of their (presumed) wishes. In general, this means that public expenditures have to be decreased (compared to the trend), helping to reduce inflation, which in turn makes it *ceteris paribus* more likely that the referenda are decided according to the government's wishes.

This interdependent politico-economic model has been empirically tested for Switzerland and the period 1950–75, with satisfactory results. It turns out, as theoretically expected, that *ceteris paribus* the government significantly reduces public expenditure when the support by the electorate is low, while it is increased when the government enjoys a high support by its citizens, measured by a high share of referenda being decided as proposed.

Democracy by party competition

According to Schumpeter (1942) and subsequently Downs (1957) the essence of representative democracy is that parties strive for the vote of the citizens. If there are only two parties, each of which attempts to maximize the share of votes received, and the voters' preferences are distributed along a spatial scale representing a particular political issue, under somewhat restrictive assumptions the following result obtains: both parties offer the same programme and chance decides which one will form the government; both party programmes focus on the median voter's preference, and the outcome is Pareto-optimal. This model provides an intuitive rationale for the observation that in representative democracies the programme of the government and the opposition are often quite similar.

The model of party competition can, however, be criticized on various grounds:

(1) There are very few countries and periods in which only two parties compete against each other. For that reason, the model of party competition has rarely, if ever, been empirically tested (at least in a satisfactory way). As soon as there are more than two parties, or if there is the *threat* of a third party entering, the median voter result breaks down. The extension of the model to more than two parties has been confronted with grave difficulties because the possibilities of coalition formation must be considered, and so far no satisfactory results have been achieved.

(2)   Parties can only be expected to maximize votes if political competition is very intensive (perfect): in that case the political survival constraint dominates government behaviour completely, and the government has no leeway for discretionary actions to further its own utility.

While the competition between parties is certainly an important and even essential ingredient of representative democracy, it is unrealistic to base the politico-economic relationships exclusively on this concept.

Representative democracy

In a representative democracy with discontinuous elections every third to fifth year, the government can be considered to be in a special position of power similar to that of a monopolist. It has various advantages in comparison to the opposition, the most important of which is the opportunity to influence the course of the economy before elections. The government has considerable discretionary power which it can use to carry out its ideological programmes. In the limiting case in which political survival is seriously threatened, government is forced to undertake a vote maximizing policy at election time, i.e. the model of monopolistic government includes as a *special* case the model of party competition, and that only an election time. The normal case is, however, that the government is free to pursue its ideologically motivated goals, but that the need to be re-elected constitutes an important constraint.

The behaviour of such a government in a representative democracy has been modelled both in the context of a Phillips-curve framework and of the whole economy. The best known model is by Nordhaus (1975) (see also MacRae, 1977; Lindbeck, 1976), who assumes that the government maximizes its vote share V at election time T. This vote share depends on the past experience of the voters with unemployment U and inflation p. The voters are thus taken to make the government responsible for the course of the economy. Past economic experiences have less influence on the vote decision; the discount factor ϱ thus measures the speed with which voters forget. The government's vote share at election time accumulated over the election period (O, T) is

(1) $V(T) = \int_{O}^{T} u[U(t), \dot{p}(t)]e^{\varrho t}dt,$

where u measures the instant evaluation of the government's policy, an increase of unemployment and inflation damaging, of course, the government $(u_U < 0, u_{\dot{p}} < 0)$

The government has control over the rate of unemployment, but is constrained by the (expectations) augmented by unemployment-inflation trade-off.

(2) $\dot{p} = f(U) + a\dot{p}^e; f'(U) < 0, 0 < a < 1$

(3) $\dfrac{d\dot{p}^e}{dt} = b(\dot{p} - \dot{p}^e); b > 0.$

Maximizing the vote share at election time (1), subject to the constraint of the economic system (2), (3), leads to the government's optimal policy: the unemployment rate is increased immediately after the election in order to push down both inflation and inflation expectations, thus shifting the Phillips-curve towards the origin. Before the election unemployment is reduced, and the cost in terms of an outward shifting Phillips-curve arises only after the election. The government thus is able to increase its vote share by deliberately destabilizing the economy, a phenomenon known as 'political business cycle'.

The fact that the government may find it advantageous actively to produce a business cycle stands in stark contrast to the 'Keynesian' notion of a benevolent government which as a matter of course has an interest in economic stabilization.

Since Nordhaus's pathbreaking study, a large theoretical and empirical literature on the political business cycle has emerged. For example, Kirchgaessner (1979) has derived the specific features of politico-economic cycles when governments pursue ideological goals subject to an election constraint, and when voters are not myopic and learn to understand the creation of the cycle. Paldam (1981) has made extensive empirical tests and has found strong evidence of a political business cycle in aggregate real and price variables. For OECD countries and the period 1948–75 the growth of real national income is largest in the second year after the elections, this being the first opportunity where the newly (re)elected government can redeem its election promises. With few exceptions such promises require increases in public expenditures, leading to an upswing. This explanation of the political business cycle adds a new aspect to the discussion.

On the basis of a complete macroeconometric model of the USA,

Fair (1975) has derived the vote-maximizing policy of a president. According to his estimates, the presidential vote share depends on the growth rate of real GNP only (a result which has not been found by other researchers). Moreover, voters only consider GNP in the election year, i.e. they completely discount the state of the economy in previous years. Under these conditions, it turns out that it is advantageous for the president to create a marked politico-economic cycle: the president maximizes votes and his re-election chance if he undertakes a strongly restrictive policy in the first part of the election period, and a strongly expansionary policy in the second part. It turns out, however, that US presidents in the post-war periods have not followed such a policy, i.e. the vote-maximizing use of instruments has weak explanatory power.

A different course is followed by monopolistic models constructed to *explain* the actual behaviour of governments in representative democracies of industrialized countries. As they can be considered the prototype of econometrically estimated politico-economic models, they will be discussed more extensively below.

Pressure group democracy

There are institutional conditions giving great power to organized interests, at least in some areas. The dependence of governments on pressure groups has not been at the forefront of politico-economic modelling, probably because the public choice scholars engaged in the area tend to apply the concepts they are familiar with from economics, and they therefore stress aspects of competition rather than of 'power'. (Traditional political scientists are exposed to quite a different tradition, pressure groups playing a central role in the writings of Bentley (1908) and Truman (1958).) Nevertheless, there are politico-economic models stressing the activity of organized interests (van Winden 1981, Borooah and van der Ploeg, 1983) and there are at least three areas in which the influence of pressure groups on the government has been specifically studied by politometric research:

(1) It has been shown that the position interest groups take on specific economic policy issues has a significant effect on referenda outcomes in Switzerland, *ceteris paribus* (Schneider and Naumann, 1982). Not surprisingly, those interest groups with large numbers of members (trade union confederation, farmers' union) have more impact at *this* level of the polity than those with only few members (which find it advantageous to exert pressure at

different levels of the political process, mainly through the public bureaucracy).

(2)   Trade union behaviour is not independent of purely political factors as has been demonstrated by Gaertner (1981) for the case of the Federal Republic of Germany and the period 1960–76. The rate of increase of wage rates moves cyclically with elections: the trade unions *ceteris paribus* ask for smaller wage increases if the party in power (social democrats) is ideologically close to them. This behaviour can be explained by an effort to contribute to keeping a government in power which is basically favourable to the trade union interest. On the other hand, if the government is politically right-wing, the trade unions see no reason to restrict their wage demands; they may even be particularly aggressive in order to reduce the government's re-election chance.

(3)   An area in which organized interest groups are particularly active and successful is tariffs. Within the framework of a newly developing international political economy based on public choice (for a survey see Frey, 1984), tariff setting has been analysed as the result of a 'game' between protectionist and free trade interests (Findlay and Wellisz, 1982; 1983). Politometric research has been able to show that the activity of interest groups strongly contributes to explaining the temporal development as well as the structure between industries of existing tariffs, particularly for the USA (see, for example, Caves, 1976; Baldwin, 1976; Magee 1982).

This discussion shows that there are fruitful (preliminary) efforts to integrate the behaviour of pressure groups into empirically estimated politico-economic models.

Authoritarian polities

The *general* relationship found between economic conditions and government for the various forms of democracy also obtains for polities with an authoritarian structure: no government, not even the most dictatorial, is completely independent of the support by the population. *Every* government has therefore an interest to meet the population's economic desires *up to a certain point*. In a dictatorship, the government has more possibilities to suppress the population's wishes, but it must nevertheless consider the fact that it may be overthrown if the population is all too dissatisfied with the reigning economic conditions. In that case it must step up repressive measures in order to keep down the likelihood of a revolt. Such a policy requires resources in terms of manpower (police, soldiers, informers) and finance, which cannot be used for other purposes. Even an authoritarian government is therefore forced to decide whether it is not more advantageous in terms of its own goals (utility maximization) to reduce the danger of being overthrown by improving the economic conditions, rather than to use additional resources to increase suppression.

A politico-economic model along these lines has been developed for the socialist countries of Eastern Europe for the period 1961–76 (Lafay, 1979). In these countries, the government's popularity with the population cannot be measured by election outcomes as the voters effectively have no choice between competing programmes and policies, nor are there any public opinion surveys available. An indirect indicator of the government's popularity is the frequency with which the politicians in power change. A frequent change of the members of the government is a sign of trouble and may therefore be taken to indicate that there are increased tensions between the government and the population. It is indeed found that a decrease in the growth rate of real wages is followed by more rapid changes among the members of the government. The governments of the planned East European countries tend to react to such mounting dissatisfaction in the population by easing their investment programmes. The capital investment plans are revised downwards in order to make it possible to grant the population a more rapid rise in real wages. When these measures are successful the population is (relatively) more supportive of the government. Once the situation of the government is stabilized, the orthodox plans are again re-established by curtailing the growth of real incomes in order to raise investment. The interaction between the government and the population thus leads to a politico-economic cycle which is comparable to the political business cycle found in Western industrialized democracies.

POLITOMETRICS OF REPRESENTATIVE INDUSTRIALIZED DEMOCRACIES

As has been pointed out in the last section, the most advanced theoretical and empirical work on politico-economic models has been done for representative democracies of economically advanced Western countries. This section presents some quantitative estimates of the interaction between the economy and the polity, using the example of the UK. The purpose is to show how the ideas outlined above can be subjected to politometric testing, and that the resulting empirical politico-economic models yield forecasts which are superior to those of alternative models of government.

The politico-economic model simplifies real life by considering just two decision-makers (voters and government), two areas (the economy and the polity) and two links of interdependence (the evaluation function and the policy function). Figure 6.1 portrays the model diagrammatically. The two functional links will now be discussed in turn.

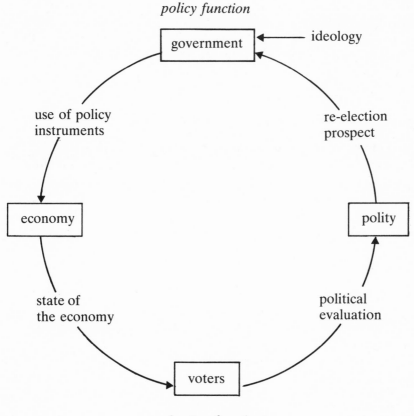

Figure 6.1 Basic outline of a politico-economic model

Voters: popularity function

It is assumed that voters tend to turn against the government when they realize that economic conditions worsen, that is when the rates of unemployment and inflation increase, and when the rate of growth of real disposable income falls. The government's position *vis-à-vis* the voters is measured by government popularity, which is the only (reasonably) reliable indicator of its standing with the voters available to the government between elections on a monthly basis. Besides economic conditions, there are political influences: government popularity wears off during the time in office ('depreciation') and it moreover follows an autonomous 'pure election cycle' (which is unexplained from an economist's view). It has been observed that the voters tend, after some time, to turn away from the government until the middle of the election period; but when the election approaches, they gradually return to support the government.

For the UK, where in the period dealt with there were only two parties effectively contending for office, the Conservative and the Labour parties, the difference between the popularity of the government and the main opposition party (the so-called 'lead') is explained. The lead function is estimated with quarterly data for the period 1958.1 to 1976.3 (see Frey and Schneider, 1978; 1981a):

$LEAD$ (t) = 11.6+
    +0.59 $LEAD$ $(t-1)$
    (7.09)
    −0.51 *change in the rate of inflation* (t) ⎫
    (−1.90)   ⎪ *economic*
    −1.21* *rate of unemployment* (t) ⎬ *influences*
    (−2.56)   ⎪
    +0.22* *rate of growth of real disposable income* (t) ⎭
    (2.13)
    −0.36* *popularity depreciation* (t) ⎫
    (−3.01)   ⎬ *political influences*
    −0.70* *pure election cycle* (t) ⎪
    (−2.34)   ⎭

$\bar{R}^2$ = 0.70, h = 1.38, $d.f.$ = 69.

(Figures in parentheses are t-values; *denotes t-values significantly different from zero at the 5 per cent level.)

All the parameters have the theoretically expected signs. In particular, government lead decreases with a rise in the rate of unemployment and increases with a rise in the growth rate of real disposable income (the change in the rate of inflation just misses being statistically significant). 'Popularity depreciation' is captured by a set of (dummy) variables which continually increase over the election period; the corresponding parameter is therefore negative. The 'pure election cycle' is captured by a set of (dummy) variables which continually increase until the middle of the election period, and then continually decrease until the next election; the corresponding parameter is therefore negative. The equation 'explains' (in the statistical sense) 70 per cent of the variance, and the h-test suggests that there is no autocorrelation of residuals. The equation thus performs well, judged according to the conventional statistical tests.

Government: policy function

The politicians in power are assumed to pursue their (ideological) selfish goals; for example, a Conservative government prefers lower public expenditures than a Labour government, measured as a share in GNP. The government's actions are restricted by political and economic constraints. As the government politicians are unable to pursue their ideological goals when they are not in power, they will make a great effort to be re-elected. They endeavour to practice an economic policy which will ensure that they receive a sufficient share of the votes. For the period investigated (1958–76) simulations with the lead function indicate that – provided inflation does not increase very quickly – an expansionary economic policy will most probably increase the government's lead. Therefore, if government fears that its lead is not sufficient for remaining in office and the next election is close, it finds it advantageous to practice an expansionary policy. If, however, the government is confident of winning the forthcoming election, it is free to practice an ideologically oriented policy. In both cases, the policies cannot be instantaneously changed, as an adjustment period is needed. Moreover, the government must consider economic constraints in the form of the balance of current account and of cost factors (real wage level).

The policy function estimated over the same period as the lead function (1958.1 to 1976.3) is shown here for the most important government policy instrument, real (exhaustive) government expenditures:

EXPENDITURES (t) = 0.16

+0.02* *Lead-deficit* $(t-1)$
(2.70)
+0.83* *adjustment to value desired*
(28.07) *for re-election* $(t-1)$

} *in case of re-election effort*

+0.01* *Conservative ideology* $(t-1)$
(2.11)
+0.03* *Labour ideology* $(t-1)$
(3.66)
+0.53* *adjustment to value desired*
(25.60) *for ideological reasons* $(t-1)$

} *in case of ideologically oriented policy*

+0.02* *balance of current account*
(3.6)
+0.02* *real wage rate* $(t-1)$
(5.90)

} *economic and financial constraints*

$\bar{R}^2 = 0.99, h = 1.19, d.f. = 68.$

The equation's test statistics meet the conventional requirements, and the estimated coefficients have the theoretically expected signs. Given a lead deficit, the government increases its expenditures in order to lower unemployment and to increase growth, in order to improve the likelihood of re-election, but time is needed to adjust. On the other hand, when there is a lead surplus, a Conservative government aims at a lower public expenditure share in GNP than a Labour government, again after a time of adjustment. Similar equations have been estimated for subsidies to households.

The popularity (lead) and its policy function describe in simple terms the interaction between the polity and the economy, and between the two sets of decision-makers, government and voters, for the particular case of the UK and the period from the end of the 1950s to the mid-1970s. Despite the considerable abstractions and simplifications of reality, this model is able to predict quite well the future course of government expenditures. In order to demonstrate this, true ex-post forecasts have been made which extend beyond the estimation period (1958.1–1976.3). Using the observed values for the economic variables contained in the lead function, government expenditures are predicted for the period 1976.4–1979.3.

In order to assess whether the politico-economic model developed brings useful insights, its estimation and forecasting performance is compared to a *competing model* which has been constructed to explain government policy in the UK. The crucial test is therefore not whether the politico-economic model is in an absolute sense 'good' (this would be a mistaken endeavour) but rather whether it is able to perform *better* than another non-trivial explanation of the same phenomenon.

The competing model used here has been developed by two British scholars, one an economist, the other a political scientist (Chrystal and Alt, 1981). The two authors specify a *policy function* which differs fundamentally from the politico-economic model discussed above. They assume that economic variables directly influence government policy and that there is no need to model the political sector. The two economic factors assumed to influence the use of the policy instruments are the level of national income (in real terms) and the lagged level of government expenditures.

Estimated over the same period (1958.1 to 1976.3) as the politico-economic model, the policy function is:

$$EXPENDITURES\,(t) = -2.623$$
$$+0.0806^*\ real\ GNP\,(t)$$
$$(3.06)$$
$$+0.759^*\ Expenditures\,(t-1)$$
$$(14.01)$$
$$R^2 = 0.99, h = 1.50, d.f. = 76.$$

Judging from the test statistics, the Chrystal-Alt version of the policy function looks satisfactory. Real GNP and lagged expenditures have a statistically significant effect on real (exhaustive) government expenditures. This means that the quality of the econometric estimation does not allow any discernment between the 'politico-economic' model as presented above, and the 'economic' model as developed by Chrystal and Alt.

The situation is different when the true ex-post forecasts are compared. In order to allow the comparison of the predicting power of the two models, the two equations of the 'politico-economic' model and that of the 'economic' model were estimated with data extending only up to 1976.3. Table 6.1 shows the forecasts for the subsequent period 1976.4 to 1979.3 whose data have *not* been used for the estimation.

Table 6.1   *Comparison of forecasts between a 'politico-economic' and an 'economic' model for exhaustive government expenditures and subsidies in the UK.*
Estimation period: 1958.1–1976.3
Forecasting period: 1976.4–1979.3

| | | | Measures of deviation between actual and predicted values | | |
			Theil's inequality coefficient	*Average absolute percentage deviation (per quarter)*	*Result*
Exhaustive government expenditures	1	Politico-economic model	0.38	1.10	Politico-economic model
	2	Economic model	0.78	2.68	superior
Subsidies	1	Politico-economic model	0.33	1.24	Politico-economic model
	2	Economic model	0.87	2.15	superior

Politico-economic model: Frey and Schneider (1981)
Economic model: Chrystal and Alt (1981)

Two measures of forecasting performance are given:

(1)   Theil's inequality coefficient T

$$T = \frac{\sqrt{\frac{1}{n}\sum(PV - AV)^2}}{\sqrt{\frac{1}{n}\sum PV^2 + \frac{1}{n}\sum AV^2}}$$

where n = number of forecasted periods
    PV = predicted values
    AV = actual values

T is one of the most often used measures for judging the quality of forecasts. If it takes the value O, one has a 'perfect' (without error) forecast, and if it takes the value 1, one has a 'bad' prediction, such as a naive trend extrapolation.

(2)   Average absolute percentage deviation between the actual and predicted values. The closer this value is to O, the better is the forecast.

As may be seen from table 6.1, the politico-economic model yields superior forecasts for both exhaustive government expenditures and subsidies: Theil's inequality coefficient and the average mean error of deviation between predicted and actual values are considerably smaller in the case of the politico-economic model.

Comparing the forecasting capacities of the model for the United Kingdom as well as for other countries (see Frey and Schneider, 1982) the analysis reaches the result that the politico-economic model more adequately predicts the actual values of the variables than competing models. The analysis suggests that:

(1)   *Macroeconomic variables* such as (the growth of) GNP, unemployment and inflation are not well suited to serve as *direct* determinants of government behaviour.

(2)   Government behaviour (also) depends on *politics*. The basic proposition of the politico-economic model that governments are interested in putting their selfish goals into practice in the political contest, i.e. to be re-elected, fares well compared to the competing proposition that governments are interested in the state of the economy (presumably to further the welfare of the population). The analysis may thus be interpreted as a test of the 'economic model of behaviour' – that actors are primarily pursuing their *own* goals, especially survival – applied to politics compared to the model of a 'benevolent dictator' (see Buchanan, 1977) – that actors pursue the 'good' of society. It should, however, be noted that these behavioural propositions are only indirectly tested, by interpreting revealed behaviour.

(3)   Government behaviour is not solely determined by the need to survive, but also by *ideological considerations*. The differentiation between the state of a popularity deficit before an election in which the government is forced to employ a popularity-increasing policy in order to be re-elected, and the state of a popularity surplus in which the government can allow itself to pursue ideologically motivated objectives, seems preferable to the crude (but still popular) assumption that the government constantly employs a vote-maximizing policy.

(4) *Economic variables* do influence government behaviour, but they do so indirectly by determining (part of) the *constraints* within which the government can act. These constraints differ between countries and periods; for example, the balance of payments constraint proves not to be relevant for the USA, but was so for the UK, 1958–79.

(5) Governments are part of politico-economic interaction in which a *multitude of actors* participates. In the policy functions of the politico-economic models estimated, the influence of public administration on government can be identified to lie in the incapacity of governments to change their policy instruments promptly to the value desired. The public administration has an interest in a conservative policy which enhances their position.

To summarize: neither the 'pure' economists' assumption that economic variables alone explain government behaviour, nor the assumption that governments maximize votes only, seem to be adequate. A satisfactory model of government behaviour and politico-economic interdependence requires that a more complex model be considered.

The models developed and the results sketched constitute only the beginnings of empirical research in political economy, and especially in the study of the interaction between the economy and the polity in a representative democracy. In order to evaluate the present state and future prospects of this type of research, we shall now discuss its shortcomings and achievements.

Shortcomings

(1) The politico-economic models so far developed do not adequately deal with some of the important decision-makers. It is in particular necessary to integrate the public bureaucracy, interest groups (business, trade unions) and parliament (the relationship between president and Congress in the USA for example) more fully.

There is at present research underway in this direction. It has been shown that the model used for the government (utility maximization subject to constraints) is also appropriate for explaining central bank behaviour, and therewith monetary policy, with the decisive constraint on the central bank being the possibility of conflicts with the government. It has been hypothesized that in the case of conflict, the government is for various reasons in a more powerful position, and the central bank has to yield to its politically motivated demands. The following propositions have been tested in this respect for West Germany, with good results; see Frey and Schneider (1981b). In the case of conflict with the government, the central bank follows government policy (with a time lag) – specifically, it employs an expansionary monetary policy in accordance with the government's expansionary fiscal policy. In the case of no conflict with the government, the central bank pursues its own utility by employing a restrictive policy, i.e. by increasing interest rates and decreasing credits in order to combat inflation.

(2) The politico-economic models do not allow for the influence of political relations between nations. This aspect is of obvious importance, especially in the age of movements towards economic and political integration such as the European community. Equally, the interaction of federal units is left out of consideration. Sub-federal units not only spend a large part of total public expenditures in many countries; they also influence the central government's policy.

(3) In the present models, government activity is reflected only through the budget. There are, however, a great many other policy areas open to the government which it can use substitutively. If the substitution possibilities are heavily employed, the policy function as sketched above may be misspecified.

(4) Informal aspects should receive more attention both with respect to voters and political actors. If, for instance, voters become increasingly aware of the fact that governments voluntarily create business cycles in order to stay in power, they may start reacting adversely to such activity. In that case, it may no longer be worthwhile for governments to create such cycles. The close relationship to the theory of rational expectation should be obvious.

Achievements

The politometric approach to studying the behaviour of government in the framework of the macro-interrelationship between the economy and polity compares favourable with the early public choice models, which had little or no empirical content. The emphasis on the dominant role of government (subject to constraints) seems to be more useful than that of models of party competition, which have become increasingly sterile and which, for good reasons, are rarely tested empirically. The politometric approach is also an advance over the systems approaches currently used in political science (going back to Easton, 1965), which are quite elaborate but which cannot be quantified with empirical data. Politico-economic models also seem to be more able to trace past government activity than pure economic models.

CONSEQUENCES

The construction of politico-economic models in which the government is an endogenous part of the system has far-reaching consequences for economics as a science. Some of the consequences are rather obvious and therefore need not be elaborated here. Thus, for *positive economics* it is clear that business cycle theory, for example, should take into account that the government does not necessarily aim at stabilizing the economy which was assumed as a matter of course by Keynes and the Keynesians (see Buchanan and Wagner, 1977), but that it may have an interest in actively producing cycles for re-election purposes. As has already been hinted at, the consequences of politico-economic models are even more far-reaching, if not revolutionary, for the *theory of economic policy*.

As the behaviour of decision-makers is here seen as being determined by the system as a whole, it is not easily influenced by actors exogenous to the interaction system, i.e. by the economist as policy adviser. (For the following, see Frey, 1983.) There are merely limited possibilities to influence the government or other decision-makers in the *current politico-economic process*. The only possibility is to inform them of the best way to reach their own goals. In the case of the government, the policy adviser will only be listened to, and his suggestions followed, if he shows the politicians in power how they can most effectively put their ideological views into practice, and, perhaps even more important, how to steer the economy to guarantee re-election. Advice based on the 'common good' (as perceived by the adviser) has little or no chance of being heard and applied in the current politico-economic process. A more effective way to influence the outcome of the performance of the politico-economic system is to *change the rules of the game*. These rules are determined by the nature of the particular institutions existent in the system, such as, for instance, the way the government is chosen. The political economy approach is thus process-oriented. If the politico-economic process works well, i.e. if it is democratic and takes individual preferences into account, the outcome is considered to be good. It should be noted that this view is analogous to the economist's view of the workings of the ideal market: the *process* of perfect competition leads to Pareto-optimality. Optimality of outcome is here a by-product of the individual actors' behaviour, i.e. it results although the common good was not the specific aim.

The benevolent dictator or social welfare function approach still dominates in modern economics despite the fact that Wicksell had already strongly rejected it in 1896. Since then even more arguments have been raised against it. To name just the most basic ones: it has been proved that no consistent social welfare function can be constructed on the basis of individual preferences; the social welfare function cannot be made operational, i.e. it is not amenable to empirical testing; the policies derived by maximizing the social welfare function are not accepted by practical policy-makers as it is not in their interest to behave this way; the approach is methodologically unacceptable because it transfers the concept of individual utility maximization to society as a whole.

Concluding remarks

There are a great many types of politico-economic models with which to capture the interdependence between the economy and the polity. A politico-economic model can only successfully mirror reality if the underlying institutional conditions are carefully considered. Accordingly, models purporting to capture the politico-economic relationships in a direct democracy, in a democracy with referenda, in a system of party competition, in a representative democracy, in a pressure group democracy and in an authoritarian system will differ greatly from each other. Some such models have been discussed and it has been shown for the particular case of the UK as a classical representative democracy of an industrial country that the politico-economic interactions are indeed significant, and that a corresponding politico-economic model performs better than a model taking only economic factors into account. It has been pointed out repeatedly that the research is only beginning, but that there are at present fascinating research efforts being made to extend and to improve the models. Even at the present stage, politometrically estimated politico-economic models have contributed profitably to extend our knowledge.

7

International Political Economy*

DAVID K. WHYNES

To many neo-classical economists, the analysis of international relations is one of their paradigm's success stories. In well under a
century, orthodox international economics has evolved from an uneasy legitimation of free trade into a sophisticated suite of models
encompassing trade and tariff policy, instability, foreign investment, currency and exchange rate adjustment and international economic integration. Moreover (it might be added), several of the most
illustrious representatives of the modern neo-classical school – men
of the stature of Harry Johnson, Richard Lipsey, Paul Samuelson
and Jacob Viner – all owe at least part of their reputations to their
formative contributions to international economic theory. One causal factor behind this expansion and refinement of knowledge must be
the scale effect, the increasing significance which economic relations
between geo-political groupings has assumed during the twentieth
century. Another might have been the realization that international
economic affairs are especially amenable to being modelled as exchange relationships, the neo-classical paradigm's particular
strength.

Not everyone has been impressed by the development of neo-
classical economic theory. There are those who share Thomas
Balogh's view, that the traditional approach to the analysis of international relations 'has produced a body of theory which is at worst
positively misleading and at best merely vacuous' (Balogh, 1973, p.
16). Such individuals have more sympathy for an alternative paradigm of geo-political analysis, international political economy. In

*Many thanks to Chris Ennew, who agreed with most of it, and to Geoff Reed, who
didn't.

common with neo-classicism, this paradigm has also been refined throughout the past century although its axioms, its methodology and, naturally enough, its conclusions are all quite distinct. In general, it owes far less to marginalism and far more to Marx.

The present essay is epistemological, being concerned with establishing the nature of political economy in the context of supranational analysis. Three steps are involved. First, and at the methodological level, I shall abstract what I take to be the defining characteristics of both neo-classicism and international political economy (hereafter NC and IPE) and juxtapose them. Second, and conceding that homogeneity in approach is unlikely to occur beyond the level of methodology, I shall consider several areas of debate within contemporary IPE. Finally, I shall comment on what I see as the value of the IPE approach.

CONTRASTING PARADIGMS

An excursion into the realms of meta-theory is always problematic. One must avoid, on the one hand, the over-generalization which rolls a dozen distinctions into one, whilst taking care, on the other hand, not to emphasize trivial or purely cosmetic differences. The conception of triviality naturally depends upon the point of reference – minor discrepancies viewed by a distant observer become substantive and irreconcilable points of difference to those immersed in the topic. Having made my disclaimer, I nevertheless believe it possible to distil from the existing literature on the analysis of international economic relations the following contrasts, at a methodological level, between NC and IPE.[1]

1. Any paradigm in social sciences will require the definition of an actor, or a unit of behaviour, to initiate activity. In most NC writing, the international actor is often taken to be the nation-state, a quasi-organic entity seemingly analogous to the individual human being who figures so prominently in NC micro-analysis. Thus, NC demonstrates how 'country A' might derive welfare gains from trade with 'country B', how 'it' might benefit from the imposition of a tariff or the depreciation of the currency, why 'it' might wish to attract external capital, why 'they' should form a customs union.

IPE theorists are, on the whole, rather uneasy about the use of the nation-state as the sole analytical unit for several reasons. To begin with, it is extremely difficult to envisage nations 'behaving', unless one views individuals as puppets whose behaviour is conditioned by a sentient social structure. Probably more important, however, is the idea that, if one is going to classify individuals into groupings (and 'nation-states' is just one example of such groupings) then it is necessary that (1) individuals within each group have more in common with each other that they do with individuals in other groups and (2) the classification scheme is valid for all individuals.

When one comes to grips with the concept of 'nation-state' it is very difficult to go beyond occupancy of geographical space as the definitional criterion. The communality of law, for instance, is often thought to be a prerequisite and, indeed, it is usually the case that all individuals living within national space are subject to the same law. It is interesting to note, however, that non-nationals are subject to the same laws (Frenchmen in Britain are not immune from prosecution), implying lack of excludability in this particular criterion. Languages, customs and religions are often common to more than one nation-state. On the other hand, there exist quite noticeable infra-national fractures which might lead us to believe that individuals have common interests across state political boundaries. Do Indian immigrants to Britain have more in common with the Anglo-Saxons with whom they live than with the Indian Indians left four thousand miles behind? Are Polish Catholics more like Italian Catholics than they are like Polish atheists? The circumstances of the Third World 'nation-states' show how the concept is being stretched to its limits. Many of these states result from the arbitrary decisions of colonial administrators – boundaries cut across earlier racial, religious or linguistic groupings and many attempt to aggregate peoples of differing traditional loyalties. There are segments in some Third World countries which are virtually divorced from their surroundings, e.g. foreign-owned extractive industries which export their outputs and whose sole internal linkage is the occasional royalty payment.

Although in principle any one of a number of groupings or actor definitions could be used, the majority of IPE writers follow Marx in interpreting the development of capitalism in terms of division of labour and the formation of classes. Further, they follow Marxist writers such as Lenin and Luxemburg in arguing that capitalism has outgrown the nation-state and become transnational. Capital has flowed to all regions of the world and it accordingly follows that we must be witnessing the division of labour on a world scale. The economic interests of individuals, it is alleged, are better seen in class terms than they are in national terms – put crudely, an American worker has more in common with a European worker than with an American capitalist.

Having accepted that grouping of individuals in terms of class (the identity of economic interests) as fundamental to IPE, the transition from 'nation' to 'class' is proving a difficult one for writers to effect. The nation-state idea is deeply entrenched in social analysis, especially in the West. Further, the tangible manifestations of global relations – trade, governments, world organizations – are all constituted in national terms. Our principal data sources are 'national accounts'. Moreover, it would be a mistake at the present time to disregard nationalism as a social fact, especially in the Western European economies. Here, the welding of a form of corporate solidarity has a very long history and actually predates the transition to capitalism. Frank, who has himself been charged with underplaying the role of class in his analyses (Brenner, 1978) suggests an additional reason why national thinking has been retained, linked to the support given by progressives to post-war national liberation movements in the Third World:

> Particularly after the war against, and the liberation of, Vietnam and other parts of Indochina, nationalism retains a deservedly large political capital of goodwill and support throughout the world.
>
> However, today – not unlike a hundred years ago – it is becoming increasingly important to question whether many nationalist and regionalist movements, independently of the subjective desires of many of their leaders and supporters, are not serving or being manipulated by essentially reactionary interests to divide and conquer popular movements of resistance to capital as it seeks to confront the new crisis of capitalism. (Frank, 1980, pp.174–5)

2. The single unit of behaviour makes analysis reasonably straightforward for NC theory. One simply assumes the existence of a social welfare function (the elements of which have all been appropriately weighted by the social decision-maker) and then maximizes it according to the specific set of circumstances. IPE finds the problem a little more difficult. If one adds additional units of behaviour, there must now be more than one welfare function. Presumably there will be no necessity for conditions for simultaneous optimization to exist, i.e. the mutual acceptability of outcomes to governments, capitalists, workers and whatever cannot be guaranteed. Further, IPE does not subscribe to the view that social decision-makers are neutral, acting in the 'best interests of society', simply because society cannot be thought of as completely homogeneous.

3. NC international relations theory parallels NC micro-theory in viewing interaction as a sequence of voluntaristic contracts. Actors are autonomous in that they are deemed to be capable of insulating themselves from the affairs of others should they so wish. Thus we find NC theorists drawing conclusions such as 'country A will trade with country B *if* . . .' or 'membership of a customs union would be advisable *if* . . .' or 'country C will permit foreign investment *if* . . .'. In contrast, IPE writers see actors as participants in a world system and relations between actors depend on power. An actor's power determines its abilities to influence others and also to emancipate itself from pressures imposed by others. Power has many facets – quantity and quality of natural resources controlled, industrial capacity, levels of technology, ability to inflict physical damage, the nature of alliances with other actors. The important feature about any actor's power status is its subjective rather than objective nature, how other actors perceive it relative to their own. One would expect voluntary contracts to be the predominant form of relationship between actors only when all actors perceive their power positions as equivalent. Where wide imbalances of power are perceived, coercion of one actor by another becomes much more of a possibility.[2]

4. Although NC is well-developed in the analysis of areas such as trade and integration, it seems to have little to say about other readily-observable international issues – war and military conquest, threat, deterrence, politico-economic destabilization, subversion and espionage. I suspect this is because NC theory appears to presume that international affairs are to be conducted according to certain 'rules of the game' and that all actors will 'play fair'. Such rules include (1) the recognized sanctity of actors' properties, (2) the freedom of actors to withdraw from contracts, and (3) the illegitimacy of the use of physical force. IPE writers, on the other hand, do not subscribe to the view that quasi-legal constraints are accepted by actors. They concede that rules might be established on an *ad hoc* basis to deal with specific circumstances (e.g. the formation of an economic community or a military alliance). Even so, in given circumstances with given objectives, it might prove optimal to the actor to flout the rules deliberately or, more subtly, to disregard them under the pretence of obedience.

5. NC and IPE theorists differ profoundly over the role of abstraction. NC theory tends to the view that there exists only a limited number of variables and factors which can be considered 'economic' and, therefore, significant analytically. Further, these factors are

assumed to have validity even when divorced from the historical context. Contemporary NC textbooks on international theory tend to confine themselves to finance and investment, balance of payments policy, trade theory and policy, aid and integration. IPE writers, in contrast, stress the need for breadth in the selection of causal factors and for depth in historical perspective. The Introduction to the Proceedings of the 1978 Stockholm Conference on the World Economic Order illustrates the NC position:

> If one wants to take the world economic order concept in an extremely broad sense it is of course true that any system that allows famine, instability and grossly unjust income distribution between nations is a bad and deficient system. Such a sweeping and non-economic interpretation of the international economic system is, however, not very helpful. Taking a more concrete attitude, and accepting present realities as to geographical split-up, differences in natural wealth, social history and present education levels, one arrives at the conclusion that the functioning of the international part of the economic system [i.e. the subject matter of NC theory] would not be a major obstacle for growth and prosperity in the world.

The reaction of IPE is to borrow a sentiment from Joan Robinson – NC theory is analysing the would 'by means of a model from which all relevant considerations are eliminated by the assumptions' (Robinson, 1966, p. 3). IPE theorists do not understand how the undesirability of 'famine, instability and grossly unjust income distribution' can be considered 'non-economic', nor do they see how geography, history, education and resource endowment can be divorced from the analysis of international affairs.[3]

More specifically, IPE criticisms are as follows. First, the abstractions of NC theory make its analyses extremely simplistic, both in terms of perception of what constitute actors' objectives and in terms of the isolation of causal factors. Accordingly, the analysis becomes unreal and irrelevant. Second, it is clear that much established NC theory relies on simplicity for its existence. The extensions of the formal analyses into considerations of wealth and income distribution objectives when many participants/factors of production/commodities/etc. are involved, or in cases where information and market conditions are imperfect, cause many of the basic theorems to break down (Shone, 1972). Third, most NC theory is structured as equilibrium analysis, essentially because of the root equation of the NC system which defines optimality of action by the identity of marginal benefit and marginal cost. Deviations from equilibrium will imply sub-optimality and, in the absense of market imperfection, abnormality. Thus, a balance of payments deficit will be considered transitory because (1) trading partners are unlikely to agree to the country obtaining goods without recompense, (2) equilibrating forces (e.g. pressure on the currency) will be set up. IPC generally denies that disequilibrium need *necessarily* be self-rectifying because of the existence of a multiplicity of forces in the world system. Further, the consideration of *any* set of circumstances as 'normal' would seem to imply an unacceptable linear theory of history.

Above I mentioned the importance of a concept of history in IPE and most writers, in the main, accept the version exemplified by Amin (1980). Following orthodox Marxian theory, Amin argues that, in certain regions, feudalism disintegrated and capitalism emerged. There came into existence the new class stratification of bourgeoisie and proletariat within particular nation-states. The external relations of these nation-states were influenced by the needs of capital accumulation which demanded the extension of capitalism beyond national confines. There accordingly arose the basis for the world capitalist system, characterized by the capitalist 'centre' and the 'periphery', areas where capitalism was not an indigenous development. The external relations themselves were essentially those of unequal exchange – political and economic power permitted the transfer of value to the centre from the periphery, resulting in the relative impoverishment of the latter. Amin stresses the difference in historical experience between the two areas. First, the capitalist mode of production was forced onto the periphery and therefore deformed the indigenous feudal mode (at the centre, the former emerged from the latter). Second, class alliances were not internal but were transnational, i.e. an alliance between international capital and the local ruling class. Finally, development at the periphery was directed by imposed external relations; external relations did not evolve with the development of the internal economy.

Amin sees this, the first phase of imperialism, as ending with the victory of national liberation movements in many regions of the periphery. Almost without exception, the new national governments followed import substitution policies, creating severe strains on the scarce resources within their control. Agriculture, in particular, was neglected and economic development continued to be constrained by the ability to export (usually primary products) to the centre. In spite of its notional political independence, the periphery remained dominated by the centre, in terms of loans, investment, aid, trade and technology. The growing realization of the failure of attempts at internal development within the periphery has lead, most recently, to calls for a 'new international economic order'.

Remaining within these very broad terms, the differences between Amin and other IPE writers are not great. Virtually all make use of the distinction between the capitalist centre and the Third World periphery although Frank (1967) prefers the terms 'metropolis' and 'satellite' and Wallerstein (1974) uses 'core' in the place of 'centre'. Some dispute remains, however, over the usefulness of these concepts. Whilst the centre/periphery generalization might prove convenient from the point of view of description, can such a broad category really be adequate for analytical purposes?

Even the most superficial examination of Africa, Asia and Latin America seems to attest to tremendous heterogeneity. In terms of natural wealth endowments, some Third World economies seem richer than many capitalist nations. Some have undergone rapid industrialization whereas others remain predominantly agricultural. Geography, climate, population density, religion, form of government, links with other economies and, presumably, values, ideals and aspirations, all vary from country to country. The aggregation of all Third World countries into one analytical category would seem to imply the neglect of a substantial volume of specific information, and a similar case might be made against over-generalization of the centre.

There appear to be two reactions to the question posed. First, writers such as Amin stress that there remain important similarities between peripheral economies, and important differences between them and central capitalist economies, which allow them to be considered together. These include inadequate industrialization embodying inappropriate production techniques, the creation of unemployment leading to reliance on the tertiary sector, the gearing of the peripheral economy to the needs of the centre, and the diminution and eventual elimination of economic autonomy (Amin, 1976). Perceived differences between peripheral economies are indicative of their specific pre- and post-imperial experiences, although these differences do nothing to alter their 'peripheral' nature.[4]

The second response is to concede that the label is adequate only at the general level, providing a frame of reference. Much modern writing on the centre, for instance, does not dispute the existence of this centre nor the nature of its relations with the periphery. It is the nature of relations *within* the centre which is disputed and three theories are current. First, the more 'traditional' line, held by IPE writers with specific Third World interests, is that the centre consists of a coalition between imperialist blocs – the USA, Western Europe and Japan – which collaborate in the exploitation of the Third World. The Organization for Economic Co-operation and Development (OECD) in Paris should perhaps therefore be seen as a 'committee for managing the common affairs of the whole bourgeoisie'. Second, Magdoff (1969) holds the view that the economic power of the USA will enable it to enter and eventually dominate the other central economies. This being the case, the centre will eventually unify under US control (Rowthorn, 1980). Third, writers such as Galtung (1973) believe that Europe is capable of responding to the American challenge. The centre is therefore likely to become less stable as interbloc competition increases.

Summarizing briefly, throughout IPE literature there run a number of themes – the rejection of nationality as the sole definition of the actor, the recognition of power, coercion and the multiplicity of goals, the appreciation of historical context and the belief in interdependence within the world system. Having emphasized the broadly-common methodology, let us turn to more specific issues.

CONTEMPORARY ISSUES IN IPE

IPE writers seldom dispute the characterization of centre/periphery relations as imperialistic, nor do they disagree that the capitalist expansion which began as piracy and plunder has now evolved into trade and investment flows. At the aggregate level, IPE writers now appear to be concerned to find answers to the following questions: 1. what is the driving force behind, or the motivation for, imperialism? 2. is imperialism progressive or regressive? 3. is imperialism exclusively a capitalist phenomenon? These questions are considered below.
1. The three fundamental works on economic imperialism all appeared within a decade of one another – John Hobson's *Imperialism* (1902), Rudolf Hilferding's *Finance Capital* (1910) and Rosa Luxemburg's *Accumulation of Capital* (1913). Hobson viewed imperialism as a reaction to underconsumption, arguing that the polarization of income and wealth between capitalists and workers depressed domestic demand and obliged capital to seek better opportu-

nities abroad. Luxemburg followed the more orthodox Marxian line by suggesting that, as the sources of surplus value dried up in one country (as they were bound to do as a result of accumulation) capital would be driven to look for new sources to exploit. Hilferding's approach was perhaps the most ambitious. He believed that the simple competitive capitalist economy described by Marx was being transformed into one characterized by monopoly, cartels and vertical and horizontal integration. Of particular significance was the merging together of financial and manufacturing interests. Economies of scale in the widest sense meant that the nation-state was no longer sufficient to contain growing capitalist enterprises. Indeed, 'national policy' was becoming a vehicle for the nurturing of such enterprises. Protectionism, political alignments and even military conquests were designed both to forestall the detrimental effects of competition at home and to allow entry into foreign markets.

Any attempt to reconcile these theories with the contemporary evidence convincingly demonstrates the complexity of the imperialism concept. Taking the case of Britain, the dominant nineteenth century economic power, there appears to be a very clear distinction between imperialism as investment and imperialism as conquest. During the nineteenth century, Britain established political control over much of Africa and Asia although most of its foreign investment went to North and South America. Further, trade with colonies declined in importance throughout the century relative to trade with other capitalist nations (Fieldhouse, 1973). Capital outflows from Britain were undoubtedly directed by expectations of high profits (from Latin American railways, US industry and gold) although there is no reason to believe that an internal investment crisis was necessarily occurring. The London capital market of the nineteenth century was far better geared to overseas investment than it was to domestic industry, the latter still favouring profits and bank loans as sources of investment funds. The stock market proved to be a most expensive place to raise domestic capital and was more often employed to float large foreign loans. In addition, 'most merchant bankers had *émigré* origins and had greater knowledge of conditions overseas than in the Midlands or the North' (Cottrell, 1975, p. 54). Clearly, Hilferding's alliance of financial and physical capital was not in evidence in nineteenth century Britain, nor, it seems, was Hobson's underconsumption driving capital abroad. Given that the 'essential point of her [Luxemburg's] analysis is that capitalism necessarily *demands* the existence of non-capitalist territories for its own survival' (Bronner, 1981, p. 85) it becomes difficult to reconcile her theory with the very high proportion of international investment flowing *between* capitalist economies.

With the passing of time these theories appear to have a lot more to offer. We are nowadays well aware of Hobsonian underconsumption in the form of the US depression of the 1930s. At present, the dominant vehicle of production is the giant corporation which has strong ownership links with the financial sector. The parent companies of the 60 largest US-based multinationals own around one-half of the US private sector.[5] As Luxemburg foresaw, we have observed some transplantation of capitalism to the periphery areas.

I shall consider current attitudes to Luxemburg in the next section and note here that the views of Hobson and Hilferding have been reworked and interwoven in the important modern theory of Baran and Sweezy (1966). This theory posits that the concentration of production over the past century has consolidated the position of the capital-owning class. The major corporations now collude to ensure that revenues are maintained whilst costs are reduced, implying that the 'economic surplus' (the difference between production and costs of production) shows a tendency to rise. To avoid stagnation or even collapse, this surplus must be reabsorbed into the system, by consumption, by investment and by 'waste'. Baran and Sweezy argue that surplus-reabsorption has become an increasingly serious problem and the inherent stagnation of the domestic economy (in this case, the USA) has led the major corporations to shift capital abroad in search of higher returns.

A central problem with these theories at their particular level of generalization is that they appear to treat capitalists like lemmings, migrating from a crisis without knowing quite where to go. I think we need to know how capital chooses its destination and why, for example, it has in the past tended to flow between capitalist economies rather than travelling to the Third World. Moran (1973) offers some help here with his model of the expansion of US investment overseas, a model based on the 'product cycle' hypothesis of Vernon (1966).

Suppose a firm develops and markets a new product. Even in an oligopolistic market, the economic pressure on it is considerable – the revenue limitations of the home market, high development and set-up costs, the possibility of competition. Exporting therefore becomes attractive in view of the greatly extended market opportunities which permit gains from economies of scale. Over the longer term, however, the exporting firm will find its plans frustrated by local manufacturers who are likely to possess three distinct advantages in their own home market. First, the local factors of production might be less expensive and, second, no transport costs will be incurred. Local producers are therefore likely to have a natural cost advantage. Third, local producers could persuade their government to protect the home market, thereby eliminating the exports of the original firm either partially or entirely.[6] The obvious way to overcome these barriers is to get behind them. Once the firm becomes sited in its overseas market it will possess all the advantages of the local producers.

There exists one further benefit from the internationalization of production which, in itself, makes the analysis of such internationalization particularly difficult. Given the existence of a number of parallel operations, the parent company is obliged to decide upon the allocation of common overheads amongst them. In effect, this empowers the company to choose in which operation it will make its profits and we should predict that the least 'profit' will be made in the country with the most penal taxes. This accounting practice would contribute to the explanation of why the rate of return on foreign investment sometimes appears lower than the return on domestic investment.

It may prove instructive to consider these theories in the light of recent data – as the USA is the single largest overseas investor we shall confine our attention to trends there.[7]

Of the $2,000 billion approximate assets held by US transnational corporations in 1977, 78 per cent were held by US parents whilst the remaining 22 per cent were held by foreign affilitates. The affilitates' share had risen from 18 per cent in 1966. Capitalist economies (Canada, Western Europe, Japan, Australasia) were the homes for 72 per cent of affiliate assets in 1977, this proportion remaining unchanged from 1966. Over the period, the total money value of overseas assets increased by 405 per cent. Assets in Japan increased by 765 per cent, those in the European Economic Community (EEC) by 457 per cent. By 1977, 34 per cent of affiliates' assets were residing in the EEC, with 19 per cent in Canada and 16 per cent in Latin America.

Additional data on the location of foreign assets are provided in table 7.1. The first two columns in this table express the assets held in differing industrial sectors in either the capitalist economies (CEs) or the Third World economies (TWEs) as a percentage of total assets held by US parents. The third column is a ratio of the percentages in the first two columns, divided by the ratio of total CE investment to total TWE investment. The result is a coefficient whose value is unity

Table 7.1 *Location of US overseas capital assets, by industrial sector and by region*

	CEs (%)		TWEs (%)		Asset Distribution Coefficient (see text)	
	1966	1977	1966	1977	1966	1977
Mining	2.9		2.3		0.42	
		2.3		1.1		0.71
Petroleum	15.9		8.0		0.66	
		16.0		6.4		0.85
Manufacturing	37.2		8.3		1.50	
		33.0		8.3		1.35
Trade	6.5		1.8		1.18	
		8.9		1.8		1.65
Finance	8.7		1.9		1.49	
		10.2		6.1		0.57
Other	3.9		2.7		0.48	
		4.3		1.7		0.87

if CE:TWE investment in a specific sector is the same as CE:TWE investment as a whole. Over- or under-representation in CEs, relative to the balance as a whole, is indicated by a higher or lower figure.

These data suggest that, in 1966, US investment in TWEs was more heavily involved in oil and mineral extraction, agricultural enterprises and the service sector (these last two being the principal components of 'other' in table 7.1). Retail and wholesale trade, manufacturing and finance (including real estate and insurance) figured more prominently in CEs, and such a pattern might be taken to confirm theories such as that of Magdoff (1969) to the effect that the USA is interested in TWEs specifically as sources of raw materials. However, comparison of the representation coefficients for 1966 and 1977 show that, in four sectors, there has been a movement towards the mean – mining and petroleum investment figured more prominently in CEs whilst manufacturing became more significant in TWEs. Trade, however, seems to have moved much more into the CE province whilst finance is now very much the TWE growth area.

In interpreting the data, the following appear relevant:

(1) Extractive industries, such as mining and petroleum, must be regarded as special cases in that their location is determined by the

location of the natural resource in question. The increasing US interest in CE petroleum investment arises from the increased exploitation of EEC oil.

(2) The substantial relative growth of trading enterprises in CEs would appear to be consistent with the Moran thesis. Trading enterprises would tend to move toward rich and well-established markets.

(3) The interpretation of changes in manufacturing location is more problematic. It seems as if three forces might be at work, for the highest growth rates in manufacturing assets for the 1966–77 period occur where (a) markets are extensive and are either protected or are in danger of becoming so, e.g. Japan and the EEC; (b) wage costs are particularly low, e.g. Taiwan and South Korea; (c) there has occurred a recent and a rapid extension of wealth, e.g. the Middle Eastern oil states. In terms of total assets, the first category is by far the most significant, lending support to the Moran hypothesis.

(4) The reversal of the representation coefficient in the financial sector can be accounted for almost completely by recent activities in the Caribbean. Many of the island-states in the area have established themselves as offshore financial centres by offering taxation incentives, minimal operating restrictions and so forth. Bermuda, for example, now has the largest insurance market in the world, over 1,500 companies being registered there. In complete contrast to extractive industries, the success of financial services is not location-dependent; we should accordingly expect such services to migrate to regions where operating costs are lowest.

(5) Foreign capital *in* the USA amounts to just over one-quarter of US foreign capital. The 1977 percentage breakdown by sector was: petroleum – 20; manufacuturing – 29; trade – 24; finance – 22. Together, Holland, Canada, the UK, West Germany and Japan owned 75 power cent of foreign assets in the USA. As is the case with US companies abroad, trade is a very important activity for foreign enterprise in the USA – although US affiliates only employed about 2 per cent of all US employees in 1977, and owned well under 10 per cent of all private capital, their imports and exports were, respectively, 28 and 20 per cent of the US total. Again, such evidence appears to substantiate the Moran hypothesis.

Where do such data leave our theories of imperialism? To begin with, the argument that capital moves in search of profit does not seem disputable although there seems no necessity, at this stage, to believe that migration occurs as a direct consequence of inherent weakness in the domestic economy (other than its size limitation). Neither does the world capitalist economy appear in *imminent* danger of collapse, as in evidenced by the enthusiasm with which capitalist powers are investing in one another. Over the longer term, however, the fundamental problem remains to be confronted – if capitalism is capable of outgrowing the nation-state it must also be capable of exhausting the transnational framework into which it is presently entering. Mutual inter-investment opportunities must be finite, so then where will capital go?

2. Rosa Luxemburg was of the opinion that imperialism was inherently beneficial to the economies of the periphery. Sharing with Marx the view that the development of capitalism from feudal society was a progressive change (in that it established the preconditions for socialism) she welcomed capital mobility as a means of developing 'backward colonies'. Thus, the

> important point is that capital accumulated in the old country should find elsewhere new opportunities to beget and realise surplus value, so that accumulation can proceed. In the new countries, large regions of natural economy are open to conversion into commodity economy, or existing commodity economy can be ousted by capital. (Luxemburg, 1951, pp. 427–8)

Writing in support of the Luxemburg thesis, McFarlane (1982) draws attention to the development of productive forces which has taken place in the Third World, in countries such as Argentina, Indonesia and the Philippines. He believes that Indonesia, in particular, has broken free from the form of peripheral linkage with the centre which existed earlier – manufacturing appears to be capable of being sustained by the home market and is no longer totally dependent upon exports.

At the present time, this appears to be very much the minority view. Most IPE writers favour an approach which interprets centre/ periphery relations as 'underdevelopment' (used as a verb rather than as a noun). The captalist centre, it is believed, is developing itself at the expense of the periphery and, as a result, conditions in, and prospects for, the periphery are deteriorating. Szentes (1976), for example, identifies four major factors in the process of underdevelopment. First, the periphery has become dependent on the centre. The presence of foreign monopoly capital is the 'most marked' form of dependence for, as a result, the key branches of economic activity are under external control. Dependence is also manifested as established trade linkages (often a legacy from pre-independence times), reliance on the centre for finance and credit, and 'technical dependence', reliance on the centre for physical capital, trained manpower and 'know-how'. Second, Szentes cites evidence for a 'systematic income drain' from the periphery, both direct (in the form of the repatriation of profit from investment) and indirect (via the centre's ability to bargain for a major share in gains from trade). Third, he argues that the centre's effect upon the periphery has been to disintegrate the internal economy by the creation of a dual society (traditonal/modern). This has involved the dislocation of traditional accumulation processes and the restructuring of incentives. Finally, the impact of the centre has completely fragmented the indigenous social structures whilst failing to put anything in their place.

To reconcile these views we might, in principle, produce a catalogue of data. We should find, for instance, that, in recent years, quite a number of Third World countries – Indonesia and the Philippines included – have experienced very substantial export growth. Indeed, OECD (1982) talks of a 'new wave of industrial exporters' and notes that the conditions for success in this respect have been 'a disciplined, educated and skilled urban labour force; an active and efficient entrepreneurial class; a stable political system' (p. 26). Such economies are clearly well along the road to capitalism, or so it would seem. To counter this notion we might argue that prosperity in such economies is illusive, depending as it does on low wage costs and therefore low living standards. This is evidenced by the fact that a component of growth in the 'new wave' countries has been transfer of production from other Third World nations (especially in South-East Asia) where labour costs had begun to rise.

One dimension of this debate certainly cannot be determined by recourse of empirical evidence. Orthodox economics talks of 'underdevelopment' in terms of a set of characteristics. Countries are said to be underdeveloped (or, more euphemistically, 'developing') if they have, say, a predominance of agricultural output, high population growth or a rudimentary financial sector. IPE, however, argues that underdevelopment is a process and a relationship, and an 'underdeveloped economy' is therefore one which is going through such a process. Accordingly, an economy can still be underdeveloped even if it appears prosperous under orthodox criteria. By analogy, the fact that a slave is well-fed does nothing to alter his essential role of slave.

These problems notwithstanding, both NC and IPE literature on the global economy does seem to suggest the feeling that something might be amiss. I have yet to come across any serious advocacy of increased poverty in Africa or more serious debt burdens for Latin America. This being the case, let us consider some of the proffered solutions to the problem of the contemporary economic order.

In official circles at least, the most respectable option is what could be termed the 'New Deal' for the Third World. This approach emphasizes the harmony of interests between all economies and stresses the mutual benefits which could accrue as a result of the centre taking more account of the circumstances of the periphery. Perhaps the most famous example of writing in this genre is *North-South: A Programme for Survival* (ICIDI, 1980). Stylized in IPE terms, the arguments of this approach run as follows. First, it is accepted that global economic relations in the past have contributed to the reduction of the potential of Third World economies for participation in the world capitalist system – the development of manufacturing remains rudimentary, demand for their exports is in decline, their debt burdens are crippling and so on. Second, it is accepted that expansion possibilities in the capitalist centre are on the verge of reaching their limits. This is evidenced by the growth of protectionism and subsidization on the part of governments eager to defend home industries against fierce infra-centre competition. As further growth requires the extension of the market, and as the only remaining opportunity of any substance is the Third World, it follows that the centre should provide purchasing power to the Third World economies and develop them as potential trading partners.

On the whole, IPE writers are not sympathetic to this view. Their most common reply is that the accommodation of the Third World by the centre in the form of, of, say, international assistance or concessional trading terms, would simply perpetuate the existing structure of the world economy. Exploitation will still occur, if only in a less intense form. I would also add that, irrespective of its virtues, a worthwhile accommodation policy on the part of the rich economies would seem an unlikely course of action for them to follow. They are, after all, still benefiting from the current situation, so what incentive is there for change?

IPE writers such as Amin and Szentes have argued that the solution to the problems of peripheral economies lies in self-help. Links with the capitalist world should be broken and links based on common interests within the periphery should be established. This particular line of argument clearly has substantial weaknesses. First, it is not obvious that the various regions of the Third World would necessarily have interests in common, over and above their collective dislike of being 'dependent'. In spite of their pronouncements of solidarity with poorer economies, for example, one suspects that the Middle Eastern oil states have inflicted substantial hardship onto other Third World regions in their pursuit of economic prosperity through oil sales. Second, it seems incorrect to assume that even if the arrival of capitalism heralded all the Third World's economic problems its departure will necessarily remove them. Poverty and stagnation in Indian agriculture, for instance, would seem to owe far more to the traditional system of land tenure than they do to modern capitalist transformations which have barely touched that sector. Similarly, corruption, bribery and other abuses of political power are not exclusive to any one pre-socialist mode of production.

Third, the curtailing of linkages with the capitalist centre could impose substantial opportunity costs. A greater degree of autarky would necessitate import-substitution industrialization which, according to some IPE writers, has already proved to be of dubious value. Unpleasant though the fact might be, the capitalist centre is capable of producing certain desirable commodities such as capital equipment and consumer durables relatively cheaply. Finally, if IPE is going to assert that peripheral economies are tied to the centre by means of a powerful nexus of political and economic bonds, then the corollary of the position must also be faced. Regions which are powerless are 'policy-takers' and not 'policy-makers'. It is very difficult to imagine, for example, how one of the small Central American states could permanently sustain an independent policy against US wishes in view of the pressure which could be brought to bear. Economic sanctions could be enforced (the curtailing of trade, aid and investment) on both a bilateral and, given US influence in the international agencies, a multilateral basis. Political destabilization could be effected. Armed force could be employed. In any event the small state is, as Vital (1971) argues,

> faced with mutually contradictory imperatives. Only intransigence offers it hope of retaining a measure of influence over the environment. But the more effective an opponent it becomes for the great power the heavier will be the resources the latter applies to its own political ends; and, by extension, the harder will the position of the minor power become. For once the conflict develops into a contest in the application of force, the minor power stands only to lose. (p. 124)

It is important to appreciate that, in power struggles, great powers do not *always* defeat small ones. As the US incursion into Vietnam demonstrated, great powers may be subverted from their purpose if they fear incurring the wrath of equally-great powers or if internal dissension arises. Even in such cases, however, the small power *per se* will still only represent a tiny influence on policy formulation within the great powers. Depending on circumstances, it might, of course, be lucky.

3. The neglect of the Eastern economies (the Soviet bloc and China) in an essay on international economic analysis would seem unpardonable were it not for the fact that such a neglect is readily observable in the existing literature. In the NC case perhaps this is not too surprising. The orthodox linkages between the East and the rest of the world – trade, investment flows, finance – are all relatively slight and, furthermore, economic behaviour within such economies appears not to conform to the requirements of the NC paradigm. The gaze of IPE also appears to be a little less intense on this matter, partly again because of the East's insularity and partly because of the lack of unanimity about the nature of the Eastern economies. (This stands in marked contrast to the strong consensus about the nature of Western capitalism.) Some writers, such as Robinson (1970) in the case of Maoist China, detected evidence of the transition to socialism. Horvat (1982) believes the East to be *étatist*, a blend of fundamental socialism and authoritarian central control, whilst Sweezy (1980) accepts the USSR as one 'valid prototype' of post-capitalist society. Frank (1980) sees the East as a body of 'deformed worker states', transitional towards capitalism and integration into the world capitalist economy.

Because of the relative insignificance of trade and investment flows, the foreign policy of the Eastern bloc requires a different type of explanation form the one developed in the Western case. No Luxemburgist 'economic necessity' argument will explain the Soviet domination of Eastern Europe, for example. Instead, we need to contemplate the opportunity afforded to the USSR as a result of its territorial conquests during the Second World War. These enabled it to contract its *de jure* boundaries and create a buffer-zone of client states between itself and the West. For a period also it was able to extract substantial reparations from former enemy territories. Ellman (1979) argues that this period of 'socialist imperialism' was brief and has long since given way to attempts to integrate the various national economies by means of trade expansion, factor mobility, technical co-operation and plan co-ordination.

Although their present insularity limits their influence in the world economy (narrowly defined), the emergence of two great powers in the East has naturally produced some recognizable impact on the world political economy (widely defined). First, the existence of a number of great powers increases the Third World's prospects for gaining economic assistance. As is generally the case in circumstances of non-collusive multiple provision, terms of funding can vary. Thus, while the World Bank's major lending criterion appears always to have been risk of default on repayment (Frey *et al.*, 1983), 'by far the most important characteristic of Chinese aid is what is widely acknowledged to be the almost unsurpassed generosity of its terms' (Paine, 1977, p. 230). Second, the existence of great powers who interpret themselves as, in some sense, rivals can improve the small powers' bargaining positions, thereby enabling them to obtain more resources. Datar (1972) has argued that Soviet assistance to India 'strengthened India's bargaining position *vis-a-vis* other aid givers and helped India to break the monopoly of foreign firms' (p. 263). Third, although not permitting independence, the existence of competing powers means that weak states have at least some degree of policy flexibility, if only as regards choice of patron. The independence of Cuba from the US orbit would surely not have been conceivable without Cuban dependence on the USSR. Fourth, the alliance of smaller powers with great powers can extend the former's potential in their own dealings, because the great powers can be employed as reservoirs. One suspects that the Vietnamese war and the conflicts in the Middle East would have been relatively brief affairs had China, the USSR and the USA been unwilling to make the necessary resources available to the participants.

Possibly the most obvious manifestation of the emergence of rival great powers is militarism. Even a modest acquaintance with history and bargaining theory informs that, whenever ruling groups in powers of equivalent strength distrust each other, arms competition ensues. Power parity is maintained at ever-increasing cost. At present, the USA allocates around 7 or 8 per cent of its total production to military uses, the USSR (being materially poorer) perhaps twice this proportion. Together, these two countries account for over one-half of world military spending, and they are also the principal weapons' suppliers to most other countries. Given the considerable slowdown in economic growth which both regions have experienced in recent years, how long can this continue?

I think the answer must be 'indefinitely'. Arms competition is positively encouraged by the ideological gulf between East and West and the very tangible economic advantages which accrue to the ruling classes as a result of military production and sales.[8] Certainly in the West, there has been little evidence of public rejection of increased arms spending and one might conclude that the taxation potential here is far from fully exploited. In the past, the most common outcome of arms-racing was war itself. Given present technology, the possibility of deliberate war at the great power level would seem remote – nuclear wars can only be lost (even by 'winners') and are not therefore contemplated as lightly as were earlier conventional conflicts.

THE RELEVANCE OF IPE

Up to this point in my analysis of IPE explicit evaluation of the paradigm has been avoided. This is the task of the final section. The value of any paradigm needs to be appraised in two respects, both in terms of its own intrinsic merits and, probably of more importance, in terms of weaknesses within alternatives (in this case, NC). On the negative side, I shall not dwell on the self-induced technical limitations of NC international theory for they are well explored elsewhere.[9] Instead, I shall concentrate on three aspects which demonstrate IPE's analytical strength, namely, 1. its demonstration of the problems inherent in the concept of 'nation-state', 2. its stress on the multiplicity of objectives and objective functions, 3. its emphasis on the reality of power.

1. Earlier in this chapter I remarked on the central role played by the nation-state in NC theory. Nation-states are taken as 'given' and inviolate, both as abstractions ('country A') and in application (the UK or France). Although undoubtedly most useful in general discussion, the adoption of the national perspective in social analysis has serious drawbacks. In the first place, we possess no definitional criterion of the collectivity of individuals within the nation-state, nor any notion of the sequence of events which gave rise to its present form. NC theory does not even attempt to tell us, in other words, why the Greeks are Greek and how it is that they came to be Greek. One should, I think, have reservations about any economic paradigm which is disinclined to define its principal actor. Second, an exclusively nationalistic perception frustrates the analysis of transnational issues – transnational enterprise, for instance, does not necessarily belong to any one nation.

Finally, adherence to the national status quo, and to the sanctity of nation-based production, can lead to some strange conclusions, an example of which is the following. Summarizing the conventional wisdom on trade and tariffs Machlup (1977) writes:

> Many economists, at all times, recognising the imperfections of competition in domestic markets, have seen one of the greatest benefits of free or freer trade in the competition from foreign producers. Unrestrained competition from abroad can end the oligopolistic sinecures of domestic firms and force them to work with greater efficiency. (p. 82)

Thus, if free trade is opened up between x nation-states the consumers in each, rather than choosing to purchase goods from one of, say, two domestic sellers, can now choose between $2x$ suppliers. More competition should lower prices and profits and encourage a search for cost reduction. In reality such welfare propositions cannot hold because they require that competition is maintained, and the forces which created the conditions for the 'oligopolistic sinecures' in any one nation-state may eventually also bring them about at any market level, up to the including the world level. There is no necessity to assume that all the x nations will remain in production. As Marx observed, unregulated competition tends to be transitional towards monopoly – interestingly enough, the 50 largest manufacturing enterprises in the EEC (a free trade area of a sort) increased their market share from 15 to 25 per cent between 1965 and 1976 (Locksley and Ward, 1979).

Although it is not interpreted as the paramount actor in global affairs the nation-state is nevertheless of interest to IPE writers Appreciating the close correspondence of polity and economy, IPE sees the nation-state as a context for a specific stage in capitalist development. Indeed, it occupies the same role for capitalism as did the tribe for pre-industrial peoples or the city-state for feudalism. It therefore needs to be studied as an organizational structure, a vehicle for a particular mode of production. In common with other such structures before it, the nation-state is transitory. As I argued above, we are presently at an analytical crossroads for a 'combination of international, economic and technological developments cast doubt on the viability of the state itself as the fundamental unit of politics' (Dyson, 1980, p. 282). Capital is now outgrowing the boundaries which initially nurtured it.

2. The characteristics of actors in IPE emerge from the analysis of economic structures and processes, i.e. the identification of position and relationship. Several lines of research are currently being followed, of which the following are examples.

First, the analysis of constitutions of organizational structures indicates the scope of actors' activities in specific circumstances. The contemporary literature on behaviour within bureaucracy is all constructed in this vein, and the EEC has formed a splendid case study for transnational bureaucratic activity. In the earlier stages of EEC operations, it appears that considerable power was given to, literally, individuals to effect binding policy changes on governments. Instances include decisions relating to agricultural policy, monetary union and trade preferences (Rosenthal, 1975).

Second, IPE has been putting all actors onto an equal footing by universalizing motivations. What, it is asked, motivates capital to flow from one region to another? The answer, one presumes, is private advantage; the new region provides an environment conducive to the realization of capital's objectives. Region A thus acts as a resource for region B. In the same manner, any actor might consider the world, at the limit, as a set of resources available for its own use. The public choice school can employ this notion to great effect in the analysis of government behaviour, by concluding that democratic governments, in efforts to sustain themselves and to survive, formulate foreign policies of electoral advantage to themselves but of possible disadvantage to other governments pursuing similar goals. That inter-government non-co-operation represents the current state of affairs in the Western world is not, I think, in doubt. In OECD's recent summary of world economic conditions we find the following remarks amongst the conclusions:

- many countries perceive their monetary policies as largely dictated by the stance of policies elsewhere;
- attempts by individual countries to reduce budget deficits have been made more difficult by similar attempts elsewhere . . .;
- with depressed growth of total sales, and unemployment high and rising almost everywhere, countries are increasingly facing protectionist measures in their traditional export markets. (OECD, 1983, p. 16)

The phenomenon of economies attempting to gain at the expense of others is often termed by NC writers the 'new mercantilism', although there appears little new about it. Mercantilism would seem to have been the essence of government foreign policy for a long, long time (Knapp, 1973). The novelty arises, I presume, because of the apparent return to mercantilism of the overtly protectionist sort after the halcyon days of nineteenth century free trade. However, Robinson (1966) has successfully demonstrated that free trade was simply an appropriate vehicle for mercantilism under the prevailing historical conditions.

It is quite common for NC textbooks to end with the sentiment that the present orgy of self-destruction of economies must be brought to a halt by inter-government co-operation. Using a public choice perspective we can see that there is no necessity for this to take place. Global depression actually offers distinct advantages to election-conscious governments because (a) it ensures that there exist no governments elsewhere whose economic successes could reveal to the electorate that domestic policies are deficient, (b) it offers a convenient scapegoat for policy failures.

Finally, IPE at the world level provides the context for the positioning of actors in relation to one another. Generally analysed in class terms, such relations will, for example, integrate government behaviour patterns with the interests of capital, organized labour, bureaucracy, financial and banking concerns and so on. This is, principally, the Marxian perspective adopted by state theorists (Jessop, 1982).

3. In its recognition of the significance of differential power IPE takes a profound step towards reality. All relations between actors are power relations – be they between capital and labour, government and electorate, bureaucrat and sponsor, or whatever – and all competitive outcomes are determined by power relativities. This is true of market relations, for simple inspection tells us that it is not the case that all governments, all capitals, all labour and so on are equally powerful – 'traders do not come naked into market' (Mackenzie, 1975, p. 71). Power both creates and is created by interdependence and inequality between actors.

This insight takes us a long way. It reveals that NC has much in common with an orthodox approach to political science which, says Morgenthau (1978), 'believes that a rational and moral political order, derived from universally valid abstract principles, can be achieved here and now'. The realization of this order is frustrated only by inadequate understanding, defective social institutions and the 'depravity of certain isolated individuals . . .' (p. 3). The analysis of global activity in terms of actors shorn of any empirical or historical characteristics has the effect of inverting totally the logic of scientific analysis. Reality comes to be seen as a set of rather annoying imperfections in a smoothly-functioning abstract model. Unfortunately, an awareness of the realities of power does not produce pleasing policy conclusions. If the obstacles to global harmony are brought about by imperfections created by power differentials then presumably power is required to overcome the powerful. What and where, however, is the source of such power? *Quis dominetur ipsos dominos?*

NOTES

1 A comprehensive bibliography of NC trade theory is contained in Bhagwati (1969). Machlup (1977) is an annotated bibliography of NC integration theory, although contributions on related international issues are also referenced. Principal contributions to modern IPE are referenced in Mommsen (1980); Roxborough (1979) and Seers (1981).
2 Fuller discussions of the 'power' concept are contained in Hart (1975); Knorr (1975) and Strange (1975).
3 The Stockholm proceedings appear as Grassman and Lundberg (1981), the quotation being on pp. 4–5. It should be added that one of the conclusions of the Conference was the awareness of the limited usefulness of NC theory in explaining world affairs as, indeed, the quotation suggests.
4 Smith (1980) is highly critical of these, and many other, arguments in Amin's work.
5 Estimated from US Department of Commerce, *Survey of Current Business*, 1982, 4, table 2, p. 35 and 1982, 10, table 2, p. 33.
6 An additional factor might be included – exchange rate fluctuations could drastically and uncontrollably alter sales potential in overseas markets owing to price effects.
7 All these data, including those for table 7.1, are estimated from *Survey of Current Business*, 1980, 7, table 1, p. 33; 1981, 10, table 10, p. 52; 1982, 4, tables 1, 2 and 5, pp. 36–9.
8 Although a full discussion is precluded here, militarism's influence on the *internal* economy is a central concern of modern political economy. Basic theory and evidence is discussed in Rosen (1973). Recent contributions to the debate include Griffin, Wallace and Devine (1982) and Domke, Eichenberg and Kelleher (1983).
9 The limitations of NC trade theory are discussed by Robinson (1973) and Steedman (1979). NC integration theory is criticized by Nau (1979), Holland (1980) and Pelkmans (1980) Szentes (1976) opens with a critique of orthodox development theory.

8

Property and the Legal System*

ROGER BOWLES

Property plays an important role in virtually all economies, and yet, with the exception of Marxians, is discussed explicitly by economists only rather rarely. The definition and allocation of property rights represent a primary preoccupation, some might argue *raison d'être*, of states. A wide range of government institutions will be concerned directly or indirectly with property and property rights. The legal system is but one part of this government machinery, albeit an important one from a property perspective. As the framework within which criteria for property ownership are set down, and within which rules governing the exchange of property rights are specified, it is a crucial link between political and economic institutions. It would seem thus to be an important concern of the political economist and it is also the concern which motivates this chapter.

A PRELIMINARY DISCUSSION OF PROPERTY

In the absence of resources on a scale sufficient to meet all the demands being made of them, claims to property will inevitably give rise to conflicts. Buchanan (1975b) uses the example of the narrow footbridge which Robin Hood and Little John both wish to use at the same time. By assigning the rights to the bridge to one or other party from the beginning it should be possible to eliminate costly efforts to establish and defend a claim to the bridge. Provided that both parties

* I am most grateful to Nick Jackson and to Alan Peacock for incisive and helpful comments on an earlier draft of this paper.

honour the assignment of the private property rights, manpower that would otherwise have been expended on fighting over, guarding and attacking the bridge can be deployed in more productive ways.

In the neo-classical paradigm, property rights are essentially private in the sense of allowing the individual owner to exclude others from the use of a particular good or resource. The rights will normally be assumed to be well-defined, unambiguously assigned, exchangeable and enforceable. If and when these conditions are not met, problems in the form of market failure begin to emerge.

For the political economist there are two important sets of questions to be posed. First, at the more 'technical' end, one can investigate the consequences of, and remedies for, market failure. This is a popular pursuit and can be used to account for much of the machinery of the state. Corrective taxes, collective provision of public goods and the provision of enforcement agencies are but some of the institutions of government or the state which can be thought of in this way. The second, and in some respects more fundamental set of questions concerns the source of property and property rights rather than their substance. At this level, the political economist confronts some big questions such as why rights are distributed in the way they are. The Walrasian auctioneer need not worry about this second set of problems because his prospective customers hold a clearly-defined set of initial endowments.

Economists at different times have discussed both sets of issues, but even during the resurgence of interest in political and legal institutions over the last two decades or so, the question of the source of property, and rights in it, has been tackled only rarely. In the absence of a satisfactory account of how the initial endowment upon which the first ever auction was based, economists have been concerned mostly with situations in which there is a determinate starting point. Implicitly, at least, they have tended to assume that the system of property rights once articulated is enforced vigorously. For if such enforcement is absent all sorts of nasty things happen. A threat of coercion has to exist somewhere along the line in order to ensure that a system of private rights will be stable. Collectively sanctioned and provided agencies such as the police and the courts thus assume a role, for in the absence of such institutions a mere declaration that the rights are assigned in some particular way may carry little weight.

Efforts to chisel away at the assignment of property rights sanctioned by the government are not unknown. Individuals may often be observed seeking to arrogate the claims of others. Tax evasion, theft, looting, unlawful occupation of premises and poaching represent but a tiny sample of ways in which citizens may try and appropriate for themselves resources destined for use by others. Such efforts may take a more organized and systematic form: mass civil disobediance, revolution and *coups d'état* represent threats that property rights will be reallocated in favour of a particular class or interest. At a level somewhere between individual chiselling and mass revolt will lie efforts to redistribute or redefine rights on a more modest scale: changes in taxes or regulations as a result of elections, referenda or vigorous campaigning by sectional interests will redistribute rights, as will changes in the law brought about by either the legislature or the judiciary.

Efforts to uphold the status quo are likely also to be vigorous. The executive branch of government will have the task of ensuring that existing rules are implemented effectively. A police force will normally enforce the criminal law, offenders being prosecuted on behalf of society at large, whether in the name of a sovereign as in England, of a state or whatever.[1] Civil law on the other hand will be enforced by the judiciary at the instigation of citizens. It will be concerned mostly with situations in which the conflict or rule-breaking behaviour has effects which are felt largely by another citizen (or at most a small group of citizens). There will sometimes be circumstances in which both kinds of law may be relevant, such as the fields of industrial relations or accidents. The 'wrong' may be a contravention of criminal law, and the punishment directed at deterrence of such actions. It may in addition infringe rights in such ways that a private action, under which the injured party is able to seek compensation from the wrongdoer, is also available. In yet other cases matters may be referred to an administrative tribunal set up to arbitrate in disputes between individuals or, as often, between an individual and the state.

In addition to a police force, the state may well have armed forces at its disposal. The army generally acts as a 'backstop' to law and order. Although its primary role will normally be to defend a country against attack by other countries it may be used in the event of a serious threat to internal security. This may entail reinforcing civilian authorities but may also involve Emergency Powers or martial law. This role of backstop of course confers on the military a potentially very powerful position. It is only rarely that the army will be involved in the day-to-day protection of property rights. The use of Emergency Powers provisions or martial law will be restricted to circumstances in which there is a major threat to internal stability. If used at all frequently, the armed forces cease to fill the roll of backstop and a vacuum will result.

The argument that coercive powers will be required if the system of property rights is to be protected may seem rather melodramatic. Much of the time compliance with the rules governing the allocation and distribution of rights will be secured by reliance on non-coercive, cheaper devices. The notion that the state (and the system of property rights it establishes and seeks to maintain) is the result of an agreement between individuals concerned to avoid the prisoner's dilemma inevitably leaves contractarian models of the state relying heavily upon the threat of coercion against those who would chisel or cheat. Such economic models of the state, it must be conceded, leave open the question of how states find non-coercive means of persuading citizens to comply.

Whatever arguments are used to explain the relatively high degree of compliance with prevailing property systems, the proponent of a *laissez-faire* market system for allocating resources has little difficulty in concluding that it is desirable that the set of rights be fully specified, that there be no ambiguity as to whom they belong, that they can be traded without impediment and that their owners can be completely confident that the rights will continue to be enforceable indefinitely.

From such a starting point one can move relatively easily to the abstract world of idealized perfectly competitive markets in which it is usually assumed that all agents have perfect information about trading opportunities, can buy or sell as much as they like at prevailing market prices and so forth (Arrow and Hahn, 1971). Implicit in this Arrow/Debreu framework is the assumption that all rights and claims can be marketed and that contracts can be enforced costlessly. Institutional details are extraneous to these discussions of whether sets of prices can be found which will ensure that all markets in the economy can be cleared simultaneously. Although it is rather easy to object to some of the assumptions as being 'unrealistic', it is important to keep in mind that many of the assertions about the efficiency of market economies and about their superiority over other methods of economic organization hinge finally upon being able to demonstrate that a perfectly competitive market is able to generate a unique and stable set of equilibrium prices.

As far as property and the legal system in such a world are concerned, most of the interesting problems are assumed away. The assumptions of the model require the existence of complete markets in contingent claims, and indeed in all claims. This means that everything of relevance must be owned by someone and be tradeable. It also requires that trading contracts of a great variety of exotic forms must be available, since the contracts entered today have to specify what is to happen in the event of any possible state of the world prevailing in the future. The principal requirement of the legal system is that it is perfectly predictable and can be relied upon with complete confidence. If the substance of the legal rules should change, a new set of equilibrium prices will have to be calculated.[2] At this level of abstraction a law or rule can be characterized as relating an agent's wealth to a state of the world. Changes in the rules will alter this relation and will thus influence behaviour and choices. Provided that the rules and the domain of possible rules are known there are no insurmountable problems. Speculation about changes in the rules may absorb resources however and this may prompt the observation that the frequency of changes should be minimized. A direct analogue may thus be established between the views of Milton Friedman and the new classical school who advocate simple, fixed rules for taxation and monetary growth[3] and the view that legal rules should remain fixed and predictable wherever possible.[4]

There are of course many issues which the Arrow-Debreu model leaves unanswered for the person interested in law and property. Being based upon an initial endowment of all resources it avoids the question of how we got where we are now. The other important matter is the question of what will happen if some of the assumptions are not met. Positive transactions costs for example may be sufficient to ensure 'gaps' in some of the markets. These transactions costs may come in several guises. It may be that agents find it prohibitively expensive to enter contracts which list exhaustively (even when taken in conjunction with a well-developed set of case law) how various contingencies are to be dealt with. Alternatively it may be that the costs to agents of acquiring all the information required to satisfy the full-information condition would be too great.

Progress on the relation between prices, markets, property and law has, for these and other reasons, been confined largely to a partial rather than a general equilibrium setting. Relaxation of the assumptions of complete information and zero transactions costs accounts for many of the recent interesting developments in economics.

Much of the path breaking work was concerned with the existence of externalities and public goods, although more recently attention has switched to circumstances where information or related problems arise in an essentially private context. The externalities debate was concerned principally with the question of how to devise instruments capable of dealing with (or internalizing) the costs of activities generating 'side effects', whilst the public goods debate was concerned with the allocation of resources in circumstances where it is difficult or inexpedient to exclude from consuming a good those who do not contribute towards the costs of its production.[5]

One obvious omission from the discussion thus far is the question of how property or property rights are to be defined. The economist who looks at the law will find a rather different notion of property rights from the one he is accustomed to using. In the economic model the idea of ownership is treated as a straightforward matter: what matters is that a claim that 'this is my pen' or 'this is my house' can be maintained and recognized. Such claims seem to be all-embracing and economists tend to treat with scepticism efforts to 'attenuate' rights, for example by regulation which imposes restrictions on the uses to which rights may be put. In the legal model property rights are often defined or depicted in a narrower kind of way. Rights need not be exclusive for example, so that several individuals may have a right to use the same piece of land. Similarly, a right may be acquired for a short time only, as when someone takes a short-term lease.

There is not necessarily any incompatibility between these different notions of property. Perhaps the important point to make is that economists are inclined to treat property rights in a relatively abstract way which embraces the well-developed, idiosyncratic forms which are a feature of the legal system as a special case. If a piece of land has a right of way across it, it will be treated differently than it will if there is no such right. One way of thinking about this is to treat two pieces of land, which are similar save for whether they have a right of way across them, as two different goods. They are different goods because different bundles of rights are involved in each case. If this seems rather arbitrary, it is worth remembering that the considerable difference in value between a freehold and leasehold piece of land resides in the bundle of rights (in the sense of the duration of the rights) attaching to it. The markets for bundles of rights which are very similar will usually be highly interdependent, but so long as there are perceptible differences which influence the value of the bundles, they can be treated as different goods. By analogy with the problem of identifying whether a differentiated good is sufficiently distinctive as to give its producer a monopoly one might suggest a cross-elasticity of demand test which could establish whether variations in the bundles of rights attaching to otherwise similar goods were of significance. For the remainder of the chapter we lapse back into the economist's normal approach of avoiding any precise definition of property or property rights and focus on instances where there is no ambiguity.

A distinction may be drawn also in reviewing contributions to the property rights literature between those works which are concerned with the *substance* of rules and institutions that bear upon trade and exchange and those which are concerned with their *source*.

Some economists focus largely on substance, as the considerable literature on liability rules testifies. The substance of rules is important because it may have allocative consequences: one assignment of liability may be more attractive than another because it entails lower aggregate costs. The considerable literature on accident compensation is a good example of the concern with substance: see for example Calabresi (1970) and Diamond and Mirrlees (1975). Elsewhere, source represents the principal focus. Buchanan (1975b) for example is not concerned with questions like whether liability is best imposed on motorists or pedestrians. Rather, his concern is to establish that the creation of a system of property rights can be expected to result from an agreement between individuals seeking a co-operative solution to the prisoner's dilemma which anarchy represents. Others argue that property rights are best treated as endogenous to the economy, the form which rights take being updated and adapted from time to time in the continuing struggle for more efficient resource use (Posner, 1977). There are of course many instances where both structure and source are discussed together.

From these preliminary observations on property rights it is possible to identify two strands amongst contemporary work by economists. On the one hand there is work in which property rights considerations are used to enrich traditional price theory. On the other hand there are efforts to face up to some of the fundamental problems the classical political economists confronted. If there is one feature more than any other which helps distinguish these latter contributions it is that they treat legal, economic and political institutions as an integral (and thus variable) element in development. They do not treat legal and political institutions as a *deus ex machina* or simply as a backdrop against which Walrasian auctions are conducted. If the term 'political economy' is to be understood to refer to a tradition which is somehow broader than neo-classical economics, then study of legal institutions seems to be a prime contender for inclusion in it and the area of property rights in particular becomes a matter of key importance.

ESTABLISHING AND ALLOCATING RIGHTS

In modern capitalist economies, rights of many kinds are traded on markets which operate relatively smoothly. There are exceptions as disputes over fishing rights in deep-sea waters and controversy over the use of space and planets testify. Nevertheless, day-to-day social political and economic life usually runs without major disruption in the form of conflicting claims to resources. There is agreement in most areas as to who holds which property rights. The source of such stability is an elusive matter: it is possible to imagine circumstances in which a major threat to the existing distribution of rights could materialize. But it seems clear that in most societies, most of the time, there is sufficient measure of agreement that any major change would be for the worse as to prevent major upheaval. The argument about the nature of the agreement between citizen and state has taken numerous forms. In this section we examine very briefly just a few strands of the debate.

The two facets of the debate on which we concentrate here are, first, the characterization of the transition from a state of nature or chaos to order, and secondly, the resolution of conflict between freedom (or rights) and welfare. Both represent central issues in political philosophy and both are also central to the development of a theory of property rights. They are however rather different sorts of questions, and each has been approached in a variety of ways.

From chaos to order   The transition from disordered chaos to organized society has been a concern of political philosophers for a long time. There are two popular kinds of device which are used as an engine for this transition. Each relies on the individual finding it expedient to assume a series of obligations to others in return for the offer of certain rights.

The first device is to posit the emergence of a sovereign who claims to be the ultimate owner or guardian of all propery rights. Such claims may be based in turn upon claims by the sovereign to be the representative of some higher authority. The legal system constructed to protect the position and interests of the sovereign may itself be claimed as an independent product of the higher authority's wishes. The sovereign, in efforts to get the best value from his position, will normally enter agreements of various kinds with his subjects under which property rights are exchanged for obligations. He has to find ways of motivating his subjects to work and to defend the 'natural order'. This may entail making it clear to each individual that he will be better off accepting the deal offered by the sovereign than striking out on his own.

A second approach, and one which is more consistent with the axioms of rational behaviour upon which economists are wont to rely, treats the emergence of society from anarchy as the result of a pact between individuals. Anarchy is treated as the non-co-operative solution to a prisoner's dilemma.[6] All participants can improve their lot provided that they can secure co-operative behaviour on the part of others. Under such a social contract, individuals agree to co-operate with one another rather than with a self-appointed sovereign. The contract may sometimes be termed a constitution since it will contain agreements and rules about how day-to-day decisions are to be made subsequently. It has the function of allowing the creation of a means of enforcing agreements which individuals want to make with one another and of specifying and promising protection of a set of rights and obligations accepted by all. Buchanan (1975b) proposes a model of the social contract along such lines, although the basic approach has been in use for several centuries.

It is far from clear quite what status is to be accorded to these two devices. They may be interpreted as efforts to produce one or other of: a simplified account of historical processes, an account of how one might want to set about organizing a society or a prediction about the sorts of things which might happen if existing arrangements were to break down as a result, let us say, of an atomic catastrophe.

But if there are difficulties in 'getting things started' there are also difficulties in sketching in the detail of constitutions and institutions once a society of some kind is posited to have emerged. One of the better known efforts to eliminate the institutional void is to be found in Rawls's *Theory of Justice* (Rawls, 1971) in which are imposed a series of relatively restrictive assumptions upon the knowledge and preference orderings of the participants in the original position. Not only are individuals put behind a veil of ignorance as to the innate qualities (and thus income-earning power) with which they will be born but also they are assumed to apply a maximin criterion when evaluating the alternative social states between which they are asked to choose.

These restrictions enable some of the more difficult problems with social contracts to be avoided. The veil of ignorance behind which individuals are placed has the effect of eliminating any information about initial endowments. Without such information, participants are unable to give way to the temptation they might feel if circumstances were different to press for those decisions most conducive to their own circumstances.

This search for 'justice' is attacked by other writers on a variety of grounds. Perhaps the most important general criticism is that models of the kind developed by Rawls have an interventionist bias as a result of the restrictive (and implausible) assumptions upon which they rely. Prominent among contemporary proponents of this view is Nozick whose *Anarchy, State and Utopia* (1974) sets out to show that it is folly to argue that individuals will ever agree to surrender voluntarily to an arrangement giving the state a role any more extensive than that of nightwatchman. On such a view, most redistributive policies followed by government such as the use of a tax system are readily shown to be coercive and sub-optimal. The rich (or those with high ability) cannot in general be expected to agree to a policy under which they are forced to pay high taxes in order that income supplements can be given to those on low incomes or with low ability. To the extent that a social contract must attract unanimous support if it is to succeed, one many argue that a Rawlsian type programme will never emerge if some of the participants in the process know that they are or will be rich. Redistributive policies cannot normally be 'saved' in this context by positing some degree of non-selfishness. Only if there is unanimity amongst the rich that they wish to make gifts to the poor via the tax sytem will any systematic redistribution be permitted.

The debate about the appropriate degree of restrictiveness to impose on the original position illustrates quite clearly the maxim that what you reap depends on what you sow. Richer social contracts require more restrictions. There seems little prospect of resolving the issue of how restrictive it is appropriate to be: empirical evidence is unlikely to be available which will readily discriminate amongst the alternatives.

Rights and utility   We move next to consider an issue which will arise in the context of discussion of sovereigns and social contracts, but will arise also if we choose to ignore the starting position and confine ourselves to the design of institutions 'downstream'. The discussion, at least in the economic literature, no longer relies on the notion of co-operation but exploits instead some of the recent work on the economics of information.

Rawls (1971) considers that rights are to be considered as a distinct, and more fundamental, concern than utility. This has consequences for the design of a social contract just as it has implications for decision-making in a more mundane, day-to-day context. Such a view runs contrary to conventional welfare economics but is attracting some notable adherents, who reach it by a variety of routes. The argument is not specific to the social contract context, and indeed has mostly been cast in terms of decision-making in a more general policy setting.

Dasgupta (1982) following the lead of earlier work by Marschak and Radner (1972) on the theory of teams and by Mirrlees (1971) on the structure of an optimal system of income tax, investigates the implications of assuming that individuals have information about their own abilities and preferences which is superior to that held by the central authorities. He suggests that there is a presumption that it will normally be desirable, in terms of the set of consumption possibilities, to allow the individual some discretion in decision-making.

In a brief, informal section at the end of his paper Dasgupta instances the system of rationing sometimes used when goods are in short supply during wartime. The central authority lacks information about the value different citizens put on a good, and in the interests of distributive justice allocates claims equally to citizens. These claims are not generally negotiable either for money or for claims to other goods, a restriction on use which will have the effect of keeping the aggregate welfare derived by the community from the good below the level which could be reached if exchange were permitted and the good allowed to find its way more easily into the hands of those placing greatest value on it.[7]

The conclusion that allowing a free market in the good is the best means of allocating it can be reached by a route which is rather different from Dasgupta's reliance on informational asymmetries. Once such route is to argue that individuals place a value on being in a position to exercise choice, even if this entails significant opportunity costs. Rowley and Peacock (1975) are amongst those who would advocate those arrangements according greatest freedom of action or rights to the individual. In this extreme form of liberalism, freedom of the individual to make choices is an important objective, irrespective of its consequences for material wealth.

Proponents of this view are inclined to claim that the potential conflict between freedom and the pursuit of rising wealth will be minimal. More significantly however they will argue that in the event of there being a trade-off they will assign much greater (sometimes absolute) weight to the freedom component.

This liberalist approach is widely recognized as running counter to Paretian welfare economics, in which the criterion for selecting among actions or decisions is the effect upon welfare. Welfare is viewed as deriving from individual utility functions which are generally written as an increasing function of the individual's level of consumption. Hahn (1982a) notes that the liberal approach including that of Rawls may be characterized by considering the policy being used as well as the consumption level to which it gives rise. The utility functions used as the basis for selecting a policy are thus written in the form $U_i(p, C_i(p))$ for the i-th individual where p refers to a policy and $C_i(p)$ to the consumption level i will enjoy in the event of policy p being pursued. A rather stark illustration of this is the choice of a slave who opts for freedom when offered it, knowing that this will leave him worse off in material terms.

The implicit purpose of efforts to resolve the balance between utility and rights and to establish the parameters of a social contract is usually to provide a starting point from which it is possible to imagine a Western-type economy deriving. This purpose is important for various reasons. From the economist's standpoint it is relevant because it will provide at least a skeleton within which property rights, central as they are to the development of exchange and markets, can be generated. But further than that, it provides a foundation for exploring notions such as the state and political institutions. The obvious way of pursuing such enquiries is to treat most activities of the state including the legal system as a response to market failure: this is essentially the kind of approach outlined in Whynes and Bowles (1981). The formation of a state, entailing agreements about criminal law and the enforcement of civil contracts and so on, is the first stage and represents the outcome of bargaining within a co-operative game setting. The second stage, the institutional superstructure, represents a response to difficulties encountered as the market economy gets into full swing. Thus we see collective provision, and the associated development of government spending and taxation, as a response to public goods; the law of tort plays its part as a means of resolving certain kinds of externality problems whilst regulatory agencies are established to watch over the possible abuse of monopoly power.

Whilst useful for some purposes, this two-stage analysis has a number of weaknesses. One of the most important is the implicit assumption that markets can function adequately without a state. Just because state-like institutions may be thought of as responses to market failure it cannot be inferred that states are themselves the product of market failure. The circularity of the argument is pinpointed by the question: can property rights, and thus effective markets, exist if there is no paraphernalia to ensure enforcement? The answer to this question is presumably 'no', but in that case the state has to be seen as a precondition for the operation of a market system rather than as a response to imperfections in its operation.

If this inconsistency continues to create problems for 'big bang' political economists and philosophers who would rely on an original position, it is less of a difficulty for those who rely on an 'evolutionary' approach in which a time origin is not explicitly defined. Rather than the state emerging from a once for all agreement, all institutions, be they legal, political or economic are conceived as responses to pressure for improvement in the efficiency with which resources are allocated. The following section is concerned with just a few of the contributions which pursue this search for a unified theory.

EVOLUTIONARY APPROACHES

The work by orthodox economists on property rights began in earnest with the publication of the paper concerned with social cost by Coase (1960). The point that the substance of liability rules would have a neutral effect on the allocation of resources in the absence of transactions costs was readily absorbed. But as economists began to explore the ramifications of this finding they came to construct more ambitious models in which transactions costs were allowed to play a role and in which the legal rules were treated as endogenous. These models were used in a reappraisal of the notion of market failure, for one of the key arguments which emerged was that *any* form of economic organization entails costs. Much of the time, the decentralized market mechanism will be the least costly form of resource allocation: but not always. A system of liability rules will be superior to the operation of a market in certain circumstances, but equally the costs of running, let us say, a tort system based on negligence may be greater than those of a system of strict liability. Once the costs of operating any of the systems comes to be taken seriously there can be no a priori grounds for the presumption that one set of arrangements is superior to any other: a case by case approach is indicated. Criteria, based usually on cost-minimization, can be derived for making a choice between the various modes of allocation and thus between different ways of assigning the relevant property rights.

Consider, as an example, the keeping of animals. A contracting or market solution in which the owner of animals concludes a bargain with all those whose welfare may be reduced by the occasional straying of the animals could be very costly. A tax system could be used in efforts to internalize the externality, but that would require some very detailed knowledge on the part of government. A third, and in these circumstances attractive, solution is a liability rule assigning responsibility for damage caused by animals to either the owner of the animals or the owner of the assets at risk. The Coase theorem makes the assignment a matter of indifference in the absence of transactions costs. A little thought about the costs that different liability rules would impose enables a presumption in favour of strict liability to be derived. It will normally be cheaper for the animal owner to keep his animals under control than it will be for others to protect themselves from the risk of damage by animals. The imposition of (strict) liability on animal owners, that is to say, enables inefficient damage to be avoided at least cost.[8] In other circumstances of course the conclusion will be different: the passenger in a car who fails to wear a seat belt is open to more serious injury than if he were to wear one. Making the drivers of cars involved in accidents in which unprotected passengers are injured liable for such unnecessary and inefficient extra damage will not usually make sense, with the result that a system of contributory negligence will be likely to be superior.

The argument that clues to the choice between alternative legal instruments and between legal and non-legal instruments can be found in the relative costs of using the different instruments has been pressed considerably further by a number of authors with interesting results. In the work of Posner (1977) it is suggested that a wide variety (if not all) legal institutions are best thought of as efforts to reduce costs and to increase the value or wealth being generated in the economy. In the work of Coase (1974) it is suggested that the debate about the provision of public goods can be illuminated by arguments drawn from a property rights perspective.[9] Another intriguing observation is that a link can be traced back to the earlier work by Coase (1937) on the nature of the firm. In that paper Coase attributes the existence of firms, in which factors of production are hired and used in fixed amounts, to the fact that this will enable cheaper production. The larger number of transactions which would be required if each individual worked on his own account would generate organizing or transactions costs in excess of the losses a firm might sometimes incur as a result of having 'too many' or 'too few' factors under contract. Such arguments are powerful because they can be used to explain why firms may be of different size, why firms in some industries may find it expedient to engage in vertical integration and so on.

Following the earlier work of Samuelson[10] it had become common practice in welfare economics and public finance to identify goods with public characteristics of non-rivalness in consumption and non-excludability as likely candidates for collective provision. Coase (1974) was concerned to show that goods like lighthouses, which had been used as examples of public goods, could and were provided privately in some instances. The basis of Coase's argument was that although it might be costly to establish and enforce private property rights in such goods it was not impossible. He went further and argued that public provision gives rise to costs of its own, with the consequence that private provision, or some kind of public/private mix, might be superior.

The original argument in favour of public provision had relied on the difficulty a lighthouse owner might have in identifying users of the lighthouse beam and charging them a toll. It was suggested that these difficulties would make it impossible for owners to collect a level of revenue which would match the value of the services being provided, leading to underprovision of lighthouses. The counter-argument relied on the difficulty a public agency would have in predicting demand for such a service, and thus its value. By assuming also that lighthouse owners will be ingenious if motivated by profit whilst public agencies will suffer from poorly motivated staff it is possible to reach the view that private provision is more attractive. The issue is by no means resolved as the debate over the appropriate method of delivering health care testifies. The notion of universal and inevitable superiority attaching to collective provision is however undermined.

The pioneering work of Posner on the application of economic analysis to law owes a considerable debt to the earlier work of Coase. The basic hypothesis underpinning Posner's work is that almost all law can be seen as an effort to achieve an efficient allocation of resources and thereby to increase wealth. The extent of the ambition held for the approach is illustrated by a recent paper on primitive society (Posner, 1980) in which efforts to improve material wealth are detected in a wide range of institutions lying in many cases well outside the areas of traditional concern to economists. Even societies in which trade and exchange play a relatively small role and in which law custom and practice take very different forms from those encountered in the sophisticated economy of today are made to yield to economic analysis.

Posner's analysis of primitive society can be thought of as an extension of some of the earlier work on property rights. Demsetz (1964) had argued that as economic circumstances changed, so the definition and assignment of property rights would adjust and adapt accordingly. On this view for example, the fencing or enclosure of land which brings to an end a system of common grazing or common use represents a response to changing economic conditions. Improvements in agricultural technology and increasing demand for products make more intensive use of land profitable. Shifting to a system of private rights in such circumstances is desirable, one might argue, because it more effectively discourages overuse of the land than would the communal solution. The creation of private rights gives rise to a market and thus to a market price. This price will be interpreted as an opportunity cost by farmers, but it will also perform the function of relating the value of the rights to the way in which they are exercised. Exhausted land is less valuable than land which has been used with care with the result that landowners face an incentive to weigh carefully how intensively to farm. That is not to say that communal ownership will necessarily lead to overuse. The key to prevention of the latter is to find some way of inducing the individual, who will wish to use the facility as intensively as possible, to respect the fact that by doing so he will be reducing the value of the resource. Private rights are one way of setting about providing such inducements, but not of course the only way. Communal agreement may be relatively cheap to achieve and enforce in a small, stable rural society even if it verges on the impracticable in most spheres of contemporary life. Indeed the existence of clubs, through which individuals buy access to facilities which are provided communally for members, suggests that communal use at least of a limited kind sometimes represents the best solution.[11]

In Posner's economic theory of primitive society, institutions such as brideprice, polygamy and gift-giving 'can be explained as direct or indirect adaptations to the high cost of information'. The characteristic feature of primitive (or strictly, pre-literate) societies for Posner's purposes is that information is very costly to produce with the consequence that institutions will be designed to economize on the amount of it which is required.

Rather than pursue here a more detailed account of work on primitive society, we conclude this section by taking up one of the points raised by Posner in passing which relates to a fairly well-established body of literature on the transacting process and the functioning of the law of contract. Posner cites a recent paper by Geertz (1978) which analyses trading in bazaars with the help of the economics of information. The inclination of buyers to transact repeatedly with the same seller, and to bargain intensively with one seller rather than to visit many, is treated as a response to the high costs of compiling information about the distribution of prices across a market.

A similar strand of reasoning is to be found in the analysis (often by non-economists) of the way in which traders in contemporary markets conduct transactions and resolve conflict in the event of a transaction breaking down. The law of contract lays down criteria for contracts being legally enforceable and it contains, accumulated in the case law or laid down by statute, principles which will be applied in settling cases coming before the court. Macaulay (1963) investigated trading practices and discovered that commercial practice bore no ready resemblance to what might have been expected by someone whose experience was limited to having read a book on the law of contract. Later work by Beale and Dugdale (1975) in England confirmed that firms very often traded in ways that would make it unlikely that their agreements would be accorded legally-enforceable status, contracts were often incomplete and disputes often resolved by reference to the custom and practice of the trade rather than by reference to the remedies which would be available at law. The reasons are not hard to find: making agreements which are water-tight from a legal standpoint is very costly. In day-to-day transactions involving a relatively small number of traders, custom and reputation may be much cheaper and equally effective devices. Obviously, in larger one-off transactions such as syndicated bank loans of enormous sums the story is quite different: extensive use is made of lawyers in drafting agreements and if necessary in pursuing legal remedies in the event of default.

The net result is that instead of the law of contract being used continually in trade, a whole variety of informal institutions have sprung up in the search for ways of reducing the costs of trade. This enables one to go beyond the results of the Coase theorem type: whilst one may argue that it does not really matter what rules the courts will imply in a contract in the absence of an express agreement, one may argue also that the law of contract taken as a whole is a relatively minor concern because of the propensity of traders to find superior informal devices with which to underpin their relations.

It seems reasonable to predict that the recent developments in the application of economic analysis to law will be extended to areas of the law and history which have not yet been attacked. The notion that markets are but one manifestation of the search for wealth and the legal system another portends an increasingly imperialistic theory of the economy. It is this sense that all institutions can be traced back to some deep-seated drive for prosperity and greater wealth which prompts one to bracket the strands of thought developed in this section and to term them evolutionary. The 'survival of the fittest' epithet seems destined for application to institutions and even to whole societies. Whatever next?

LAW, PROPERTY AND POLITICAL ECONOMY

At the outset it was observed that a Walrasian auctioneer would require a complete set of mutually exclusive and completely defined property rights already allocated amongst the agents participating in his market-clearing exercise. In the later stages it was shown that much of the recent work by economists on property rights and on the role of the legal system goes about matters quite differently. Writers in both areas would concede the importance of prices and markets, but they might have conflicting conceptions of the process of economic development.

Any effort to establish the boundaries and substance of political economy has to come to terms with the coexistence of these various approaches. The technocratic models of general equilibrium theorists are generally cast at a level of abstraction which makes institutional concerns look petty whilst the pragmatism of some of those who take the institutions themselves as the appropriate subject for study rules out much need for an analytical base. The tradition of political economy, deriving from Adam Smith and the classical economists, entails a relatively broad-based conception of the appropriate domain of study but a unified mode of argument. Contemporary work by economists on the legal system can be claimed to be directed at a legitimate element in the classical programme and to be using an analytical armoury which has its origins in the early work on prices and markets.

A view about how best to define political economy is probably derived more appropriately from a view about the sorts of questions one wants to address than from a commitment to one or other set of analytical tools. The economists concerned with law and property will usually have an interest in some of the bigger issues of the day. Are health care facilities best provided directly by government under a social insurance scheme, by private profit-making institutions, by charities or by some mixture of these agencies? How are conflicting claims to resources such as fishing grounds and outer space to be reconciled between nations? Are the laws regulating land tenure arrangements conducive of the best spreading of risk and of the best level and pattern of production?

Some economists would argue that such issues are inescapably political matters and entail judgements which (*qua* economists) they are not competent to make. They would urge a narrower focus and application of the Pareto criterion as a guide to policy recommendations. That this impasse has inhibited economists during the twentieth century is beyond doubt. Efforts to avoid it take various forms. Rejection of the Pareto criterion in favour of a Hicks-Kaldor or wealth maximizing criterion is one route and efforts to produce a positivist economic theory of democracy another. Much of the writing on property rights and the legal system sets out to avoid the normative barrier by treating economic efficiency, wealth maximization or whatever as a *putative* objective. This is consistent with the positivist approach, which most of these writers espouse, to the extent that it produces hypotheses which are in some respects falsifiable. The argument is thus turned around from asking questions such as 'is social insurance the best method of providing health care?' to investigating assertions of the kind 'economic efficiency would prompt the provision of health care by means of social insurance if and only if the following conditions are met . . .', followed by an effort to establish where such conditions prevail and whether modes of provision actually observed conform with those indicated by the theory. The problem with this kind of interpretation is that it encourages a selective testing of hypotheses, and because of the relatively detailed information needed before anything like a hypothesis can be proposed it can easily degenerate into little more than a description of what is observed. To argue for example that high information costs will dictate that efficient outcomes are those which economize on informational inputs may enable one to interpret history in a new and interesting way, but it must be doubtful whether such exercises can be classed as positive. In order to use such theories to predict what will happen tomorrow assumptions have to be made about how much information will cost in the future, and there is unlikely to be a method of establishing this independently of knowledge about how the economy is going to develop.

Consider, for example, usury laws. In some essentially market economies usury is still forbidden, whilst there still exist in most Western economies important relics of the usury laws of earlier days. Compound interest for example will not be awarded on damages by the courts of many countries including England.[12] Such practices would normally be termed inefficient by economists since they impose constraints on the capacity of courts to allow opportunity cost type arguments full expression. The economist who would explain legal rules by reference to efficiency criteria can find ways out of this apparent contradiction by arguing that risks of what might appear to be undercompensation can be discounted. Feinting of this kind may be rationalized as an element in a sophisticated treatment of a tricky issue, but it is not conducive to consumer confidence. Alternative treatments, in which non-efficiency criteria are accorded a place or usury laws are regarded as a device for reducing the cost of servicing the national debt, may seem preferable to being forced to argue that such vestiges represent either a passing, insignificant relic or that they continue to play a wealth-maximizing role.

Property has played a less prominent role in the writings of economists than one might have expected. To some extent this is compensated by the relative importance accorded it in other disciplines such as political philosophy. Often, it is treated as something which, thank goodness, is simply there. Less often is it treated as a matter of concern. Similar sorts of remarks might be made about the concern of economists with the legal system, whether in the context of property or more generally.

The last two decades however have seen economists take up many of the issues lying at the boundary of their subject, in some cases to the extent of pushing into areas traditionally the preserve of others. The legal system had long been treated as a part of 'the environment' in which economic decisions are made. As such it was principally of interest only if it were changed. The source of any change was of little concern, as was the process by which it was implemented. The upsurge of interest in the legal system on the part of economists was prompted by the observation that legal rules may on occasion perform functions which would in other circumstances be performed by bargaining and market transactions. This prompted discussion of the relation between non-market institutions of different kinds such as legal rules, regulation and taxes particularly in reference to matters such as pollution and consumer protection. It also prompted renewed discussion of the relation between public and private provision of goods and services.

The links and overlap between economics and politics became stronger, not least because economists found that their property rights analysis could be extended to discussion of constitutions, social contracts and other grand designs. Law represented a second subject area towards which overtures were made. Property rights generally have a legal foundation and expression and as interest grew in liability rules as allocative devices some cross-fertilization took place.

As an appreciation developed of the potential economic significance of legal institutions, one strand of thought emerged which was characterized by the notion that the legal system, like other institutions, can be viewed as playing an essential role in economic development. Rather than being a *deus ex machina*, which is simply 'out there', the legal system comes to be treated as a device employed by man in the search for increasing material wealth. This notion of the law as an engine of efficency ranks alongside the notion that collective action and political behaviour generally are also motivated by a pursuit of wealth.

The implications of all this for political economy are rather more profound than seems to be widely realized. Markets become just one constituent of a portfolio of institutions used in the pursuit of man's objectives. Much of the analysis developed for application in a market setting can be applied to the non-market institutions like clubs, states, alliances, legal systems, custom and practice and so forth, but the market itself as embodied in the process of explicit transacting assumes a more minor role. The subject area of property rights has played a central role in bringing the legal system onto the economic stage and there are no signs of an imminent exit.

NOTES

1 Historically speaking, police forces are a relatively recent invention. In earlier times criminal law did not exist as a distinctive entity as it does today. For an intriguing discussion of the means by which laws prohibiting theft, murder and so on were enforced in Anglo-Saxon times see Whitelock (1952), especially chapters II and VII.

2 Unless one presses the modelling of alternative states of nature to include different sets of legal rules.

3 Friedman has been urging such views for a long time: see for example his 'A Monetary and Fiscal Framework for Economic Stability' in Friedman (1953). The new classical school views were developed in a series of papers published in the 1970s. For a selection of these works see Lucas and Sargent (1981).

4 Any introductory legal text will emphasize this point. Judges are particularly inclined to refer to the primary importance of certainty in commercial transactions.

5 The externalities debate, and in particular the role played by legal institutions, was triggered by the seminal paper of Coase (1960).

6 Buchanan (1975b) uses such a game-theoretic characterization: for a more thorough treatment of some of the analytical aspects see Taylor (1976).

7 The loss of consumer surplus inherent in prohibiting the sale or exchange of entitlements to a rationed commodity has for long led economists to the view that markets have a useful role to play in allocating commodities even when they are very scarce and 'necessary'.

8 The notion of the cheapest cost avoider was first developed by Calabresi (1970) and has been widely adopted. Strict liability upon animal owners in England is contained in statute, namely the Animals Act 1971: for details see Hepple and Matthews (1980, chapter 10.4).

9 For further argument along similar lines see the paper on 'The Limitations of Public Goods Theory: The Lighthouse Revisited' in Peacock (1979).

10 The original papers by Samuelson were published in 1954–5. For a summary see Samuelson (1969).

11 An economic theory of clubs is proposed in Buchanan (1965).

12 For further discussion of the statute prohibiting English courts from awarding compound interest on damages see Bowles and Whelan (1981).

Concluding Comments

It is not normally an editor's job to provide an additional commentary on the work of the contributors; such an occurrence would be regarded, quite rightly, as lese-majesty. In the case of this particular collection, however, I believe that one or two further remarks might be excused because, as I noted in the Introduction, the contributions both represent statements in their own right and form specific source material integral to the entire debate currently growing up over the nature of political economy. To fuel the fire further, I offer below some speculations of my own based on the assembled material.

In reading through the accounts of various approaches to political economy one cannot help but be struck by the impression of a common epistemology. 'Common' is perhaps most easily interpreted in the negative sense because there appears to be substantial agreement over the deficiencies of neo-classical economic methodology. For example, charges of irrelevance to real-world issues or an obsession with technique at the expense of analysis are regularly made by all species of political economist.

The majority of political economists would, I believe, accept Latsis's (1976) characterization of neo-classical method as *conventionalism*, a conventionalist being one who holds that theories and concepts are simply convenient and 'conventional' descriptions of affairs which, in themselves, are neither true nor false. However, it is the separation of high-level theory from low-level reality which, to the political economist, is the cause for concern.

> Direct empirical confrontation of the theory's postulates with low level statements is excluded. Empirical anomolies i.e.,

clashes between the theory's consequences and experiential statements, are accommodated by means of a battery of conventionalist strategms such as the appeal to 'special circumstances'. Finally, those empirical successes, if any, which the theory secures are hailed as triumphs and used as arguments for putting up with its intuitive implausibility and its empirical inadequacy. (Latsis, 1976, p. 14)

Examining the 'common' epistemology in the positive sense, whether a truly unified method of political economy actually exists, and what the precise nature of it might be, are harder questions to answer. Unfortunately, these are questions infrequently asked because, on occasions, it appear that political economists can have as little time for the adherents of a rival political economy school as they have for mainstream economics. My own impression is that there exists far more ground than is often thought and that political economists tend towards the epistemology of *essentialism* (some, it must be said, more than others).

In his extensive survey of methodology, Blaug (1980) interprets essentialism as a 'methodological standpoint that regards the discovery of the essence of things as the central task of science and defines the essence of a thing as that element or set of elements without which the thing would cease to exist' (p. 226). Translated into the context of the social sciences, essentialism must tend to embrace *verstehen*, the dictate that, as scientists, we need to understand human behaviour in human, rather than reified or mechanical, terms. These notions are, of course, extremely general but they do become concrete when we home in one some of the methodological parallels between the political economy variants.

The obvious starting point is attitudes towards assumptions in analysis. Political economists object to the neo-classical paradigm not because of its use of assumptions *per se* but because of the nature of these assumptions. Marxians, for instance, complain that orthodox economists treat capital exclusively as a thing and completely ignore the implicit property and power relationship. Institutionalists argue that the extreme methodological individualism of the orthodoxy completely overlooks the social determinants of human behaviour. Both the Austrian and the public choice schools emphasize subjectivism – behaviour is dictated by that which makes sense to the actor, and not by that which makes sense to the observer in terms of some preconceived notion of 'rationality'. Placed within the context of essentialism, political economists are, for obvious reasons, quite unwilling to enter into abstractions which necessitate a total divorce between idea and reality. What purpose can be served by assuming away imperfect information and knowledge, uncertainty (in the sense of 'random' as opposed to 'probabilistic'), power differentials and other conditional behavioural influences when even the most superficial contact with the real world indicates all are present? The standard plea in reply to this question is 'simplification of reality to facilitate understanding' but an essentialist must counter-argue that an abstraction which removes the defining elements of the essence is not a simplification but a distortion. Indeed, it will become the image of a 'reality' with no independent existence outside the mind of the observer. Marx provides an eloquent statement of the methodology which, I believe, the majority of political economists would accept:

> The premises from which we begin are not arbitrary ones, not dogmas, but real premises from which abstractions can only be made in the imagination. They are real individuals, their activity, and the material conditions under which they live, both those which they find already existing and those produced by their activity. These premises can thus be verified in a purely empirical way. (Tucker, 1980, p. 32)

The proposition that political economy is essentialist has additional corollaries consistent, it seems to me, with a number of the arguments of the papers in the collection. The objective of genuine explanation leads naive prediction (i.e. exclusive concern with forecasting) and description to be played down. Forecasting ability is not seen as the *only* relevant consideration in hypothesis appraisal, and some political economists go so far as to deny outright the possibility of forecasting owing to the necessary complexity of explanatory models. Much of neo-classical theory is dismissed because of its tautological and descriptive nature. Joan Robinson's famous remark, for example – 'utility is the quality in commodities that makes individuals want to buy them, and the fact that individuals want to buy commodities shows that they have utility' (Robinson, 1964, p. 48) – carries the implication that the neo-classical 'explanation' of purchasing behaviour in terms of utility maximization is merely an alternative way of describing what is seen to take place. The conventionalist argument is circular and, from the point of view of communicating information about the world, meaningless (Katouzian, 1980, provides many other examples). There is accordingly reluctance (especially on the part of Marxians and Austrians) to contemplate purely hypothetical end-states, such as 'competitive equilib-rium', because it is the *process* which requires the explanation. It is indicative to note that, in pursuit of explanation, no school of politic-al economy recognizes constraints upon its enquiries. There appears to be general rejection of any arbitrary distinction between 'econo-mic' and 'non-economic' facts or ideas when it comes to searching for solutions to particular problems.

A criticism commonly levelled at modern political economists is that they have an 'anti-empirical' bias (although such an accusation has, at one time or another, be made against virtually all methodolo-gies!). Were any such anti-empirical potential to be realized then I think we should have to have serious reservations about political economy, given the stress placed on the understanding of reality. In appraising such a criticism, however, we need to bear in mind the transition in meaning through which the term 'empirical' has lately travelled. Our modern conception of empiricism, argues Ions (1977), amounts solely to 'conclusions based on the statistical manipulation of aggregated data' (p. 150). Empirical means experimental with, implicitly, a 'natural science' methodological stereotype in mind. That such a form of evidence generation is important cannot be doubted, but this exclusive definition of 'empirical' is artificially limiting. In earlier times, the concept had both experimental *and* experiential connotations, aspects of which I have already touched on in the context of assumptions. With these twin connotations, an empirical science can be distinguished from an abstract science, a body of deductively-established propositions derived from an axiom set. This, of course, is political economy's vision of economics. It would seem to me inconceivable that experience and experiment could ever be legitimately banished from the method of political economy because no *genuine* explanation of reality can ever be inconsistent with reality.

This having been said, there might be more merit in the criticism at the personal, as opposed to the theoretical, level. Because of the extreme difficulty of communicating a holistic perception of experi-ence, an analysis of the essentialist type can sometimes seem occult, even mystic, when assessed by individuals who have not shared that experience. Without doubt, this difficulty could provide ample scope for self-delusion and deception, although difficulty *per se* will never constitute grounds for invalidating a methodology on logical grounds. Whether individual practitioners practice what they preach is another matter. All that can be said here is that 'care should be exercised' when undertaking or when appraising an analysis, but this is obviously true for all methodologies including that of neo-classical economics.

In the Introduction I posed the question whether a new paradigm was emerging. The answer, I think, is that political economy is both old and new. On the one hand, we can certainly recognize the innovations made by the political economists of recent times, public choice analysis, Sraffa's production models and 'poleconometrics' being examples. On the other hand, the essentialist character of political economy seems to root it in a venerable methodological tradition which predates the modern bifurcation into politics and economics. This tradition surfaces again and again in the history of method, appearing as it does in the work of Marx, Vico, Hobbes, Bacon and the Socratic thinkers. Arguably, therefore, we are more in need of an explanation for the emergence of 'economics' than we are for the persistence of 'political economy'.

Such an explanation is unlikely to be simple and only a few dimensions of the problem will be stated here. Given that the transition in common usage between our two key terms – economics and political economy – appears to have occurred in the late nineteenth century, perhaps we might begin our search with the so-called 'marginal revolution' of the period. In this context, the following considerations will be relevant.

First, dissatisfaction with the analyses of the 'old school' – the phrase is J. S. Mill's although he was perhaps the old school's most distinguished alumnus – had begun to emerge by the middle of the nineteenth century. Some formative contributions made by Continental thinkers (such as Cournot and Gossen) were embodied in the arguments of the later English marginalists (such as Jevons) but their principal objections to the classical approach were not levelled at its epistemology. Rather, it was the theories themselves, such as the wage-fund doctrine and the natural wage theory, which were held to be inadequate (Hutchison, 1978). The methodological critique was the province of the 'historical school' in Germany and the growing ranks of economic historians in England. Both disputed the validity of the hypothetico-deductive method on the grounds of anti-empiricism and ideological bias. Thus, in 1857, we find Marx objecting to the old school presenting production 'encased in eternal natural laws independent of history, at which point *bourgeois* relations are then quietly smuggled in as the inviolable natural laws on which society in the abstract is founded' (Marx, 1973, p. 87).

Second, the exclusion of the political element from the emerging 'economics' was by no means rapidly accomplished. 'Political' in this context is taken to imply (1) the normative evaluation of policy objectives and (2) the analysis of processes by means of which objectives are formulated. Such concerns were certainly important to an old school anxious for practical political reform and the creation and preservation of a competitive market economy (Hutchison, 1981). The evaluation of policy outcomes, however, was conspicuous in the work of the early marginalists. Jevons and Sidgwick devoted much attention to cases of what we nowadays term market failure (e.g. public goods and externalities) using broadly similar ethical criteria to indicate the failure of markets as the old school had used to indicate success. Marshall was concerned especially about the material and spiritual improverishment which the prevailing economic structure appeared to generate. In 1907 he wrote: 'the State alone can bring the beauties of nature and art within the reach of the ordinary citizen' (in Hutchison, 1978). One could be forgiven for mistaking this for a quotation from Aristotle.

Finally, it is clear that, over the period being considered, the whole subject did undergo a character change, from Ricardian plutology (the study of wealth) to Marshallian catallactics (the analysis of exchange). How, asks Hicks (in Latsis, 1976), do we explain the rise of catallactics? An answer at the broadest level of abstraction is provided by Frohock and Sylvan (1983). They argue that the schism between economics and politics resulted from the emergence of Western liberal capitalism, a mode of production in which subsistence and production was effectively partitioned from political action. Political and economic theory became divorced, in other words, because political and economic practice were becoming divorced. Robinson and Eatwell (1973) have suggested that catallactics was more readily received because it preached equilibrium and harmony instead of strife and conflict between social classes. Presumably this feature would make it as acceptable in the USA, where catallactics received a great deal of attention in the post-war period, as it was in the UK. Hicks's own answer to his question is perhaps less profound but it is, in my view, particularly appealing. John Stuart Mill's remark in his *Principles of Political Economy*, to the effect that the theory of the subject was complete, hardly constituted tidings of great joy to the growing band of purely academic economists. Catallactics was new and it possessed most attractive intellectual qualities. There was clearly considerable scope for mathematical operations and the analysis of exchange systems appeared far more manageable and tidy than a holistic multi-faceted science of wealth.

It provided a new way of taking up the economic problem; not just a new theory but a new approach which was capable of much development. It was not . . . in the main a reaction to contemporary events. The possibility of a utility theory had been there all the time; what the catallactists showed was that something could be done with it. (in Latsis, 1976, p. 215)

There is clearly much potential for debating the origins of the modern conception of economics although I doubt whether we shall ever be able to find a location more precise than 'around the end of the nineteenth century'. However, the first authoritative statement of the new attitude can be identified with more accuracy. This was John Neville Keynes's *Scope and Method of Political Economy*, published in 1891. Having lived through the protracted methodological controversies of the 1870s and 1880s, Keynes was anxious to arrive at some form of reconciliation. Furthermore, he was anxious to demonstrate that the pedigree of his discipline was both continuous and respectable.

The result was very much in the spirit of Marshall's *natura non facit saltum* and just about every disputant in the controversies found accommodation. The question of whether political economy was a pure science, a policy science or a code of ethics was resolved by the answer that it embodied all three elements. There was the element of 'economic science' proper, concerned with objective 'laws or uniformities', paralleled by a science of regulation 'relating to criteria of what ought to be and concerned therefore with the ideal as distinguished from the actual'. The ethical aspect was also considered part of political economy although, interestingly enough, Keynes held it to be 'non-economic'. With equal dexterity, the conflict between the historical school's preference for empirical/inductive methods and the mathematical school's partiality for 'pure', deductive theory was also resolved – Keynes held that both methods had valid roles to play because they were, in fact, complementary to one another. However, whilst appearing to accept the legitimacy of virtually all contemporary attitudes to political economy, Keynes did regard the advance of economic science as the economist's foremost task. The establishment of a 'body of systematised knowledge' was, he believed, the logical prerequisite for empirical research and policy formulation (Deane, 1978, pp. 102–3).

One must not doubt the influence of John Neville Keynes. His notions about the scope of political economy are the source of many modern views, not least that of Lord Robbins given in the Introduction. With Keynes's blessing, generations of neo-classical economists have been continually adding to the box labelled 'Pure Economic Science'. For the reasons noted above, the modern political economist must regard the Keynesian 'synthesis' as papering over the cracks. The questions have not been answered, they have been avoided. What can the contents of this box be, other than a series of mutually reinforcing, circular definitions severed from reality? In the words of Phyllis Deane (1983, p. 11): 'There *is* no one kind of economic truth which holds the key to fruitful analysis of *all* economic problems, no pure economic theory that is immune to changes in social values or current policy problems.'

Bibliography

Akerlof, G.A. (1980) 'A theory of social custom, of which unemployment may be one consequence', *Quarterly Journal of Economics* 1966, vol. 94, no. 4, pp. 749–76.

Alexander, K.J.W. (1975) Editorial Foreword in Arun Bose, 1975.

Althusser, L. (1969) *For Marx*, London, Allen Lane.

Amin, S. (1976) *Unequal Development*, New York, Monthly Review Press.

(1980) *Class and Nation, Historically and in the Current Crisis*, London, Heinemann.

Arrow, K.J. and Hahn, F.H. (1971) *General Competitive Analysis*, Edinburgh, Oliver & Boyd; San Francisco, Holden; Day Inc.

Ayres, Clarence E. (1943) 'The Significance of Economic Planning', in Seba Eldridge (ed.), *Development of Collective Enterprise*, Lawrence, University of Kansas Press.

(1944) *The Theory of Economic Progress*, Chapel Hill, University of North Carolina Press.

(1946) *The Divine Right of Capital*, Boston, Houghton Mifflin Company.

(1952) *The Industrial Economy*, Boston, Houghton Mifflin Company.

(1953) 'The Role of Technology in Economic Theory', *American Economic Review*, May.

Azariadis, C. (1975) 'Implicit contracts and underemployment equilibria', *Journal of Political Economy*, pp. 1183–1202.

(1981) 'Implicit contracts and related topics: A survey', in Z. Hornstein, J. Grice and A. Webb (eds), *Economics of the Labour Market*, London, HMSO, pp. 221–48.

Baily, M.N. (1974) 'Wages and employment under uncertain demand', *Review of Economic Studies*, vol. 41 (I), no. 125, pp. 37–50.

Baldwin, Robert E. (1976) *The Political Economy of U.S. Trade Policy*, Center for the Study of Financial Institutions, Graduate School of Business Administration, New York University, Bulletin 1976–4.

Balogh, T. (1973) *Fact and Fancy in International Economic Relations*, Oxford, Pergamon Press.

Baran, P.A. and Sweezy, P.M. (1966) *Monopoly Capital*, New York, Monthly Review Press.

Barry, N.P. (1979), *Hayek's Social and Economic Philosophy*, London, Macmillan.

(1981), 'Austrian Economists on Money and Society', *National Westminster Bank Review*, pp. 20–31.

(1982), 'The Tradition of Spontaneous Order', *Literature of Liberty*, pp. 7–58.

Beale, H. and Dugdale, A. (1975) 'Contracts between businessmen: planning and the use of contractual remedies,' *British Journal of Law and Society*, vol. 2, pp. 45–60.

Becker, S. (1976) *The Economic Approach to Human Behaviour*, Chicago and London, University of Chicago Press.

Becker, G.S. and Stigler, G.J. (1977) 'De gustibus non est disputandum', *American Economic Review*, vol. 67, pp. 76–90.

Bentley, Arthur F. (1908) *The Process of Government*, Chicago, University of Chicago Press.

Bergstrom, Theodore C. and Goodman, Robert P. (1973) 'Private Demands for Public Goods', *American Economic Review*, vol. 63, June, pp. 280–96.

Bhagwati, J. (1969) 'The Pure Theory of International Trade: A Survey', in American Economic Association, *Surveys of Economic Theory*, London, Macmillan, vol. 2, pp. 156–239.

Black, D. (1948a) 'On the Rationale of Group Decision Making', *Journal of Political Economy*, vol. 56, pp. 23–34.

(1948b) 'The Decisions of a Committee Using a Special Majority', *Econometrica*, vol. 16, pp. 245–61.

(1958) *The Theory of Committees and Elections*, Cambridge, Cambridge University Press.

Blaug, M. (1978) *Economic Theory in Retrospect*, Cambridge, Cambridge University Press.

(1980) *The Methodology of Economics*, Cambridge, Cambridge University Press.

Böhm-Bawerk, E. (1896, 1975), *Karl Marx and the Close of His System*, London, Merlin.

Borcherding, Thomas E. and Deacon, Robert T. (1972) 'The Demand for the Services of Non-Federal Governments', *American Economic Review*, 62, December, pp. 891–901.

Borooah, Vani K. and van der Ploeg, Frederic (1983) *Political Aspects of the Economy*, Cambridge, Cambridge University Press.

Bose, Arun (1975), *Marxian and Post-Marxian Political Economy*, Harmondsworth, Penguin.

(1977), *Political Paradoxes and Puzzles*, Oxford, Clarendon Press; Delhi, Oxford University Pres.

(1980a), *Marx on Exploitation and Inequality: An Essay in Marxian and Analytical Economics*, Delhi, Oxford University Press; Oxford, Oxford University Press.

(1980b), *Exploitation, Social Classes and Contradictions in Agriculture in Modern India* (to be published).

Bowles, R.A. and Whelan, C.J. (1981), 'Judgment Awards and Simple Interest Rates', *International Review of Law and Economics*, vol. 1, pp. 111–14.

Bradley, Ian and Howard, Michael (1982a) 'An Introduction to Classical and Marxian Political Economy' in *Classical and Marxian Political Economy*, Ian Bradley and Michael Howard (eds), London, Macmillan, pp. 1–43.

(1982b) 'Piero Sraffa's "Production of Commodities by Means of Commodities" and the Rehabitation of Classical and Marxian Political Economy' in *Classical and Marxian Political Economy*, Ian Bradley and Michael Howard (eds), London, Macmillan, pp. 229–54.

Brennan, G. and Buchanan, J.M. (1980) *The Power to Tax*, Cambridge, Cambridge University Press.

Brenner, R. (1978) 'The Origins of Capitalist Development: a Critique of Neo-Smithian Marxism', *New Left Review*, vol. 104, pp. 25–92.

Breton, A. (1974) *The Economic Theory of Representative Government*, Chicago, Aldine-Atherton.

Bronner, S.E. (1981) *A Revolutionary for our Times: Rosa Luxemburg*, London, Pluto Press.

Broome, J. (1978) 'Trying to Value a Life', *Journal of Public Economics*, vol. 9, pp. 91–100.

(1983a) 'Utilitarianism and Separability', *Discussion Paper*, University of Bristol.

(1983b) 'Uncertainty and Fairness', *Discussion Paper*, University of Bristol.

Buchanan, J.M. (1954) 'Individual Choice in Voting and the Market', *Journal of Political Economy*, vol. 62, pp. 334–43.

(1964) 'What Should Economists Do?', *Southern Economic Journal*, vol. 30, pp. 213–22.

(1965) 'An Economic Theory of Clubs', *Economica*, vol. 32, February, pp. 1–14.

(1975a) 'Public Finance and Public Choice', *National Tax Journal*, vol. 28, pp. 383–94.

(1975b) *The Limits of Liberty: Between Anarchy and Leviathan*, Chicago, University of Chicago Press.

(1977) *Freedom in Constitutional Contract. Perspective of a Political Economist*, College Station, Texas, Texas A. & M. University Press.

(1982a) 'Individual Choice Behaviour in Private, Agency, and Collective Decision Roles', *Mimeo*, Center for Study of Public Choice.

(1982b) 'Order Defined in the Process of its Emergence', *Literature of Liberty*, vol. V, p. 5.

Buchanan, J.M. and Faith, R.L. (1980) 'Subjective Elements in Rawlsian Contractual Agreement on Distributional Rules', *Economic Inquiry*, vol. 18, pp. 23–38.

Buchanan, J.M. and Thirlby, G.F. (eds) (1973) *LSE Essays on Cost*, London, Weidenfeld and Nicolson.

Buchanan, J.M. and Tullock, G. (1962) *The Calculus of Consent*, Ann Arbor, University of Michigan Press.

Buchanan, M. and Wagner, R.E. (1977) *Democracy in Deficit. The Political Legacy of Lord Keynes*, New York, Academic Press.

Bush, Paul D. (1981–2) 'The Normative Implications of Institutional Analysis', *Economic Forum*, Winter, pp. 9–30.

Calabresi, G. (1970) *Costs of Accidents*, New Haven, Yale University Press.

Caves, Richard E. (1976). 'Economic Models of Political Choice: Canada's Tariff Structure', *Canadian Journal of Economics*, vol. 9, pp. 278–300.

Chow, Gregory C. (1973) 'Problems of economic policy from the viewpoint of optimal control', *American Economic Review*, vol. 63, December, pp. 825–37.

Chrystal, Alec K. and Alt, James E. (1981) 'Some Problems in Formulating and Testing a Politico-Economic Model of the

United Kingdom', *Economic Journal*, vol. 91, September, pp. 730–36.

Clark, John M. (1957), *Economic Institutions and Human Welfare*, New York, Alfred A. Knopf.

Coase, R.H. (1937) 'The Nature of the Firm', *Economica*, n.s. IV, pp. 386–405.

(1960) 'The Problem of Social Cost', *Journal of Law and Economics*, vol. 3, pp. 1–44.

(1974) 'The Lighthouse in Economics', *Journal of Law and Economics*, vol. 17, October.

Cochran, Kendall P. (1983) 'The Instrumentalist Foundation for Institutionalist Economic Thought', paper presented at the Third World Congress of Social Economics, Fresno, California, August, pp. 1–15.

Cohen, Morris (1931) *Reason and Nature*, New York, Harcourt Brace and Company.

Commons, John R. (1968) *Legal Foundations of Capitalism*, Madison, University of Wisconsin Press.

(1934, 1961) *Institutional Economics, Its Place in Political Economy*, Madison, University of Wisconsin Press.

(1950) *The Economics of Collective Action*, New York, Macmillan Co.

Cottrell, P.L. (1975) *British Overseas Investment in the Nineteenth Century*, London, Macmillan.

Crotty, J.R. (1973) 'Specification Error in Macro-Econometric Models: The Influence of Policy Goals', *American Economic Review*, no. 5, pp. 1025–30.

Culbertson, William P. (1978) 'The Preconception of Institutional Economics', *The Social Science Journal*, January, pp. 7–12.

Dahl, Robert A. and Lindblom, Charles E. (1953) *Politics, Economics, and Welfare*, New York, Harper & Brothers.

Das Gupta (1982) Review of Arun Bose's, 'Marx on Exploitation and Inequality: An Essay in Marxian Analytical Economics, in *India Quarterly*, New Delhi, January–March, pp. 112–14.

Dasgupta, P. (1982) 'Utilitarianism, information and rights' in A. Sen and B. Williams (eds), 1982.

Datar, A.L. (1972) *India's Economic Relations with the USSR and Eastern Europe, 1953 to 1969*, Cambridge, Cambridge University Press.

Deane, P. (1978) *The Evolution of Economic Ideas*, Cambridge, Cambridge University Press.

(1983) 'The Scope and Method of Economic Science', *Economic Journal*, 93, pp. 1–12.

Demsetz, H. (1964) 'Toward a Theory of Property Rights', *American Economic Review*, vol. 57, May, pp. 347–59.

Dewey, John (1928) *The Philosophy of John Dewey*, edited by Joseph Ratner, New York, Henry Holt and Company.

(1939) *Theory of Valuation*, Chicago, University of Chicago Press.

(1949) *Reconstruction in Philosophy*, New York, The New American Library.

Dewey, John and Tufts, James H. (1932), *Ethics*, New York, Henry Holt and Company.

Diamond, P.A. (1967) 'Cardinal Welfare, Individualistic Ethics, and Interpersonal Comparisons of Utility: Comment', *Journal of Political Economy*, vol. 75, pp. 765–6.

Diamond, P.A. and Mirrlees, J.A. (1971) 'Optimal taxation and public production', *American Economic Review*, 61, March, pp. 8–27 and 61, June, pp. 361–78.

(1975) 'On the Assignment of Liability: The Uniform Case', *Bell Journal of Economics*, 6, 2, pp. 487–51.

Dobb, Maurice (1968) 'Classical Political Economy', in D. Horrowitz (ed.) *Marx and Modern Economics*, London, MacGibbon and Kee.

Domke, W.K., Eichenberg, R.C. and Kelleher, C.M. (1983) 'The Illusion of Choice: Defense and Welfare in Advanced Industrial Economies 1948–1978', *American Political Science Review*, 77, pp. 19–35.

Dorfman, Joseph, *et al.* (1963) *Institutional Economics: Veblen, Commons, and Mitchell Reconsidered*, Berkeley, University of California Press.

Dowd, Douglas, (ed.) (1958) *Thorstein Veblen: A Critical Reappraisal*, Ithaca, Cornell University Press.

(1964) *Thorstein Veblen*, New York, Washington Square Press.

Downs, A. (1957) *An Economic Theory of Democracy*, New York, Harper Row.

(1967) *Inside Bureaucracy*, Boston, Little Brown.

Dumont, Louis (1980) 'Agriculture and the Birth of Classical Economics: The *Docteur* Quesnay', in E.J. Hobsbawm and others (ed.) *Peasants in History*, Calcutta, Oxford University Press.

Dyson, K. (1980) *The State Tradition in Western Europe*, Oxford, Martin Robertson.

Easton, D. (1965) *A System Analysis of Political Life*, New York, Wiley.

Edgeworth, F.Y. (1881) *Mathematical Psychics: An Essay on the Application of Mathematics to the Moral Sciences*, London, Routledge.

Edgley, Roy (1982) 'Philosophy', in David McLellan (ed.) *Marx: The First Hundred Years*, Fontana, pp. 239–302.

Elliott, John E. (1980) 'Fact, Value, and Economic Policy Objectives', *Review of Social Economy*, April, pp. 1–20.

Ellman, M. (1979) *Socialist Planning*, Cambridge, Cambridge University Press.

Elson, Diane (1979) 'The Value Theory of Labour', in Diane Elson (ed.) *Value: The Representation of Labour in Capitalism*, London, CSE Books.

Elster, J. (1978) *Logic and Society: Contradictions and Possible Worlds*, Chichester, Wiley.

(1982) 'Sour Grapes – Utilitarianism and the Genesis of Wants', in A. Sen and B. Williams (eds), 1982.

(1983) *Explaining Technical Change*, Cambridge, Cambridge University Press.

Engels, Frederick (1844, 1975) 'The Condition of England. I The Eighteenth Century', in K. Marx and F. Engels, *Collected Works*, vol. 3, Moscow, Progress Publishers, pp. 469–88.

(1874, 1950) 'Prefatory Note to Peasant War in Germany', in K. Marx and F. Engels, *Selected Works*, 2-volume ed., vol. 1, Moscow, Foreign Languages Publishing House.

(1884, 1949) 'The Origin of the Family, Private Property and the State', in K. Marx and F. Engels, *Selected Works*, 2-volume ed., vol. ii, Moscow, Foreign Literature Publishing House.

(1894, 1947) *Anti-Dühring*, Moscow, Foreign Languages Publishing House.

(1895) Engels to Schmidt, in *The Correspondence of Marx and Engels*, ed. Dona Torr, London, Lawrence and Wishart, pp. 527–8.

Fabricant, Salomon (1952) *The Trend of Government Activity in the United States since 1900*, New York, National Bureau of Economic Research.

Fair, Ray C. (1975) 'On controlling the economy to win elections', *Cowles Foundation Discussion Paper*, 397.

Feyerabend, P.K. (1975) *Against Method: Outline of an Anarchistic Theory of Knowledge*, London, New Left Books.

Fieldhouse, D.K. (1973) *Economics and Empire, 1830–1914*, London, Weidenfeld and Nicolson.

Findlay, Ronald and Wellisz, Steven (1982) 'Endogenous Tariffs, the Political Economy of Trade Restrictions and Welfare' in Jagdish N. Bhagwati (ed.), *Import Competition and Response*, Chicago, University of Chicago Press, pp. 223–43.

(1983) 'Some Aspects of Political Economy of Trade Restrictions', *Kyklos*, forthcoming.

Foster, J. Fagg, (1981) 'The Papers of J. Fagg Foster', *Journal of Economic Issues*, December, pp. 857–1012.

Frank, A.G. (1967) *Capitalism and Underdevelopment in Latin America*, New York, Monthly Review Press.

(1980) *Crisis: In the World Economy*, London, Heinemann.

Frankena, William K. (1967) 'Value and Valuation', in *The Encyclopedia of Philosophy*, vol. 8, New York, Macmillan and Free Press.

Freeman, R.B. and Medoff, J.L. (1979) 'Two Faces of Unions', *The Public Interest*, Fall, pp. 69–93.

Frey, Bruno S. (1978) *Modern Political Economy*, Oxford, Martin Robertson.

(1983) *Democratic Economic Policy. A Theoretical Approach*, Oxford, Martin Robertson.

(1984) 'The Public Choice view of international political economy', forthcoming in *International Organization*.

Frey, Bruno S. and Schneider, Friedrich (1978) 'A Politico-Economic Model of the United Kingdom', *Economic Journal*, 88, June, pp. 243–53.

(1981a) 'A Politico-Economic Model of the U.K.: New Estimates and Predictions', *Economic Journal*, 91, September, pp. 737–40.

(1981b) 'Central Bank Behaviour. A Positive Empirical Analysis', *Journal of Monetary Economics*, 7, April, pp. 291–315.

(1982) 'Politico-Economic Models in Competition with Alternative Models: Which Predicts Better?', *European Journal of Political Research*, 10, pp. 241–54.

Frey, Bruno S. *et al.* (1983) *A Formulation and Test of a Simple Model of World Bank Behaviour*, Institute for International Economic Studies, Stockholm, Seminar Paper 240.

Friedman, M. (1953) 'The Methodology of Positive Economics', *Essays in Positive Economics*, Chicago, University of Chicago Press.

(1977) 'Nobel Lecture: Inflation and Unemployment', *Journal of Political Economy*, no. 3, pp. 451–72.

Frohock, F.M. and Sylvan, D.J. (1983) 'Liberty, Economics and Evidence', *Political Studies*, 31, pp. 541–55.

Fusfeld, Daniel R. (1972) 'The Rise of the Corporate State in America', *Journal of Economic Issues*, 6, March, pp. 1–19.

Gaertner, Manfred (1981) 'Politik und Arbeitsmarkt. Eine Uebersicht ueber ausgewaehlte Markrotheorien', *Zeitschrift fuer die gesamte Staatswissenschaft*, 137, June, pp. 252–83.

Galbraith, John K. (1957) *The Affluent Society*, Boston, Houghton Mifflin Company.

(1971) *The New Industrial State*, Boston, Houghton Mifflin Company.

(1973) *Economics and the Public Purpose*, Boston, Signet.

(1983a) Interview, 'The Anatomy of Power', *Challenge*, July/August, pp. 26–33.

(1983b) *The Anatomy of Power*, Boston, Houghton Mifflin Company.

Galtung, J. (1973) *The European Community: A Superpower in the Marking*, London, George Allen and Unwin.

Geertz, C. (1978) 'The Bazaar Economy: Information and Search in Peasant Marketing', *American Economic Review*, vol. 68, Papers and Proceedings, May.

Giddens, A. (1979) *Central Problems in Social Theory: Action, Structure and Contradiction in Social Analysis*, London, Macmillan.

Gordon, D.F. (1974) 'A Neoclassical theory of Keynesian unemployment', *Economic Inquiry*, vol. 12, pp. 431–59.

Gordon, R.J. (1982) 'Why U.S. wage and employment behaviour differs from that in Britain and Japan', *Economic Journal*, March, pp. 13–44.

Gram, Harvey and Walsh, Vivian (1983) 'Joan Robinson's Economics in Retrospect', *Journal of Economic Literature*, June, pp. 518–50.

Gramsci, Antonio (1975) *Selections from The Prison Notebooks*, New York, International Publishers.

Grassman, S. and Lundberg, E. (eds) (1981) *The World Economic Order*, London, Macmillan.

Griffin, L.J., Wallace, M. and Devine, J. (1982) 'The Political Economy of Military Spending: evidence from the United States', *Cambridge Journal of Economics*, 6, pp. 1–14.

Gruchy, Allan G. (1947) *Modern Economic Thought: The American Contribution*, New York, Prentice-Hall.

(1972) *Contemporary Economic Thought: The Contribution of Neo-Institutional Economics*, Clifton, Augustus M. Kalley.

226 BIBLIOGRAPHY

Hahn, F. (1982a) 'On some difficulties of the utilitarian economist', in A. Sen and B. Williams (eds), 1982.

(1982b) 'Reflections on the Invisible Hand', *Lloyds Bank Review* April, pp. 1–21.

(1982c) 'General Equilibrium Theory', in D. Bell and I. Kristol (eds), *The Crisis in Economic Theory*, New York, Basic Books, pp. 123–38.

Hall, R.E. and Lilian, O. (1979) 'Efficient wage bargains under uncertain supply and demand', *American Economic Review*, no. 5, pp. 868–79.

Hamilton, Walton (1953) *Newtonian Classicism and Darwinian Institutionalism*, Albuquerque, The University of New Mexico Press.

(1957), *The Politics of Industry*, New York, Alfred A. Knopf.

Hamlin, A.P. (1983) 'Procedural Individualism and Outcome Liberalism', *Scottish Journal of Political Economy*, vol. 30, pp. 251–63.

(1984) 'Constitutional Control of Processes and their Outcomes', *Public Choice*, vol. 42, pp. 133–46.

Hammond, P.J. (1981) 'Ex-ante and Ex-post Welfare Optimality under Uncetainty', *Economica*, vol. 48, pp. 235–50.

(1982) 'Utilitarianism, Uncertainty and Information', in A. Sen and B. Williams (eds), 1982.

Harcourt, G.C. (1982) 'The Sraffian Contribution: An Evaluation' in *Classical and Marxian Political Economy*, Ian Bradley and Michael Howard (eds), London, Macmillan, pp. 259–75.

Harsanyi, J.C. (1976) *Essays on Ethics, Social Behaviour and Scientific Explanation*, Dordrecht, Reidel.

Hart, J. (1976) 'Three approaches to the measurement of power in International Relations', *International Organisation*, 30, pp. 289–305.

Hayek, F.A. von (1931, 1935a) *Prices and Production*, London, Routledge.

(1935b) *Collectivist Economic Planning*, London, Routledge.

(1939) *Profits, Interest and Investment*, London, Routledge and Kegan Paul.

(1941) *The Pure Theory of Capital*, London, Routledge and Kegan Paul.

(1944) *The Road to Serfdom*, London, Routledge and Kegan Paul.

(1948) 'Economics and Knowledge' in *Individualism and Economic Order*, London, Routledge and Kegan Pual, pp. 33–56.

(1955) *The Counter-Revolution of Science*, Glencoe, The Free Press.

(1960) *The Constitution of Liberty*, London, Routledge and Kegan Paul.

(1967) *Studies in Philosophy, Politics and Economics*, London, Routledge and Kegan Paul.

(1973) *Law, Legislation and Liberty*, vol. i, *Rules and Order*, London, Routledge and Kegan Paul.

(1976a) *Law, Legislation and Liberty*, vol. ii, *The Mirage of Social Justice*, London, Routledge and Kegan Paul.

(1976b) *The Denationalisation of Money*, London, Institute of Economic Affairs.

(1978a) 'Competition as a Discovery Procedure', in *New Studies in Philosophy, Politics, Economics and the History of Ideas*, London, Routledge and Kegan Paul, pp. 179–190.

(1978b) 'The Campaign Against Keynesian Inflation', *New Studies in Philosophy, Politics, Economics and the History of Ideas*, pp. 191–231.

(1979) *Law, Legislation and Liberty*, vol. iii, *The Political Order of a Free People*, London, Routledge and Kegan Paul.

Heilbroner, Robert L. (1970) 'On the Possibility of a Political Economics', *Journal of Economic Issues*, December, pp. 1–22.

Hepple, B.A. and Matthews, M.H. (1980) *Tort: Cases and Materials*, 2nd edition, London, Butterworths.

Hill, Lewis E. (1978) 'Social and Institutional Economics: Toward a Creative Synthesis', *Review of Social Economy*, December, pp. 311–24.

Hinich, Melvin J. (1977) 'Equilibrium in Spatial Voting: The Median Voter Result is an Artifact', *Journal of Economic Theory*, 16, December, pp. 208–19.

Hobbes, Thomas (1951, 1974) *Leviathan*, ed. C.B. Macpherson, Harmondsworth, Penguin.

Holland, S. (1980) *Uncommon Market*, London, Macmillan.

Hollerman, L. (1982) 'Japan's Economic Impact on the United States', *Annals of the American Academy of Political and Social Science*, 460, March, pp. 127–35.

Hollis, M. (1981) 'Economic Man and Original Sin', *Political Studies*, no. 2, pp. 167–80.

Hollis, M. and Nell, E.J. (1975) *Rational Economic Man: A Philosophical Critique of Neoclassical Economics*, Cambridge, Cambridge University Press.

Honderich, E. (1976) *Three Essays on Political Violence*, Oxford, Basil Blackwell.

Horvat, B. (1982) *The Political Economy of Socialism*, Oxford, Martin Robertson.

Howard, Michael and King, J.E. (1976), Introduction in *The Economics of Marx*, Harmondsworth, Penguin, pp. 9–45.

Howe, R.E. and Roemer, J.E. (1981) 'Rawlsian Justice as the Core of a Game', *American Economic Review*, vol. 71, pp. 880–95.

Hutchison, T.W. (1978) *On Revolutions and Progress in Economic Knowledge*, Cambridge, Cambridge University Press.

(1981) *The Politics and Philosophy of Economics*, Oxford, Basil Blackwell.

ICIDI (Independent Commission on International Development Issues) (1980) *North-South: A Programme for Survival*, London, Pan Books.

Ions, E. (1977) *Against Behaviouralism*, Oxford, Basil Blackwell.

Jessop, B. (1982) *The Capitalist State*, Oxford, Martin Robertson.

Johr, W.A. and Singer H.W., (1949) *The Role of the Economist as Official Adviser*, London, George Allen and Unwin.

Journal of Public Economics (1976) Special issue on 'Taxation Theory', 6, July–August, pp. 1–169.

Kafoglis, M. and Cebula, R. (1981) 'The Buchanan-Tullock Model: Some Extensions', *Public Choice*, vol. 36, pp. 179–86.

Katouzian, H. (1980) *Ideology and Method in Economics*, London, Macmillan.

King, J.E. (1982) 'Value and Exploitation Some Recent Debates' in *Classical and Marxian Political Economy*, Ian Bradley and Michael Howard (eds), London, Macmillan, pp. 157–87.

Kirchgaessner, Gebhart (1979) 'Zur Struktur politisch-oekonomischer Konjunkturzyklen', in Carl Christian von Weizsaecker (ed.), *Staat und Wirtschaft*, Schriften des Vereins für Socialpolitik, N.F. vol. 102, Berlin, Duncker and Humblot, pp. 427–50.

Kirzner, I. (1973) *Competition and Entrepreneurship*, Chicago, University of Chicago Press.

(1979) *Perception, Opportunity and Profit*, Chicago, University of Chicago Press.

Knapp, J. (1973) 'Economics or Political Economy?', *Lloyds Bank Review*, 107, January, pp. 19–43.

Knorr, K. (1975) *The Power of Nations: the Political Economy of International Relations*, New York, Basic Books.

Kolakowski, Leszek (1977) *The Socialist Idea: A Reappraisal*, ed.

Leszek Kolakowski and Stuart Hampshire, London, Quartet Books.

Kregel, J.A. (1973) *The Reconstruction of Political Economy: An Introduction to Post-Keynesian Economics*, New York, John Wiley & Sons.

Kuhn, T.S. (1970) *The Structure of Scientific Revolutions*. Chicago, University of Chicago Press.

Lachmann, L. (1976) 'From Mises to Shackle: An Essay on Austrian Economics and the Kaleidic Society', *Journal of Economic Literature*, vol. 14, pp. 54–62.

(1977) *Capital, Expectations and the Market Process*, Kansas City, Sheed Andrews and McMeel.

Lafay, Jean-Dominique (1979) 'Empirical analysis of politico-economic interaction in the East European countries', in *mimeo*, Université de Poitiers. To appear in *Soviet Studies*.

Lakatos, I. (1978) 'The Methodology of Scientific Research Programmes', in J. Worral and G. Currie (eds), *Philosophical Papers*, vol. 1, Cambridge, Cambridge University Press.

Lampedusa, Giuseppe di (1958, 1974) *The Leopard*, London, Fontana/Collins.

Latsis, S.J. (ed.) (1976) *Method and Appraisal in Economics*, Cambridge, Cambridge University Press.

Lenin V.I. (1894, 1960) 'What the "Friends of the People" are and how they fight the Social Democrats', in V.I. Lenin, *Collected Works*, vol. 1, Moscow, Foreign Languages Publishing House, pp. 129–332.

(1899, 1956) *The Development of Capitalism in Russia*, Moscow, Foreign Languages Publishing House.

Lerner, A.P. (1944) *The Economics of Control*, New York, Macmillan.

Lewis, C.I. (1947) *An Analysis of Knowledge and Valuation*, LaSalle, Ill. Open Court Press.

Lindbeck, Assar (1976) 'Stabilization policy in open economics with endogenous politicians', *American Economic Review, Papers and Proceedings*, 66, May, pp. 1–19.

(1977) *The Political Economy of the New Left: An Outsider's View*, New York, Harper and Row.

Lippincott, B. (1938) *On the Economic Theory of Socialism*, New York, McGraw-Hill.

Littlechild, S. (1981) 'Misleading Calculations of the Social Costs of

230   BIBLIOGRAPHY

Monopoly Power', *Economic Journal*, vol. 91, pp. 348–63.

(1982) 'Equilibrium and Market Process', in I. Kirzner (ed.), *Method, Process, and Austrian Economics*, Lexington, Lexington Books, pp. 85–102.

Loasby, B.J. (1976) *Choice, Complexity and Ignorance*, Cambridge, Cambridge University Press.

Locksley, G. and Ward, T. (1979) 'Concentration in manufacturing in the EEC', *Cambridge Journal of Economics*, 3, pp. 91–7.

Lovell, Michael C. (1978) 'Spending for Education: The Exercise of Public Choice', *Review of Economics and Statistics*, 60, November, pp. 487–95.

Lowe, Adolph (1965) *On Economic Knowledge*, New York, Harper and Row.

(1980) 'The Veblen-Commons Award', *Journal of Economic Issues*, June, pp. 241–54.

Lucas, R.E. and Sargent, T.J. (eds) *Rational Expectations and Econometric Practice*, London, George Allen and Unwin.

Lukes, S. (1973a) *Individualism*, Oxford, Basil Blackwell.

(1973b) 'Types of Individualism' in *Dictionary of the History of Ideas*, vol. 2, New York, Scribeners, pp. 594–604.

(1974) *Power: A Radical View*, London, Macmillan.

Luxemburg, R. (1913, 1951) *The Accumulation of Capital*, London, Routledge and Kegan Paul.

Lynd, Robert S. (1948) *Knowledge for What?*, Princeton, Princeton University Press.

Macaulay, S. (1963) 'Non-contractual relations in business: a preliminary study', *American Sociological Review*, vol. 25, pp. 55–69.

McFarlane, B. (1982) *Radical Economics*, London, Croom Helm.

Machlup, P. (1977) *A History of Thought on Economic Integration*, London, Macmillan.

Mackenzie, W.J.M. (1975) *Power, Violence, Decision*, Harmondsworth, Penguin.

MacRae, Duncan C. (1977) 'A political model of the business cycle', *Journal of Political Economy*, 85, April, pp. 239–63.

Madan, G.R. (1979) *Western Sociologists on Indian Society: Marx, Spencer, Weber, Durkheim, Pareto*, London, Routledge and Kegan Paul.

Magdoff, H. (1969) *The Age of Imperialism*, New York, Monthly Review Press.

Magee, Steven P. (1982) 'Protectionism in the United States', in mimeo, Department of Finance, University of Texas at Austin.

Marglin, S.A. (1974) 'What Do Bosses Do? The Origins and Functions of Hierarchy in Capitalist Production' *Review of Radical Political Economy*, Summer, pp. 61–112.

Marschak, J. and Radner, R. (1972) *Economic Theory of Teams*, New Haven, Yale University Press.

Marsden, D. and Saunders, C.T. (1981) *Pay Inequalities in the European Community*, London, Butterworths.

Marx, Karl (1842, 1975) 'Debates on the Freedom of the Press', in K. Marx and F. Engels, *Collected Works*, vol. 1, Moscow, Progress Publishers, pp. 132–81.

—— (1843, 1975) 'Contribution to the Critique of Hegal's Philosophy of Law', in K. Marx and F. Engels, *Collected Works*, vol. 3, Moscow, Progress Publishers, pp. 5–129.

—— (1844a, 1975) 'Letters from Deutsch-Französische Jahrbücher, in K. Marx and F. Engels, *Collected Works*, vol. 3, Moscow, Progress Publishers, pp. 133–45.

—— (1844b, 1975) 'Contribution to the Critique of Hegel's Philosophy of Law, Introduction', in K. Marx and F. Engels, *Collected Works*, vol. 3, Moscow, Progress Publishers, pp. 175–87.

—— (1844c, 1975) 'Critical Marginal Notes on the Article by A Prussian', in K. Marx and F. Engels, *Collected Works*, vol. 3, Moscow, Progress Publishers.

—— (1844d, 1975) 'Economic and Philosophic Manuscripts of 1844', in K. Marx and F. Engels, *Collected Works*, vol. 3, Moscow, Progress Publishers.

—— (1846–7, n.d.) *The Poverty of Philosophy*, Moscow, Foreign Languages Publishing House.

—— (1847, 1950) 'Wage Labour and Capital', in K. Marx and F. Engels, *Selected Works*, 2-volume ed., vol. i, Moscow, Foreign Language Publishing House, pp. 66–97.

—— (1848, n.d.) 'Lecture on Free Trade', in K. Marx, 1846–47, n.d., pp. 234–53.

—— (1857, 1973) *Grundrisse*, Harmondsworth, Penguin.

—— (1859, 1970) *A Contribution to the Critique of Political Economy*, Moscow, Progress Publishers.

—— (1861–3, 1954, n.d.) *Theories of Surplus Value*, Part I, Moscow, Foreign Languages Publishing House.

—— (1862, 1971) *Theories of Surplus Value*, Part III, Moscow, Foreign Languages Publishing House.

—— (1862, 1971) *Theories of Surplus Value*, Part III, Moscow, Foreign Languages Publishing House.

—— (1863–6, 1976) 'Results of the Immediate Process of Production', in K. Marx, 1867, 1956, pp. 943–1084.

(1865, 1950) 'Wages, Price and Profit', in K. Marx and F. Engels, *Selected Works*, 2-volume ed., vol. i, Moscow, Foreign Languages Publishing House, pp. 361–405.

(1867, 1958) *Capital*, vol. 1, Moscow, Foreign Languages Publishing House.

(1867, 1976) *Capital*, vol. 1, Harmondsworth, Penguin.

(1869, 1950) 'The Eighteenth Brumaire of Louis Bonaparte', in K. Marx and F. Engels, *Selected Works*, 2-volume ed., vol. i, Moscow, Foreign Languages Publishing House, pp. 221–311.

(1875, 1949) 'Critique of the Gotha Programme', in K. Marx and F. Engels, *Selected Works*, 2-volume ed., vol. ii, Moscow, Foreign Language Publishing House.

(1893, 1957) *Capital*, vol. 2, Moscow, Foreign Languages Publishing House.

(1894, 1959) *Capital*, vol. 3, Moscow, Foreign Languages Publishing House.

(1913) *A Contribution to the Critique of Political Economy*, Chicago, Charles H. Kerr and Co.

(1964) *Pre-Capitalist Economic Formations*, ed. E.J. Hobsbawm, London, Lawrence and Wishart.

(1979) 'The Eighteenth Brumaire of Louis Bonaparte', in K. Marx and F. Engels *Collected Works*, vol. 11, London, Lawrence and Wishart.

Marx, Karl and Engels, Frederick (1845–6, 1976) *The German Ideology*, Progress Publishers.

(1848, 1950) 'Manifesto of the Communist Party', in K. Marx and F. Engels, *Selected Works*, 2-volume ed., vol. i, Moscow, Foreign Languages Publishing House.

Medio, Alfredo (1972) 'Profits and Surplus Value: appearance and reality in capitalist production', in E.K. Hunt and J.G. Schwartz (eds), *A Critique of Economic Theory*, Harmondsworth, Penguin.

Menger, C. (1870, 1950) *Principles of Economics*, translated by James Dingwell and Bert Hoselitz, Glencoe, Free Press.

(1883, 1963) *Problems of Economics and Sociology*, translated by Francis J. Nock, Urbana, Illinois University Press.

Mill, J.S. (1970) *The Principles of Political Economy*, edited by D. Winch, Harmondsworth, Penguin.

Mirrless, J.A. (1971) 'An Exploration in the Theory of Optimum Income Taxation', *Review of Economic Studies*, 38, pp. 175–208.

(1982) 'The Economic Uses of Utilitarianism', in A. Sen and B. Williams (eds), 1982.

Mises, L. von (1912, 1971) *The Theory of Money and Credit*, New York, Foundation for Economic Education.

(1936) *Socialism*, London, Jonathan Cape.

(1949, 1972) *Human Action*, Yale, Yale University Press.

(1956, 1972) *The Anti-Capitalistic Mentality*, Illinois, Libertarian Press.

(1962, 1978) *The Ultimate Foundation of Economc Science*, Kansas, Sheed Andrews and McMeel.

Mitchell, Wesley C. (1950) *The Backward Art of Spending Money and Other Essays*, New York, Augustus M. Kelley.

Mommsen, W.J. (1980) *Theories of Imperialism*, London, Weidenfeld and Nicolson.

Moran, T.H. (1973) 'Foreign Expansion as an "Institutional Necessity" for US Corporate Capitalism', *World Politics*, 25, pp. 369–86.

Morgenthau, H.J. (1978) *Politics among Nations*, 5th edition, New York, Knopf.

Mueller, D.C. (1976) 'Public Choice: A Survey', *Journal of Economic Literature*, vol. 14, pp. 395–433.

(1979 *Public Choice*, Cambridge, Cambridge University Press.

Myrdal, Gunnar (1954) *The Political Element in the Development of Economic Thought*, Cambridge, Cambridge University Press.

(1960) *Beyond the Welfare State*, New Haven, Yale University Press.

Nagel, Ernest and Newman, James R. (1968) *Gödel's Proof*, New York, New York University Press.

Nau, H.R. (1979) 'From integration to interdependance: gains, losses and continuing gaps', *International Organisation*, 33, pp.119–47.

Newman, James R. (1965) 'Gödel's Proof', in *International Encyclopedia of Science*, vol. 2, London, Nelson, pp. 52–3.

Niskanen, W.A. (1971) *Bureaucracy and Representative Government*, Chicago, Aldine-Atherton.

(1975) 'Bureaucrats and Politicians', *Journal of Law and Economics*, vol. 18, pp. 617–43.

Nordhaus, W.D. (1972) 'The Worldwide Wage Explosion', *Brookings Papers on Economic Activity*, no. 2, pp. 431–64.

(1975) 'The Political business cycle', *Review of Economic Studies*, 42, April, pp. 169–90.

Nozick, R. (1974) *Anarchy, State and Utopia*, New York, Basic Books; Oxford, Basil Blackwell.

O'Driscoll, G. (1977) *Economics as a Co-ordination Problem*, Kansas, Sheed Andrews and McMeel.

(1982) 'Monopoly in Theory and Practice', in I. Kirzner, *Method, Process, and Austrian Economics*, pp. 189–213.

OECD (1982) 'A New Wave of Industrial Exporters', *OECD Observer*, 119, November, Paris, OECD, pp. 26–30.

OECD (1983) *OECD Economic Outlook*, 33, July, Paris, OECD.

Oswald, A.J. (1982) 'The Microeconomic Theory of the Trade Union', *Economic Journal*, September, pp. 576–95.

Paine, S. (1977) 'China's Economic Relations with Less Developmed Countries', in D. Nayyar (ed.), *Economic Relations between Socialist Countries and the Third World*, London, Macmillan.

Paldam, Martin (1981) 'An essay on the rationality of economic policy: The test case of the electional cycle', *Public Choice*, 37, November, pp. 287–305.

Pattanaik, P.K. (1968) 'Risk, impersonality and the social welfare function', *Journal of Political Economy*, December. Reprinted in E.S. Phelps (ed.), *Economic Justice*, Harmondsworth, Penguin, 1973.

Peacock, A.T. (1979) *The Economic Analysis of Government*, Oxford, Martin Robertson.

Pelkmans, J. (1980) 'Economic Theories of Integration Revisited', *Journal of Common Market Studies*, 18, pp. 333–54.

Perry, G.L. (1975) 'Determinants of wage inflation around the world', *Brookings Papers on Economic Activity*, no. 2, pp. 403–35.

Peterson, Wallace C. (1976) Review of *The Political Authority and the Market System*, by Robert A. Solo, *Journal of Economic Issues*, 10, December, pp. 977–81.

Phelps Brown, H. (1975) 'A Non-Monetarist View of the Pay Explosion', *Three Banks Review*, March, pp. 3–24.

Pindyck, Robert S. (1973) *Optimal Planning for Economic Stabilization*, Amsterdam, North Holland.

Pommerehne, Werner W. (1978) 'Institutional Approaches to Public Expenditure: Empirical Evidence from Swiss Municipalities', *Journal of Public Economics*, 9, April, pp. 255–80.

Pommerehne, Werner W. and Schneider, Friedrich (1978) 'Fiscal Illusions, Political Institutions, and Local Public Spending', *Kyklos*, 31, pp. 381–408.

Popper, K.R. (1963) *Conjectures and Refutations: The Growth of Scientific Knowledge*, London, Routledge and Kegan Paul.

Posner, R.A. (1977) *Economic Analysis of Law*, 2nd edition, Boston, Little-Brown.

(1980) 'A Theory of Primitive Society with Special Reference to Primitive Law', *Journal of Law and Economics*, XXIII, pp. 1–53.

Rae, D.W. (1969) 'Decision Rules and Individual Values in Constitutional Choice', *American Political Science Review*, vol. 63. pp. 40–56.

(1975) 'The Limits of Consensual Decision', *American Political Science Review*, vol. 69, pp. 1270–94.

Rawls, J. (1971) *A Theory of Justice*, Cambridge, Mass., Harvard University Press, 1971; London, Oxford University Press, 1972.

Ricardo, David (1817, 1951) 'On the Principles of Political Economy and Taxation', in *Works*, ed. P. Sraffa, vol. i, Cambridge, Cambridge University Press.

(1951) 'Notes on Malthus', in *Works*, ed. P. Sraffa, vol. ii, Cambridge, Cambridge University Press.

Robbins, L. (1981) 'Economics and Political Economy', *Papers and Proceedings of the American Economic Association*, 71, pp. 1–10.

Robinson, J. (1964) *Economic Philosophy*, Harmondsworth, Penguin.

(1966) *The New Mercantilism*, Cambridge, Cambridge University Press.

(1970) *The Cultural Revolution in China*, Harmondsworth, Penguin.

(1973) 'The Need for a Reconsideration of the Theory of International Trade', *Collected Economic Papers*, vol. 4, Oxford, Basil Blackwell, pp. 14–24.

Robinson, J. and Eatwell, J. (1973) *An Introduction to Modern Economics*, Maidenhead, McGraw-Hill.

Roemer, J.E. (1982a) 'Exploitation, Alternatives and Socialism', *Economic Journal*, vol. 92, pp. 87–107.

(1982b) *A General Theory of Exploitation and Class*, Cambridge, Massachusetts, Harvard University Press.

Romer, Thomas and Rosenthal, Howard (1979) 'The Elusive Median Voter', *Journal of Public Economics*, 12, June, pp. 143–70.

Roosevelt, Frank and Hymer, Stephen (1972) 'Comment' in Lindbeck, 1977, pp. 119–37.

Rosen, S. (ed.) (1973) *Testing the Theory of the Military-Industrial Complex*, Lexington, Heath.

Rosen, S.J. and Kurth, J.R. (eds) (1974) *Testing Theories of Economic Imperialism*, Lexington, Heath.

Rosenthal, G.G. (1975) *The Men behind the Decisions*, Lexington, Heath.

Rothbard, M.N. (1962) *Man, Economy and State*, Los Angeles, Nash.

(1978) *For a New Liberty*, New York, Collier-Macmillan.

Routh, G. (1975) *The Origin of Economic Ideas*, London, Macmillan.

Rowley, C.K. and Peacock, A.T. (1975) *Welfare Economics: A Liberal Restatement*, London, Martin Robertson.

Rowthorn, B. (1980) *Capitalism, Conflict and Inflation*, London, Lawrence and Wishart.

Roxborough, I. (1979) *Theories of Underdevelopment*, London, Macmillan.

Sachs, J. (1979) 'Wages, profits and macroeconomic adjustment: A Comparative Study', *Brookings Papers on Economic Activity*, no. 2, pp. 269–319.

Samuelson, Paul A. (1952) 'Comment', on Kenneth E. Boulding, 'Welfare Economics', in Bernard F. Holey (ed.), *A Survey of Contemporary Economics*, vol. II, Homewood, Ill., Richard D. Irwin.

(1959) 'A Modern Treatment of the Ricardian Economy: The Pricing of Goods, of Labour and Land Services' in *Quarterly Journal of Economics*, May, pp. 1–35.

(1969) 'The Pure Theory of Public Expenditure and Taxation, in J. Margolis and H. Guitton (eds), *Public Economics*, London, Macmillan.

(1982) 'Quesnay's Tableau Economique as a Theorist would Formulate it Today' in *Classical and Marxian Political Economy*, Ian Bradley and Michael Haward (eds), London, Macmillan, pp. 45–78.

Say, J.B. (1803, 1949) 'A Treatise on Political Economy' (extracts) in K.W. Kapp and Lore L. Kapp (eds), *History of Economic Thought: A Book of Readings*, New York, Barnes and Noble, pp. 289–99.

Scanlon, T.M. (1982) 'Contractualism and Utilitarianism', in A. Sen and B. William (eds) 1982.

Schneider, Friedrich and Naumann, Jörg (1982) 'Interest Group Behaviour in Democracies: An Empirical Analysis for Switzerland', *Public Choice*, 38, June, pp. 281–304.

Schneider, Friedrich, Pommerehne, Werner W. and Frey, Bruno S. (1981) 'Politico-economic interdependence in a direct democracy: the case of Switzerland', in Douglas A. Hibbs and Heino Fassbender (eds), *Contemporary Political Economy*, Amsterdam, North Holland, pp. 231–48.

Schumpeter, Joseph A. (1942) *Capitalism, Socialism and Democracy*, New York, Harper and Row.

(1954) *History of Economic Analysis*, London, George Allen and Unwin.

Seers, D. (ed.) (1981) *Dependency Theory: A Critical Reassessment*, London, Frances Pinter.

Sen, A. (1976) 'Rational Fools: A critique of the behavioural foundations of Economic Theory', *Philosophy and Public Affairs*, no. 6, 1976/7, pp. 317–44.

(1979a) 'Personal Utilities and Public Judgements: Or What's Wrong With Welfare Economics', *Economic Journal*, vol. 89, pp. 537–58.

(1979b) 'Utilitarianism and Welfarism', *Journal of Philosophy*, vol. 76, pp. 463–89.

(1983) 'The Profit Motive', *Lloyds Bank Review*, January, pp. 1–20.

Sen, A. and Williams B. (eds) (1982) *Utilitarianism and beyond*, Cambridge, Cambridge University Press.

Shackle, G.L.S. (1972) *Epistemics and Economics*, Cambridge, Cambridge University Press.

Sharkansky, Ira (1967) 'Government expenditures and public services in the American States', *American Political Science Review*, 61, December, pp. 1066–77.

Sharpe, Myron E. (1974) *John Kenneth Galbraith and the Lower Economics*, White Plains, International Arts and Sciences Press.

Shell, Karl (1967) *Essays in the theory of optional economic growth*, Cambridge, Mass.; London, MIT Press.

Shone, R. (1972) *The Pure Theory of International Trade*, London, Macmillan.

Smith, Adam (1776, 1937) *An Inquiry into the Nature and Causes of the Wealth of Nations*, ed. E.R.A. Seligman, vol. 1, London, J.M. Dent.

(1970) *The Wealth of Nations*, Harmondsworth, Penguin.

Smith, S. (1980) 'The Ideas of Samir Amin: Theory or Tautology?', *Journal of Development Studies*, 17, pp. 5–21.

Solo, Robert A. (1974) *The Political Authority and the Market System*, Cincinnati, South-Western Publishing Co.

Solow, Robert M. (1967) 'A Rejoinder', *Public Interest*, 9, Fall, pp. 118–19.

Sraffa, Piero (1960) *Production of Commodities by Means of Commodities*, Cambridge, Cambridge University Press.

Steedman, Ian (1977) *Marx after Sraffa*, London, NLB.

(ed.) (1979) *Fundamental Issues in Trade Theory*, London, Macmillan.

(1980) 'Economic Theory and Intrinsically Non-Autonomous Preferences and Beliefs', *Quaderni della Foundazione G. Feltinelli*, no. 7/8.

(1982) 'Marx on Ricardo' in *Classical and Marxian Political Economy*, Ian Bradley and Michael Howard (eds), London, Macmillan, pp. 115–56.

Strange, S. (1975) 'What is economic power and who has it?', *International Journal*, 30, pp. 207–24.

Sweezy, P.M. (1980) *Post-Revolutionary Society*, New York, Monthly Review Press.

Szentes, T. (1976) *The Political Economy of Underdevelopment*, 3rd edition, Budapest, Akademiai Kiado.

Taylor, M. (1976) *Anarchy and Cooperation*, New York, Wiley.

Theil, Henri (1968) *Optimal decision rules for government and industry*, Amsterdam, North Holland.

Tinbergen, Jan (1956, 1963) *Economic Policy: principles and design*, Amsterdam, North Holland.

Tool, Marc R. (1977) 'A Social Value Theory in Neoinstitutionalist Economics', *Journal of Economic Issues*, December, pp. 820–43.

(1979) *The Discretionary Economy: A Normative Theory of Political Economy*, Santa Monica, Goodyear Publishing Company.

(1980) 'The Social Value Theory of Orthodoxy: A Review and Critique', *Journal of Economic Issues*, June, pp. 309–26.

Truman, David B. (1958) *The Governmental Process*, New York, Knopf.

Tucker, D.F.B. (1980) *Marxism and Individualism*, Oxford, Basil Blackwell.

Tullock, G. (1965) *The Politics of Bureaucracy*, Washington, Public Affairs Press.

(1967) *Toward a Mathematics of Politics*, Ann Arbor, University of Michigan Press.

(1971) *Logic of the Law*, New York, Basic Books.

Ulph, A.M. (1982) 'The Role of Ex Ante and Ex Post Decisions in the Valuation of Life', *Journal of Public Economics*, vol. 18, pp. 265–76.

Vaughn, K. (1979) 'Does it Matter that Costs are Subjective?' *Southern Economic Journal*, vol. 40, pp. 702–15.

Veblen, Thorstein (1899) *The Theory of the Leisure Class*, New York, Macmillan.

(1906) 'The Socialist Economics of Karl Marx and his Followers'

Quarterly Journal of Economics, 20, pp. 575–95 and 21, 299–322.

(1906) *The Theory of Business Enterprise*, New York, Charles Scribner's Sons.

(1919) *The Vested Interests and the State of the Industrial Arts*, New York, B. W. Huebsch.

(1921) *The Engineers and the Price System*, New York, Viking Press.

(1923) *Absentee Ownership and Business Enterprise in Modern Times*, New York, Viking Press.

(1914, 1964) *The Instinct of Workmanship*, New York, Augustus M. Kelley.

Vernon, R. (1966) 'International investment and international trade in the product cycle', *Quarterly Journal of Economics*, 80, pp. 190–207.

Vital, D. (1971) *The Survival of Small States*, London, Oxford University Press.

Wallerstein, I. (1974) *The Modern World System*, New York, Academic Press.

Walsh, Vivian and Gram, Harvey (1980) *Classical and Neoclassical Theories of General Equilibrium: Historical Origins and Mathematical Structures*, Oxford, Oxford University Press.

Whitelock, D. (1952) *The Beginnings of English Society*, Hardmondsworth, Penguin.

Whynes, D.K. and Bowles, R.A. (1981) *The Economic Theory of The State*, Oxford, Martin Robertson; New York, St Martin's Press.

Wicksell, Knut (1896) *Finanztheoretische Untersuchungen* Jena, Gustav Fischer.

Wiser, F. van (1927) *Social Economics*, New York, Adelphi Co.

Winch, P. (1958) 'The Idea of a Social Science', London, Routledge and Kegan Paul.

Winden, Frans van (1981) *On the interaction between the state and the private sector. A study in political economics*, S'Gravenhage, Pasmans.

Wiseman, J. (1980) 'Costs and Decisions', in D. Currie and W. Peters (eds), *Contemporary Economic Analysis*, vol. 2, London, Croom Helm.

Wittgenstein, L. (1922) *Tractatus Logico–Philosophicus*, London. Routledge and Kegan Paul.

(1953) *Philosophical Investigations*, Oxford, Basil Blackwell.

Index